Dallas

THE MAKING OF A MODERN CITY

Patricia Evridge Hill

UNIVERSITY OF TEXAS PRESS
AUSTIN

The photographs on pages xxxi and 89 are from the collection of the Texas/Dallas History and Archives Division, Dallas Public Library: Images # MA 83.16/13 and # PA 81-00312, respectively.

Portions of the material in this book previously have appeared as follows: "Women's Groups and the Extension of City Services in Early Twentieth-Century Dallas," in *East Texas Historical Journal* 30 (1992): 3–10; "Real Women and True Womanhood: Grassroots Organizing among Dallas Dressmakers in 1935," in *Labor's Heritage* 5 (Spring 1994): 4–17

Requests for permission to reproduce material from this work should be sent to Permissions, University of Texas Press, P.O. Box 7819, Austin, TX 78713-7819.

∞ The paper used in this publication meets the minimum requirements of American National Standard for Information Sciences—Permanence of Paper for Printed Library Materials, ANSI Z39.48-1984.

Library of Congress Cataloging-in-Publication Data

Hill, Patricia Evridge, 1958–
    Dallas : the making of a modern city / by Patricia Evridge Hill.—1st ed.
        p.   cm.
    Includes bibliographical references and index.
    ISBN 0-292-73103-5 (c : alk. paper). —ISBN 0-292-73104-3 (p : alk. paper)
    1. Dallas (Tex.)—History. 2. Business and politics—Texas—Dallas—History. I. Title.
F394.D2157H35   1996
976.4'2811—dc20   95-52459

To Carl, my love and my guide to Dallas

CONTENTS

ILLUSTRATIONS

TABLES

ACKNOWLEDGMENTS

FROM THE DAY I FIRST PROPOSED WRITING A "NEW" history of Dallas until the completion of this book, I have been surrounded by individuals who stimulated my thinking and institutions that facilitated my work. My initial thanks, however, are to Harvey Graff, inspirational teacher and mentor and dear friend. Harvey knew that I would write about Dallas long before I did. I have since given up trying to figure out how he knows the things he knows. Gerald Soliday, Ted Harpham, and Esteban Egea joined Harvey on a dissertation committee that was a model of interdisciplinary thought and scholarship. My work at the University of Texas at Dallas was supported during 1987–1988 and 1988–1989 by dissertation fellowships from the university's School of Arts and Humanities.

The staffs of the Texas/Dallas History and Archives Division of the Dallas Public Library and the Dallas Historical Society are due considerable praise for their suggestions and advice. The knowledge, organization, and support of Gerald Saxon and Jane Boley of the Labor Archives at the University of Texas at Arlington Library made treading the virtually uncharted waters of working-class Dallas history less daunting than it would have been alone.

Robert Fairbanks, Marilynn Johnson, and Zane Miller read the unrevised dissertation and helped to guide its transition from dissertation to completed book. I appreciate their comments. An additional debt is owed to Bob Fairbanks for lunchtime conversations during which he convinced me to look more closely at the 1920s for clues to understanding Dallas's volatility in the 1930s. He was right.

In South Carolina, department chairs Gil Guinn and Robert Figueira scheduled my heavy teaching loads creatively and flexibly to allow me to complete this project, mine regional archives for materials relating to a new one, and sustain a commuter marriage. Another of my Lander University colleagues and a valued friend, Elizabeth Bethel, is a model of engaged scholarship in an environment designed to facilitate teaching. Beth deflates that increasingly politicized and ultimately false dichotomy between teaching and research. Her scholarly work enriches the classroom experiences of students in ways we need to more clearly explain to policy makers and the public.

A Travel to Collections Grant from the National Endowment for the Humanities enabled me to make a return research visit to Dallas during the summer of 1992. The Lander Foundation has provided funding for presentations at the North American Labor History Conference and the Southern Labor Studies Conference. On both occasions, I benefited enormously from the comments and encouragement of labor historians.

Theresa May, of the University of Texas Press, was open to the idea of a manuscript that combines traditional historical subfields. Leslie Tingle, who guided its transformation, has made the process more fun than I imagined it could be. Helen Simons was a helpful copy editor, and Linda Webster provided the index.

My greatest debts are to the strong women who raised me. My grandmother, Aileen Linder Crutchfield, made me believe that I could do anything I wanted to do, and my mother, Ann Hunter Evridge, showed me that I could do anything life required of me. Linda deLone Evridge has been such a cheerleader that sometimes she underestimates the impact her own considerable accomplishments have on her "little" sister.

This book is dedicated to Carl, who turns my head and warms my heart after more years than either of us wants me to type. He introduced me to Dallas and embodies both the vigor that has characterized so much of the city's past and the tolerance and openness that I hope represent its future.

Charleston, South Carolina
1995

DALLAS, "BIG D," HAS ALWAYS BEEN FOND OF SLOGANS.
Dallas substitutes a series of advertising monikers—"the city that
works," "Home to the Great State Fair of Texas," the "city of
choice"—for historical awareness or a collective memory. An "improbable city," lacking the geographical advantages that supposedly characterize prominent urban places, Dallas, now more than 150 years old,
still hesitates to inquire into its past.[1]

As newcomers are quickly told, "the business of Dallas is business."
According to the rhetoric that has prevailed since the 1940s, the
attributes of place have been determined by autonomous markets and
by the actions of businessmen who possessed the means to buy land
and build a city. Dallas's contemporary residents (and those who study
American cities) are largely unaware of the competition and cooperation that characterized urban life in Dallas between 1880 and 1920.
City builders who used labor organizations, social clubs, radical political parties, the alternative press, protest rallies, and statutes such as the
1907 charter's recall provision to mold their urban environment are
lost amid paeans to local businessmen.

Dallas: The Making of a Modern City focuses initially on Dallas during the Gilded Age and Progressive Era, when the city matured as a
commercial crossroads and regional distribution center. It then highlights the city's transition in the 1920s and 1930s from a relatively
open politics of competition and cooperation to a closed system in
which local business leaders amassed unprecedented political power
and civic influence.

Between 1880 and 1920, Dallas was much like its rivals of similar
size and age on the developing prairies.[2] Various groups competed for,
and to a significant extent shared, power. Few residents of early Dallas
or other "new" nineteenth-century towns preferred stasis or advocated

a return to a simpler time.[3] Within a general consensus on growth—virtually all of the city builders discussed in the pages that follow favored growth and were convinced that Dallas was destined to become a "great" city—competing interests presented different visions of exactly how urban expansion should occur. In formal statements of purpose or through priority given one project over another, the commercial-civic elite, clubwomen, populists, socialists, trade unionists, and municipal reformers articulated their visions of the ideal city. Competing groups formed short-lived coalitions when elements of their respective visions of growth overlapped. Local conflicts were usually resolved on the basis of "fair" compromises. Fairness, as originally articulated by Dallas populists in the 1890s to mean a larger share of the benefits of growth for "producers," became the dominant rhetorical and ideological framework within which challengers attempted to extract services and amenities from the businessmen who dominated civic affairs. Significantly, the racism of the majority of Dallas's citizens severely hampered the efforts of those who sought to unite producers or organize grassroots movements based on popular notions of fairness.

A series of bitter conflicts in the years following World War I convinced a new generation of business leaders that Dallas's continued growth was threatened by the unruly nature of urban affairs. The elite that matured in the 1920s and consolidated its power with the formation of the Dallas Citizens Council in 1937 put an abrupt end to the internecine feuding that had characterized relationships among Dallas's early leaders—airing intraclass disputes behind closed doors and presenting a united front to the public. At the same time, it relied on civic boosterism, control of the media, the mythology of frontier capitalism, prejudices and fears of the largely native, white population, and brutal repression to isolate and marginalize those who challenged its hegemony.

Joe Feagin documented the effective organization of workers and intense political activity of neighborhood-based independents in Houston during the final two decades of the nineteenth century—the same period during which Dallas's first Left-liberal coalition, that of trade unionists, the Knights of Labor, and populists, challenged the local commercial-civic elite. Feagin notes that while businessmen in early Houston, like their Dallas counterparts, were undoubtedly the most influential group in town, they did not assume complete command of civic affairs until after the "suite 8F crowd," a new, more cohesive elite, emerged in the 1920s and dominated by the late 1930s.[4] Feagin's argument mirrors my analysis of the origins of Citizens Council control in Dallas. It also raises questions as to the patterns of early urban development in other Texas cities and in those throughout the Southwest. Ironically, white middle-class voters and those workers who supported poll taxes, residency requirements, at-large elections, and other exclusionary devices intended to dilute the voting strength of blacks and Hispanics (and at least in the Dallas case to prevent further Ku Klux Klan incursions into city government) may have established electoral systems that severely limited their own options.

Political scientist Stephen Elkin considers Dallas after World War II an extreme example of the entrepreneurial political economies characteristic of Sunbelt cities, in which strong alliances developed between businessmen and public officials. The difference in Dallas was not that the city was dominated by business leaders but the extent and duration of that dominance in the postwar decades or, to use Elkin's words, "the range of actors who become active bargainers being more restricted in Dallas."[5]

The lack of research into the nature of Dallas's urban development before 1940 has resulted in the widespread assumption that early Dallas was very much like the modern city—that business interests were never seriously challenged, that local residents have always been staunchly anti-union, and that politics was always the exclusive domain of conservatives. This work is at once a response to the profoundly ahistorical transference of the characteristics of a modern city onto eighty years of largely unexplored urban development and a reinterpretation of Dallas's past. Its respective parts provide a more inclusive history of the early city and an analysis of the urban context in which dissent was accommodated, marginalized, or repressed.

My approach has been to link the intertwined stories of organized labor, women's groups, political radicals, progressive reformers, and the city's business leaders in order to achieve a cumulative understanding of Dallas's past and present. The various parts introduced in the first half of the book and blended in the final three chapters contribute to a whole—a new interpretation of Dallas's past. This work initiates a scholarly conversation about the nature of urban development in an important American city. I hope it stimulates interest, debate, and more work on Dallas.

I

Dallas grew within the context of a national model in which passive, regulatory cities developed into locally financed, service-oriented cities, and then into metropoles dependent on federal largesse and unable to rely on continued growth to ensure fiscal stability.[6] Like other cities of the Sunbelt, however, Dallas's population continued to increase well into the 1980s, allowing the city to maintain its conservative patterns of taxation and prosperous image much longer than urban areas of the North and East. Throughout the city's history, the rhetoric of loosely regulated capitalism and laissez faire individualism has prevailed. Public discourse that emphasizes the roles of market forces and those who successfully manipulate them is reinforced by a powerful myth explaining the city's origins and early growth.

Dallas's origin myth is a well-established part of local lore. According to the myth, the town surpassed its rivals in North Central Texas—most notably Fort Worth, almost forty miles to the west, but also Waco to the south and Sherman to the north—because of the hard work and salesmanship of early settlers. The identity of modern Dallas is based on images of its founders' building a prosperous city where none ought to be. Warren Leslie called Dallas a "creation of the citizens," but perhaps Holland McCombs, writing for *Fortune* magazine in 1949, best articulated the myth of Dallas's origin. McCombs described the city as a "monument to sheer determination." According to the *Fortune* article, "Dallas doesn't owe a thing to accident, nature or inevitability. It is what it is . . . because the men of Dallas damn well planned it that way."[7]

Not surprisingly, John Neely Bryan, the city's founder, is touted as the ultimate booster for his ability to persuade migrants to invest their futures in a town possessing neither a navigable river nor any other raison d'etre. The myth gives no consideration to very real geographical, political, and social aspects of settlement.

The local origin myth did not appear in early histories of Dallas, which emphasized geographical advantages and the size and fertility of the city's hinterland. One of the city's first historians, writing in 1892, claimed that railroad magnate Jay Gould predicted Dallas's rise as the commercial center of North Texas. In 1909 local historian Philip Lindsley asserted that it was "natural" for an inland city to develop along established trade routes in one of the most fertile sections of the state. Almost as an afterthought, he discussed the role of Dallas citizens in the city's growth.[8]

Two influential histories published in the late 1920s continued to emphasize Dallas's geographical advantages. Former Speaker of the Texas House of Representatives John Cochran and former Dallas school superintendent Justin F. Kimball added sections on "self-sacrificing pioneers" and the "Dallas Spirit," but neither suggested that the city had no reason to exist or was purely the product of boosterism.[9] As late as 1936, in the midst of the hoopla surrounding the Texas Centennial Exposition, a profile in the Chamber of Commerce's magazine touted Dallas as the product of its fertile hinterland, which attracted a population of over 2,000,000 to within a 100-mile radius of the city.[10]

Holland McCombs's 1949 article in *Fortune* magazine, which introduced the founders of the Dallas Citizens Council to the nation, was the first widely disseminated purveyor of the city-with-no-reason-to-exist myth. McCombs probably based his conclusions on interviews with R. L. Thornton and other members of the city's postwar elite. Thornton's ahistorical views are legendary in Dallas; as part of his argument that the city should host a centennial celebration of statehood won before John Neely Bryan built his cabin, Thornton asserted that people "weren't looking for history. . . . What they wanted was progress."[11] Although Thornton's Chamber did not create the origin myth, neither did it use the state's centennial as an occasion during which to explore Dallas's past. The year of the fair, the Chamber of Commerce's introduction in the Dallas directory contained no historical material whatsoever and the above-mentioned profile in the Chamber's magazine dispensed with history in a mere two paragraphs.[12] It is likely that McCombs came to Dallas with little or no knowledge of the city's past, noted the lack of "obvious" natural advantages (i.e. a harbor or oil wells), and relayed the infectious bravado and ahistoricism of local business leaders.

According to local lore, the town's historical origins are incidental—since no logical reason for settlement existed, it could have happened anywhere. This assumption ignores the discoveries and ambitions of

John Neely Bryan. When Bryan left Van Buren, Arkansas, in 1840, to establish a trading post on the upper Trinity River in North Central Texas, he was attracted to a site on the east bank of the river that later became Dallas's central business district. His was *not* a random choice. The Republic of Texas had already provided funds for a military highway from Austin to the Red River to cross the Trinity near the convergence of its three forks. There the width of the river valley narrowed from five miles to one, and gummy mud river banks—almost impossible to negotiate with heavy oxcarts—gave way to a limestone ridge that provided a natural river crossing. Col. William Cooke began his survey of Preston Road, as the highway was known, a year before Bryan built his first cabin in 1841. Bryan's ability to persuade three families to move to the site from Bird's Fort, a Texas Ranger stockade to the northwest, and the absence of hostile Indians convinced him to abandon his career as a frontier trader in favor of speculating on his 640-acre tract of land. By the end of 1842, other settlers had taken up residence in the new town, which was already called Dallas.[13]

Like Dallas County, organized in 1846, the town could have been named for George Mifflin Dallas, a Pennsylvanian elected vice president in 1844 partly on the issue of Texas annexation. But the town was called Dallas before the election campaign, and the future vice president had a brother who, as a naval commander, also had a well-known name. To further complicate the question, John Neely Bryan had a friend named Joseph Dallas who moved to the region from Washington County, Arkansas, and settled at Cedar Springs, three miles north of Bryan's settlement.[14] The uncertainty surrounding the town's name is indicative of both Dallas residents' ambivalence toward the past and the recent nature of local interest in the city's historical identity. For whomever Dallas the city was named, the town site was surveyed and platted by 1846. Bryan became the first postmaster, dividing his time between running a post office and store from his home, waging a campaign to have Dallas named county seat, and encouraging settlement in the new town. Dallas defeated Hord's Ridge (now Oak Cliff) in an 1852 election for county seat, and two years later Bryan sold his holdings in town to Alexander Cockrell for $7,000.

A native of Kentucky, Cockrell was an early migrant to Hord's Ridge, a settlement on the west bank of the Trinity, established in 1845 by Judge William Hord. Cockrell manufactured bricks and branched into the lumber business. His materials supplied early settlers on both sides of the river. Cockrell operated a ferry across the Trinity that linked Hord's Ridge and Dallas, and he was a principal investor in the first bridge spanning the river.

From its origins as a river crossing strategically placed along a proposed military highway, early Dallas benefited from the rapid settlement of much of its hinterland. In the United States during the 1840s, those who settled the frontier obtained land from the public domain at a minimum of $1.25 per acre or purchased it from prior owners. In the Republic of Texas, frontier land was almost free—as it had been since Stephen F. Austin first opened the country to white settlers from the United States. The Republic's last act donating land to settlers expired in 1842. Between 1842 and 1854, the period during which Dallas emerged as a county seat, most migrants to Texas had to purchase land, usually from speculators.[15] The only areas in which land remained free were the established empresario reserves—the Republic's reserves of the 1840s stemming from Austin's original contract with Mexico and the State Colonization Law of 1825. Just as the settlements of East Texas began to expand onto the blackland prairies, Texas granted William S. Peters and his associates from Louisville, Kentucky, approximately 16,000 square miles in the region of the upper Trinity. In 1841 they established the Texan Emigration and Land Company to organize settlement of what became known as the Peters Colony. Texas law prohibited an empresario from settling a colony with migrants from other parts of the state, so Peters's reserve attracted small farmers from areas to the north and east—mostly without slaves and many from free and border states. This relatively homogeneous introduction of Peters Colony settlers so close to early Dallas had a tremendous impact on the region. Committed to family farming, the Peters colonists came largely from the Ohio River valley and were slightly more prosperous than other Texas migrants. The majority grew grains and vegetables. Those growing cotton did not do so on the same scale as the plantation owners of South Texas. Many farm families granted 640 acres of free land near Dallas, and therefore possessing cash reserves, developed an interest in trade.[16] The colonists were able to support a comparatively large artisan and commercial class and attracted teachers, lawyers, doctors, and ministers virtually from the beginning of settlement.[17]

Another impetus for Dallas's rapid rise as the region's dominant town was the settlement of La Reunion, established four miles west of

Dallas. The first French settlers of La Reunion arrived in 1854 via New Orleans, and the main body of the French, Swiss, and Belgian colony arrived from Houston with a caravan of oxcarts the next year. Its leader, Victor Considerant, a disciple of the French socialist Francois Marie Charles Fourier, sought to establish a cooperative community.[18] Considerant, exiled by Napoleon III for protesting French military adventures in Italy, believed the acquisitive nature of human beings could be regulated through their organization into self-supporting groups of 1,600 individuals. Although the utopian settlements were to be primarily agricultural and cooperative, Considerant did not abolish private ownership of property. La Reunion was to be the first of many such cooperatives in Texas. All members of the community, including women, enjoyed equal political rights and the opportunity to achieve economic independence.

Initial encounters between La Reunion colonists and citizens of Dallas took place in the colony's cooperative store. La Reunion's merchants carried an unusual selection of goods, many far superior to what was available in Dallas. The cooperative store quickly developed a clientele among Texans as well as colonists. Dallas residents regarded the foreigners with more curiosity than apprehension. In spite of initial concern that parties with music might desecrate the Sabbath, many regularly accepted invitations to the Europeans' Sunday afternoon and evening dances.

Eventually numbering almost 350 persons, the La Reunion colony contained highly educated professionals as well as scientists, artists, writers, musicians, artisans, and naturalists. La Reunion, however, lacked the agricultural expertise to ensure success under primitive and strange conditions. Considerant purchased a beautiful tract on a limestone bluff that reminded him of vineyard country in France but was, in fact, the worst agricultural land in Dallas County. After a three-year struggle, the immigrants disbanded La Reunion and many of the colony's leaders, including Considerant, returned to France. Most of the European settlers remained, however, and by 1860, 160 La Reunion colonists lived in Dallas. Others purchased farms in Dallas County, and one group began a new settlement six miles south of La Reunion on Mountain Creek.

The infusion of so many skilled Europeans into a commercial crossroads serving relatively prosperous farmers further distinguished Dallas, a town of not quite 2,000 in 1860, from county seats to the north, south, and east.[19] The colonists were quickly integrated into community life—one served as the city's mayor. Another former La Reunion resident founded Dallas's first brewery. Julien Reverchon, who came to La Reunion in his teens, and Jacob Boll, who left Switzerland to join his family after it moved to Dallas, won international acclaim as naturalists. Portrait artists, piano tuners, cigar makers, jewelers, dancing masters, and the like added their talents to those of carpenters, stone masons, shoemakers, and immigrants possessing skills more practical in a frontier town to supply goods and luxury items to area farmers who, fortuitously, could afford them.

While serving as a supply center for the Confederate army west of the Mississippi River, Dallas's location shielded the town from destruction during the Civil War. The wartime demand for wheat, saddlery, and leather goods enabled residents to rebuild quickly after an 1860 fire destroyed most of the business district. As southern migrants poured into Texas after the war, Dallas County's thriving wheatlands and the city that served them became, for many, the destination of choice.

Bryan's locating the town at a natural river crossing along what would become a major thoroughfare ensured that all traffic between the United States and the heavily populated central portions of Texas would pass through its limits.[20] Unlike Fort Worth, which was located at the very edge of settlement, Dallas could rely upon a large, fertile hinterland spreading out in three directions. The blackland prairies surrounding the city to the north, south, and east make up a considerable portion of the narrow arc of easily plowed land that extends northeast from the Rio Grande to the Red River. Known as the Blackland Belt, the upper reaches of this most heavily populated section of the state were ideally suited to wheat production. Dallas began as a typical commercial city—dependent on the products of its region. The timing of its emergence coincided with that of many inland areas of the South and West. Geographical considerations, the financial resources of Peters Colony settlers who paid very little for their land, and the presence of a large number of skilled artisans provided early Dallas not only with ample reason to exist but also with an impetus for growth.

The new elite that founded the Dallas Citizens Council in the 1930s clearly enjoyed the national recognition it received from the *Fortune* article and incorporated McCombs's version of Dallas's development. The myth of Dallas as the product of local businessmen's ability to "sell" others on an indistinguishable piece of the prairie undergirded the Citizens Council's argument that the business community could represent the interests of all citizens. As recently as the early 1980s, advertising campaigns linked what was good for local business with prosperity for the city as a whole.[21] The origin myth and a lack of historical inquiry still characterize public discourse in Dallas. Together, they obscure both the contentiousness of civic affairs in the late nineteenth and early twentieth centuries and the variety of actors who built the city.[22]

II

The character of migration to the Dallas area shifted somewhat after the end of Peters Colony settlement. Between 1860 and 1880, the majority of new settlers came from Missouri, Tennessee, and Arkansas. They were joined by migrants from Louisiana, East Texas, and other southern states where lives had been disrupted by the Civil War. Most remained small-scale farmers or practiced trades in town. Unlike the Peters Colony settlers, however, southern migrants who either rented land near Dallas or purchased their own farms planted cotton instead of wheat.

The decades following the Civil War transformed Dallas from a thriving crossroads marketplace of 2,000 to the largest city in North Texas, second only to Houston in the state (see Table 1).[23] Although all of Texas experienced rapid growth (a statewide increase of just under 500 percent between 1861 and 1878), the population of Dallas County and the counties immediately surrounding it leaped by almost 1,000 percent during the same period. No other section of the state experienced growth at this rate. During the 1872–1875 triennium, which included the year of the panic, the increases in Dallas and surrounding counties were enough to offset declines in other parts of Texas and created a pattern of slight increase statewide.[24]

Dallas was insulated from the hard times because of its mixed economy and acquisition of two railroads, the Houston & Texas Central in 1872 and the Texas & Pacific the following year. During the decade of the 1870s, the city's population jumped from 3,000 to 10,358.[25] Aside

TABLE 1
DALLAS POPULATION, 1880–1940

CENSUS	POPULATION
1880	10,358
1890	38,067
1900	42,638
1910	92,104
1920	158,976
1930	260,475
1940	294,734

Source: U.S. Census Bureau

from processing wheat and cotton, the town possessed important lumber planing, publishing, and saddlery industries.[26] Dallas's production of $100,000 worth of saddles and harnesses in 1880 was roughly double that of Austin, its nearest Texas competitor.[27] The city became a regional distribution center for farm equipment, wagons, and plows as the northern-most Texas outfitting point along the Shawnee Trail. The most important Dallas County industries (in order of dollar value of goods produced) were grain milling, lumber planing, publishing, saddlery and harness making, cigars and cigarette making, foundries and machine shops, brick and tile factories, production of tin, copper, and sheet-iron ware, bakery products, the manufacture of ice, carriage and wagon building, and confectionery making. Within Texas, the total industrial output for Dallas County in 1880 trailed only that of Galveston.[28]

Like other southern and southwestern cities, early commercial Dallas was a violent place.[29] In addition to farm families, artisans, and small business owners, the city attracted a floating population of buffalo hunters, trappers, and day laborers and some of the legendary figures of the West. John B. ("Doc") Holliday practiced dentistry, Belle Starr sang in a local dance hall and supposedly fenced stolen horses from her livery stable, Sam Bass robbed trains until he was killed by the Texas

Rangers, and Frank James (Jesse's brother) worked as a salesman at Sanger Brothers.[30] Free drinks to customers from tin cups at whiskey barrels in the town's stores proved to be, necessarily, a short-lived custom. Benjamin Long, a veteran of the La Reunion colony and two-term Dallas mayor, was shot and killed in a saloon after confronting a man who refused to pay for a beer.[31] Merchants and settlers combined to subdue the most troublesome of the early drinking establishments, brothels, and gambling houses, but, as late as 1880, the city of barely 10,000 possessed fifty-two saloons.[32]

Dallas opened its first public school in 1883. Colored School No. 1 admitted students a year later. The influx of southern migrants reinforced national patterns of racial separation and limited educational as well as economic and social opportunities for the city's blacks (19 percent of the total population in 1880).[33]

A decade after the arrival of the railroads, Dallas possessed six flour mills, two grain elevators, and two cotton compresses as well as six banks, two foundries, and over seven hundred other commercial structures.[34] Between 1880 and 1890, assessed property values in Dallas jumped from just over $4,000,000 to more than $30,000,000.[35] Workers installed electric lights and telephone lines and paved Main and Elm streets with bois d'arc blocks. Traffic nearly strangled the congested downtown area. Busy streets were made even more dangerous by grade rail crossings. By 1886 six railroads operated in Dallas.[36] Building was haphazard and unregulated. Even public buildings had short life spans and, after an 1890 fire, the thirty-six-year-old county began construction of its sixth courthouse. "Old Red," as Dallas's courthouse is known locally, was constructed in traditional Romanesque style of red sandstone and granite. The structure, which recently celebrated its centennial, is one of a handful of nineteenth-century landmarks that have survived natural disasters, Dallas's leaders' preference for modern buildings, and the business district's continued expansion.[37]

In addition to the rapid construction of the physical city, Dallas residents sought to "catch up" with older American cities by imitating established forms of association. Many new migrants brought with them the Victorian penchant for establishing new organizations. Others simply founded local affiliates of groups active in their hometowns. Physicians organized the first Dallas County Medical Society in November of 1871, succeeded five years later by the Dallas County Medical and Surgical Association. County attorneys organized a Bar

Association in 1880 and claimed 150 members after just twelve years. Sports enthusiasts established an amateur baseball association in 1883. The city's upper and middle classes patterned social and literary clubs, musical societies, and charities after prestigious organizations in New York, Chicago, Boston, and Philadelphia and organized local affiliates of Masonic Orders, the Oddfellows, and the Red Cross. A combination of the transference of established cultural patterns and mimetic development characterized Dallas's social and cultural institutions well into the twentieth century.[38]

Although the majority of the frontier population attended evangelical protestant churches, Dallas residents had a variety of religious choices. In 1892, 511 members supported St. Matthew's Episcopal Cathedral downtown on Ervay Street. The city's more than 5,000 Catholics divided themselves between Sacred Heart and St. Patrick's, and the Jewish Temple Emanu-El, already seventeen years old in 1892, served 125 regular members. Organized in 1888, Emanu-El's Ladies Auxiliary attracted women from other synagogues and claimed 150 members.[39]

At the turn of the century, Dallas was a T-shaped city with a fairly even distribution of prosperous and working-class neighborhoods and separate shanty towns along flood plains inhabited by impoverished whites and blacks. The bar of the "T" included the business district and East Dallas (annexed in 1890) separated by a sparsely settled area dotted with the homes of prosperous businessmen, workers, and shopkeepers. This central area also contained one of several freedmen's districts. Neighborhoods south of the downtown area and Oak Cliff—across the Trinity River to the southwest—formed the "T's" stem (see Figure 1).[40]

The social register for 1895 lists approximately equal numbers of the city's elite south, north, and east of downtown and across the river in Oak Cliff. Many merchants, like Albert and Ben Linz, kept permanent residences downtown—in the Grand Windsor and Oriental hotels. Other prominent landholders and business leaders, including Col. Tom Kingsley, Wildy Gibbs, and J. L. A. Thomas, were long-time residents of the Oriental. The downtown residences of prosperous farmers strengthened ties to the city and especially to the business district. The proximity to downtown of The Cedars, an exclusive neighborhood immediately south of the business district, also stimulated contact between agriculturalists and local merchants.[41]

Since the State of Texas awarded Dallas its charter in 1856 (the orig-

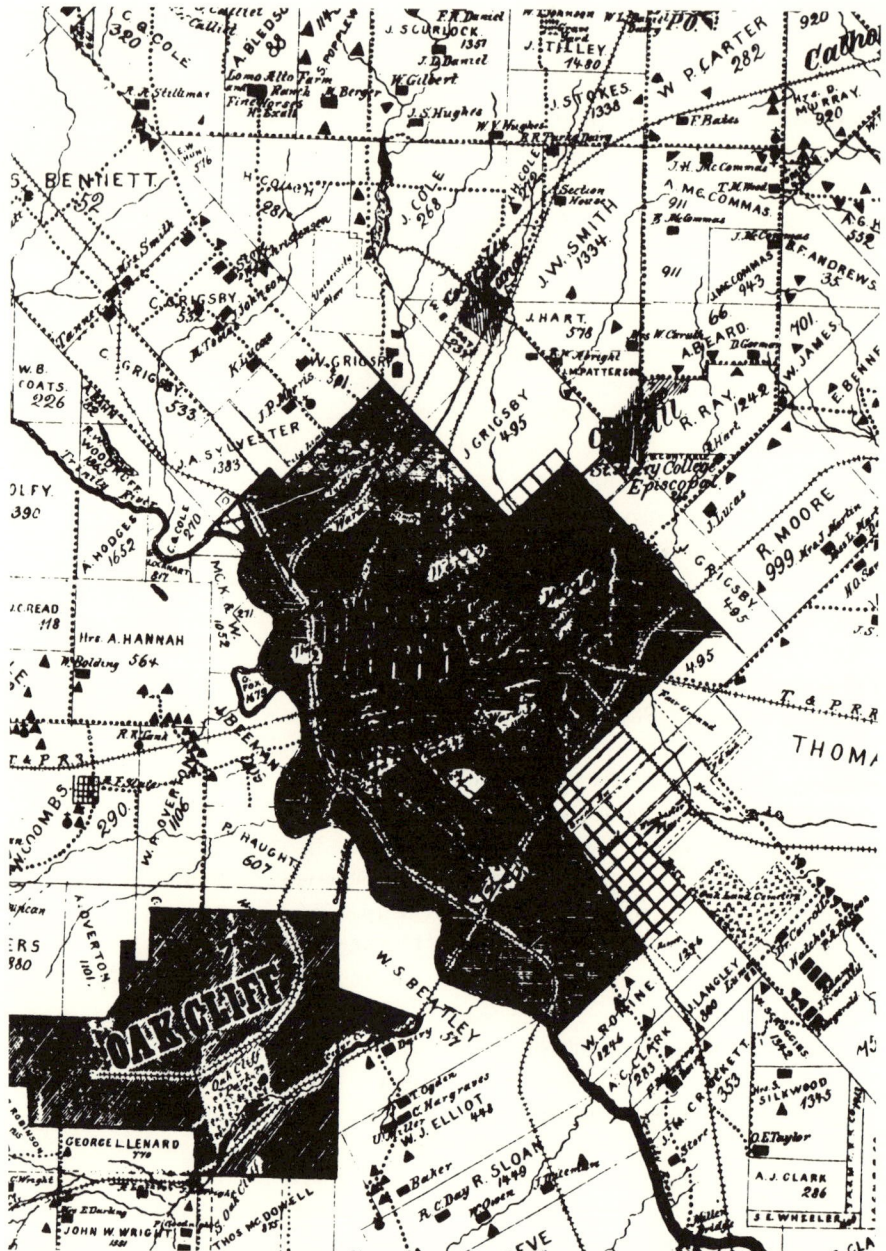

FIGURE 1: Dallas, East Dallas, and Oak Cliff (across the Trinity River to the Southwest) in 1900. The city extended approximately three miles from its center. From Sam Street's map of Dallas County, Texas. Courtesy of Texas/Dallas History and Archives Division, Dallas Public Library.

inal town charter was exchanged for a city charter in 1871), Dallas's independent and often unruly citizens were represented by a mayor and aldermen who served on a single council.[42] In 1880 two aldermen were elected from each of four wards and the mayor was elected at large. Over the next decade, the council grew to include the mayor and as many as twenty-four aldermen representing twelve wards. The number of city officials varied but generally included an elected marshal and tax assessor-collector and an appointed secretary, treasurer, attorney, engineer, and health officer.[43]

Perhaps not surprising in a commercial center catering to a vast agricultural hinterland, merchants and landowners figured disproportionately among the city's early leaders. No single interest group or class, however, could mount successful campaigns for civic improvements or establish public institutions without allies during Dallas's first eighty years. The three chapters that constitute Part One of this book analyze the agendas and activities of political groups and interests that vied for influence between 1880 and 1920. Together they provide "contribution histories" of Dallas clubwomen, populists, socialists, and trade unionists as well as a profile of the city's first commercial-civic elite.[44]

Male members of the elite established a series of local organizations dedicated to economic growth and ran for political office as Democrats in what was essentially a one-party state. Disputes among businessmen typically enlisted groups favoring increased municipal spending on a particular project against fiscal conservatives. "Organized womanhood"—often the wives, mothers, and daughters of prominent businessmen—sought to refine ostensibly laissez-faire capitalism through environmental reform and increased spending on cultural institutions and social services.[45] Through the Dallas Federation of Women's Clubs, female members of the elite exerted a powerful influence on civic affairs decades before passage of the suffrage amendment.

Between 1886 and 1917, Dallas Populists and socialists organized and maintained local chapters of national political parties. Dallas radicals emphasized cooperation, education, and the empowerment of producers. They sought to replace the prevailing economic system with policies designed to "restore" a fair balance between farmers and wage laborers and those whose livelihoods depended on the production of others. Although affiliated with national political parties, Dallas Populists and socialists functioned as local interest groups—moderating the elite's choice of candidates during their respective periods of intense activity rather than achieving consistent electoral victories. Despite their ultimate political failure, local radicals established significant and enduring urban institutions and broadened the spectrum of acceptable social, political, and economic discourse.

Dallas radicals joined local trade unionists to form the city's first Left-liberal coalitions. Although several champions of organized labor won state and local elections or were appointed to important municipal offices, Dallas unionists, like their radical allies, were unable to mount consistent political challenges to the candidates of the elite. Analyses of key strikes in 1898 and 1919 reveal both the influence of organized labor in Dallas and the limitations of a workers' movement dependent on notions of fairness shared by an aspiring middle class.

The second part of this book provides an analysis of why and how business leaders closed the door on dissent in Dallas between 1920 and 1940. The demands of local building tradesmen, the division of Dallas's middle and upper classes into camps favoring or opposing various reform and city planning measures, and the reemergence of the Ku Klux Klan made the years after World War I an especially unsettling time in Dallas. Middle-class professionals and their allies among the elite who challenged the prevailing view that growth depended on extreme fiscal restraint and minimal taxation found their relatively late blooming efforts to institutionalize social reform overshadowed by those of businessmen seeking changes in the structure of city government that would thwart the Klan's political ambitions. Reformlike reaction was perceived by influential members of the elite and by many Dallas voters as a serious threat to growth.

A new generation of leaders matured by the end of the 1920s convinced that civic coherence depended on the business community's ability to speak with a single voice. This new elite sought to "manage" the politics of competition and cooperation by ignoring those issues which fostered intraclass feuds and by promoting only those on which there was a general consensus among business leaders. Local tensions during the interwar years combined with national and international crises to make the notion of apolitical officials who would guard the interests of the entire city especially appealing to Dallas voters. During the 1930s, continued internecine feuding among members of the elite, renewed demands for fairness by local factory workers, and Dallas's financial obligations to the state's Centennial Exposition motivated the city's most powerful bankers, merchants, and utility heads to establish the Dallas Citizens Council, the forum through which they dominated civic affairs for the next forty years.

The hegemony of this group—its self-discipline, control of the local media, and repression or co-optation of challengers—and the lack of inquiry into the city's past have resulted in a view among both scholars and Dallas residents that the city has always been an "empire of consensus."[46] City building has rarely (if ever) been as simple as the city's origin myth and the rhetoric of the Dallas Citizens Council indicate. An awareness of, and appreciation for, the earlier politics of competition and cooperation could ease the way toward an urban environment in which dissent, conflict, and its resolution are perceived not as threats to civic coherence but as constructive signs of a more inclusive public life.

Part One

tions forming short-lived, single-issue coalitions whose success depended upon the support of workers, shopkeepers, and prominent women.

Female members of prosperous Dallas families also took an active role in city building and turned their fin de siècle social and literary clubs into vehicles for urban reform. Clubwomen moderated their fathers', husbands', and sons' visions of largely unrestricted growth by virtue of their status within the upper-middle or upper classes and through effective organizing and manipulation of public opinion.

A Dallas club member and reform advocate wrote in 1906, "Men have shut one eye and squinted so hard at commercial interest with the other, they see little else."[3] Elite southern women have been characterized as exercising "a sort of peripheral vision"—calling attention to early signs of urban decay that could shatter the vision of commercial progress that motivated elite men.[4] The commitment of prominent Dallas women was based on a combination of altruism and the belief that social services were requisite amenities of a progressive urban center. Disfranchised and excluded from many commercial ventures, Dallas women used both organizations and their influence within families to guide the city's growth. In addition to their work for suffrage, Dallas clubwomen between 1900 and 1920 organized successful campaigns for a public library, juvenile courts, probation officers, parks and playgrounds, a jail matron, and water-treatment facilities.

Male members of the Dallas elite, despite their common plan to build a great city, shared the individualist ethos at the core of an American middle-class system of values that developed during the nineteenth century.[5] Their fortunes were almost all relatively new. Most of the men who became prominent by virtue of their wealth and interest in civic affairs retained many of the attitudes of the farm families and shopkeepers who raised them. They cohered as a civic group while limiting social relations almost exclusively to family members and those with whom they attended church. Lynn Lawther described the relationships his father, a Dallas businessman and mayor, maintained with bankers and utility-company executives as politically based and bolstered by similar ideas about municipal spending. The younger Lawther recalled that "there was very, very little social mingling with these people. . . . In saying that, why, it sounds like maybe there was some reason that we weren't friendly people. But [there was] very little mingling, socializing in the homes."[6]

It would take Dallas's commercial-civic elite several generations to transform itself from a cadre of independent businessmen into a self-perpetuating upper class through the convergence of relevant experience and familial bonds. Late-nineteenth- and early-twentieth-century businessmen displayed a willingness to cooperate when Dallas competed with its rivals for railroads, newspapers, and a federal reserve bank. At home, however, civic aggressiveness was combined with a tendency to split into factions that limited their dominance of public affairs. In contrast, prominent Dallas women joined forces through their clubs and exerted a great deal of civic influence despite limitations imposed by traditional gender roles and their lack of experience in the public realm.

During the final decades of the nineteenth century and the first decades of the twentieth, the business community's lack of unity and clubwomen's early interest in social reform engendered an urban politics in which local radicals, workers, and middle-class reformers proved to be both competitors and necessary allies of the Dallas elite.

I

In 1870 the Houston & Texas Central railroad extended to Corsicana (Navarro County). Officials publicized plans for a route north to McKinney (Collin County) that would bypass Dallas. The city's commercial-civic elite emerged when Dallas boosters organized to raise $5,000 in cash and secure three miles of right-of-way north and south of Main Street to persuade the railroad to alter the line. Dallas voters overwhelmingly approved the inducements (167 to 11) after William H. Gaston donated 115 acres of his 400-acre tract east of the city to the railroad.[7] In July 1872 the first locomotive arrived at a depot in East Dallas. An estimated 5,000 people from throughout the county (the city's population was just over 3,000 at the time) witnessed the event.[8] East Dallas, the new community surrounding the frame depot, quickly developed into a railroad town.

At almost the same time, the state legislature approved the Texas & Pacific railroad's proposed line from El Paso to Memphis. After discussions with the group that attracted the Houston & Texas Central, State Representative John W. Lane, a former Dallas mayor and copublisher of the city's *Herald*, added a clause requiring the railroad, originally routed farther to the south, to cross the Trinity no more than a mile from Browder Springs—a site one mile south of downtown Dallas whose name would not attract the attention of rival legislators. The Texas & Pacific received a $100,000 bonus in bonds, a right-of-way through the center of the business district, and twenty-five more acres of Gaston's East Dallas land to extend the line into town. Dallas voters approved the inducements by a vote of 192 to 0, reflecting the local consensus on the benefits of urban growth.[9] Dallas became the terminus of two railways in February 1873—motivating merchants such as E. M. Kahn and the Sanger brothers who had followed the railroad north from Houston to establish dry goods and clothing houses. Dallas reaped unexpected benefits when the national financial crisis that same year halted the extension of the Texas & Pacific line to Fort Worth.[10]

The sixty-two Dallas businessmen who put up money to acquire the railroads established the Board of Trade, Dallas's first commercial organization, in 1874. For twenty years—until Dallas merchants organized the Commercial Club, forerunner of the present Chamber of Commerce—the Board of Trade supported candidates for municipal and county offices who were committed to conservative fiscal policies and the active solicitation of investment capital. Although overshadowed by businessmen and their organizations, prominent Dallas attorneys, physicians, and a few clergymen also took active roles in civic affairs.[11]

As was the case in New South cities such as Atlanta and Nashville, Dallas's commercial-civic leaders in the 1870s and 1880s had survived but not escaped the Civil War.[12] William L. Cabell, a former Confederate general, established what would become a family tradition when he was elected mayor in 1874. He served two more terms (beginning in 1877 and 1883) before retiring from public life. Cabell's oldest son, Benjamin E., followed his father's example and served as mayor between 1900 and 1904. Highly visible contemporaries of the elder Cabell, all Confederate veterans active in public life after 1872, included county tax collector and real-estate developer W. H. Prather, Sheriff James E. Barkley and Deputy Sheriff Charles H. Nichols, County Prosecutor John T. Ault, Justice of the Peace T. G. T. Kendall, District Judge George N. Aldredge, attorney Robert E. Cowart, and William Henry Gaston, the "boy captain" of Hood's Texas Brigade, who served both the town of East Dallas and the city as treasurer and was associated with thirteen local banks.[13]

Col. C. C. Slaughter, a cattleman and banker who lived in Dallas from 1874 to 1919, established the National Beef Producers' and Consumers' Association. Slaughter's ownership of over one million acres of ranchland made him the largest individual taxpayer in the state.[14] In addition to Slaughter, bankers J. T. Trezevant, William Edgar Hughes, and John Nicholas Simpson, merchants Isaac, Lehman, and Philip Sanger, and George Marcus Swink, who installed the city's first street railway, were all Confederate veterans.[15]

Like the Sanger brothers, who had immigrated to Galveston before the Civil War, many of the merchants who followed the railroads to Dallas and became part of the city's early commercial-civic elite were German Jews. Although Jews never comprised 5 percent of the city's population, Dallas elected five Jewish aldermen, all of them merchants, between 1873 and 1905.[16]

This mix of southerners, migrants from border states, European immigrants, and original Peters Colony and La Reunion settlers cooperated to lure capital and businesses to Dallas in much the same way that they attracted the railroads. Led by J. T. Trezevant, the Board of Trade courted George Bannerman Dealey in 1882 as he scouted locations for a North Texas branch of the forty-year-old *Galveston News*. The Galveston paper was Texas's oldest and most prestigious daily newspaper, and its statewide distribution network appealed to Dallas merchants who would advertise in the new North Texas affiliate. Fifty businessmen offered to purchase $25,000 of stock in the Galveston paper's parent company if Dealey convinced his employers to locate the paper in Dallas. Throughout the 1880s, St. Louis papers were popular in Dallas and provided the primary competition for the *News*'s brand of "metropolitan journalism"—ostensibly impersonal reporting, editorial independence from advertisers, and "nonpartisan" political coverage. The appeal of St. Louis papers was limited, however, because they arrived in Dallas by rail one day after publication. Dealey correctly determined that a same-day paper could win the market and located the operation, of which he was named business manager, in Dallas.[17] The *Morning News* maintained close ties with the business community and routinely received accusations from the city's many weekly and monthly papers that it served only as a mouthpiece of the men who brought it to Dallas.[18]

Like commercial-civic elites across America, Dallas leaders used annexation as a means of raising additional revenue (without raising taxes) and increasing the property values of land held for speculation.

They frequently compared municipal governments of satellite communities to small business organizations. The latter, according to the rhetoric of the era, never operated as efficiently as larger corporations and would benefit from consolidation. Ironically, East Dallas, the first major town annexed by Dallas, defied the businessmen's characterization of community government as inefficient. Containing more than 1,400 acres (an area larger than that of Dallas itself) and an estimated population of 6,000 when annexation was finalized in 1890, East Dallas possessed a sanitary water system and a $15,000 brick school building. The location of the State Fairgrounds in East Dallas ensured additional customers for neighborhood merchants, who provided a variety of goods and services. East Dallas mayor George W. Crutcher, treasurer William H. Gaston, and alderman Horatio Nelson Haskell, all of whom were Dallas bankers who lived in East Dallas and held land for speculation, favored annexation and persuaded the town council to make inquiries regarding the city's position on the issue. Not surprisingly, Dallas was eager to expand. The state constitution of 1876 allowed cities to extend their limits "whenever a majority of the qualified electors" of a territory indicated that they supported annexation. Under this ambiguous statute, new boundaries could be effected by an act of the legislature; no election giving the voters in the city or in the area to be annexed a direct voice was required.[19]

In the spring of 1889, the legislature passed a bill that revoked East Dallas's charter and made it part of the larger city. East Dallas leaders negotiated measures that would ensure them a number of aldermen equal to one-fourth of the Dallas council and relief from Dallas's bonded debt. The area also received a brick fire station, better police protection, and Dallas's promise to pave several major streets. Although East Dallas was a bastion of Populist and labor voters—its "Bloody First Ward" was said to regularly deliver the votes of more than 100 railroad men—working-class residents were pleased with the expanded services and did not oppose the actions of their council. After the legislature approved the bill, Crutcher and most of his aldermen were returned to office until annexation went into effect. East Dallas continued to reelect many of the same aldermen over the next decade.[20]

The aggressiveness of Dallas civic leaders and their allies in East Dallas aroused suspicion in Oak Cliff, across the Trinity to the southwest. The community voted to incorporate in 1890, primarily to discourage annexation attempts by Dallas. Ten years later, Oak Cliff residents voted decisively against a merger. Oak Cliff overextended itself in the first years of the twentieth century, forcing the payment of teachers in city scrip and leading popular mayor Rufus Porter to conclude that annexation was preferable to civic instability. Opponents of annexation countered Dallas's promises of financial security with concern that Oak Cliff would lose its ability to prohibit the sale of liquor and that Dallas's stock law would hurt working-class families who kept farm animals on small plots of land (Dallas residents were required to pen large domestic animals at all times, while in Oak Cliff animals could forage on undeveloped land during the day). Due largely to assurances that Oak Cliff would remain "dry" and that the stock law would not be enforced south of the river, a measure to disincorporate (a move that by this time generally preceded annexation) carried by a narrow margin in 1903.[21] Some Oak Cliff officials disavowed the election and refused to surrender city records to Dallas. When the legislature approved disincorporation and amended Dallas's charter to include Oak Cliff, the recalcitrant officials challenged the state's authority in the matter. The Texas Supreme Court ruled in favor of the legislature and Dallas the following year.[22]

On several occasions, the city tried to annex Highland Park, an exclusive residential town on high ground developed by John S. Armstrong and his son-in-law Hugh E. Prather. Armstrong, a Dallas banker and grocer, sold his meat-packing business in 1906 to Swift & Company of Chicago and used the money to purchase four adjoining tracts of land five miles north of the business district. Following a national trend and catering to the tastes and fears of an urban elite seeking relief from crowded downtown neighborhoods, Armstrong and Prather hired Wilbur David Cook, the landscape architect who designed Beverly Hills, to lay out the town with an emphasis on parks and greenbelts. The new town's deed restrictions ensured a homogeneous residential neighborhood twenty-two years before Dallas passed its first zoning ordinance. Highland Park's early advertising slogans, "Beyond the City's Dust and Smoke" and "It's Ten Degrees Cooler in Highland Park," reflect its attractiveness to Dallas's elite.[23]

The migration of many prominent families to Highland Park divided the Dallas business community—pitting those who wanted to annex the town against Highland Park residents, who enjoyed the amenities of the city but shared few of its problems. In 1917, 1925, and 1927

Dallas added amendments to its city charter that authorized the annexation of Highland Park, but the suburb's residents consistently voted to remain a separate town (by 1917, Dallas had acquired Home Rule, and the state's annexation law provided residents of incorporated towns a direct voice in matters of annexation and consolidation).[24] Members of the elite who favored the annexation of Highland Park combined civic boosterism and a local brand of manifest destiny. The Dallas *Democrat*'s editor, a six-term state senator, proclaimed, "Every suburb that is naturally a part of Dallas should be taken in."[25] Justin Kimball asserted that Highland Park residents had a "moral obligation" to join Dallas since they enjoyed the amenities of the city and depended on its sewage system.[26]

In the cases of East Dallas and Oak Cliff, Dallas prevailed by responding to concerns expressed by residents opposed to becoming part of the larger city. Highland Park's wealthy residents did not require outside assistance to keep their town solvent and could afford to provide their own city services or purchase them from Dallas. The 1927 amendment to the Dallas charter was dropped in 1968, and Highland Park remains an independent town.

As cities became increasingly associated with social problems and moral evils, the tranquillity offered by deed-restricted suburbs such as Highland Park attracted more and more urban residents with the means to move away from neighborhoods near downtown. Throughout the United States in the early twentieth century, changes in incorporation and annexation laws enabled middle- and upper-income suburbs to maintain their independence.[27] As long as the city's commercial life remained concentrated in the business district, however, residents of Highland Park retained a vital interest in Dallas's expansion and development. In this context, the presence of a prestigious, independent suburb such as Highland Park was not a threat but an irritating reminder of divisions within the elite.

In early 1906 the *Dallas Morning News* published the first of a series of calls for the city to exchange its ward-based council of aldermen for a commission government patterned on the one Galveston had adopted after a hurricane devastated the island city in 1900. Businessmen in favor of the commission plan immediately organized the Citizens Association.[28] Under the Galveston plan, a mayor and four commissioners were elected at large, with the mayor serving as the executive officer while individual commissioners were responsible for finance and revenue, waterworks and sewage, streets and public property, and fire and police. That plan promised to provide leadership based on business principles and appealed to a variety of Dallas residents who associated the corporate model with efficiency and modernity. Voters authorized a city commission by a two-to-one margin in April 1906.[29]

Majorities in favor of structural reform in nine out of ten Dallas wards could easily obscure the politics of competition and cooperation that resulted in such a decisive victory for the new charter. The Dallas Trades Assembly had opposed the commission plan because at-large elections would favor candidates with greater financial resources and mainstream appeal at the expense of those with strong backing only in a particular neighborhood or community. Dallas unionists had long associated at-large elections with property qualifications and poll taxes and demanded government by the people "and not by an official aristocracy."[30] Labor proposed the addition of direct democracy devices such as initiative, referendum, and recall to any new charter to ensure that commissioners remained accountable to the people. The *Morning News* had objected to these tools of popular democracy, calling them "fads." Sensing a backlash against structural reform, however, commission backers opened the convention that drafted the new charter to neighborhood representatives (the Texas legislature granted city charters which were generally drafted locally). Workers from the area surrounding the South Dallas cotton mill sent a socialist newspaper editor who acted as a proxy for organized labor and argued successfully for the inclusion of initiative, referendum, and recall provisions. Although the Trades Assembly continued to publicly oppose the new charter, the Dallas document—a precedent for what later became known nationally as the Des Moines plan—was a product of compromise and much more palatable to the city's workers than the Galveston plan.[31]

The Dallas charter of 1907 gave the mayor the power to appoint all city officers, although the city auditor was nominated by the presidents of major banks. The mayor possessed the authority to veto ordinances passed by the commission, but the veto could be overridden by the votes of three commissioners. The charter granted the city broad powers in the areas of revenue generation for improvements, taxation, building regulations, and police powers. The city could award franchises for the provision of natural gas and electricity, telephone and street-railway systems, and street maintenance. One of the few major restrictions on the city was a mandate that waterworks be municipally owned and operated.[32]

Debates over city planning and the expenditure of municipal funds proved to be more divisive than the new city charter or the recurring schemes to annex Highland Park. The Trinity River's record-setting flood in 1908 caused damage estimated at $2 million and forced the evacuation of 2,000 people. Dallas remained in darkness for three nights, and a malaria epidemic followed the obstruction of the city's water supply. In the wake of the disaster, the *Morning News* ran a series of articles highlighting the work of J. Horace McFarland and the American Civic Association and exposing Dallas's lack of planning. The *News*'s G. B. Dealey and Chamber of Commerce officials L. O. Daniel and John R. Babcock formed the Dallas City Plan and Improvement League (CPIL), and that body persuaded the mayor and city commissioners to hire Kansas City and St. Louis landscape architect George E. Kessler to develop Dallas's first city plan.[33]

The scope of Kessler's work, published in 1912, staggered those city leaders who focused their attention exclusively on easing downtown street congestion and developing the potentially rich Trinity bottomlands. Despite the influence of local proponents of Progressive Era reforms and the nationwide trend toward planning, a faction of the elite—including some who favored city planning as an ideal—objected to specific measures that would regulate business development or significantly affect local tax rates. Kessler, for example, proposed eliminating from downtown the tracks of the Texas & Pacific, but the railroad and merchants with shops or warehouses along its route delayed relocation of the tracks for more than a decade.[34]

In the context of a national movement to create a "city beautiful," Kessler's plan included fountain-filled parks and a downtown free from the incessant danger and noise of trains.[35] The plan also reflected Kessler's awareness of critics of the city beautiful. Ultimately, he blended aesthetic ideals with concerns for sanitation, recreation, and housing more characteristic of the newer "city practical."[36] Significantly, Kessler responded to Dallas's needs as perceived by the commercial-civic elite. He called for a network of continuous boulevards and parkways to link the important park lands already owned by the city. According to the planner, "Reaching through from the business section to all the residence districts, these lines will establish new bases for development and will enable the residents in the older sections to materially better the physical conditions of properties through which the boulevards pass, and by means of these improvements to hold and often to re-create land values."[37] With its generous inclusion of greenbelts, the Kessler plan appealed to women's clubs and those interested in reform as well as to speculators who owned land in older neighborhoods and downtown merchants whose businesses did not front alongside the railroads.[38]

Kessler lamented the "unhappy result of the individual land speculator's planning of cities"—the lack of continuity, narrow streets, long blocks, sidewalk awnings, advertisements, and other obstructions. He concluded that a history of loosely regulated development gave Dallas "a measure of village appearance, unattractive and immature."[39] Most civic leaders, however, concentrated on aspects of Kessler's plan that promised quick gains for downtown businesses. Aesthetic and environmental proposals were often ignored.

Unlike removal of the Texas & Pacific's tracks and the proposed system of interconnected greenbelts, Kessler's street-widening plans and call for consolidation of passenger rail traffic in a central terminal appealed to virtually all Dallas business leaders. Construction began almost immediately on streets in the business district, and the new Union Station opened in 1916. Consultation with Dealey and Dallas merchants made the planner aware of competition between businessmen in the eastern and western sections of downtown. In an attempt to forestall a major rift between powerful factions of the business community, Kessler sacrificed the city beautiful notion of clustering all public buildings around an impressive plaza. Nevertheless, the east end–west end rivalry continued. By 1918 a city planning writer for the *Morning News* declared the City Plan and Improvement League moribund. Soon afterward, Dealey, Charles L. Sanger, and others in the west end established the Dallas Property Owners' Association, and merchants from the eastern section of the business district formed the Central Improvement League. Members of both organizations charged that their rivals received a disproportionate share of municipal monies allocated to street improvements. In an unsuccessful attempt to offset the parochial concerns of Dallas businessmen, the Chamber of Commerce organized the Metropolitan Development Association (MDA), hired a resident engineer, and published a planning periodical. In 1920 the MDA and the two sectional groups cooperated to sponsor Kessler's return to Dallas.[40] The city's rapid growth and the ongoing need to balance factions within the business community led to the commercial-civic elite's developing a "justification for piecemeal improvements that verged on mere boosterism" and Kessler's concentration on traffic relief proposals.[41]

The divisive nature of aspects of the plan that involved large expenditures outside the business district also resulted in a sacrifice of the comprehensiveness associated with city beautiful planning. Controversial proposals were shelved because the factions that developed to promote or oppose them generally lacked enough support to carry the particular measure. Action was taken only when Kessler's recommendations were compatible with major tenets of the local elite's vision of growth. Proposals that regulated the physical expansion of the city were particularly suspect. For example, the planner's suggestion that developers of suburban properties be required to plat new streets to conform with those in the older city was rejected as a dangerous and unwarranted precedent despite the fact that the Dallas Real Estate Board agreed with the spirit of the proposal and ordered its members to secure the approval of the City Plan Commission before undertaking new development.[42] Kessler's proposed Mill Creek parkway failed because of civic leaders' disregard for aesthetic benefits and reluctance to allocate municipal monies for projects that did not immediately promote economic development.[43]

There was general agreement among Dallas businessmen as well as among clubwomen and other reform advocates that some of Kessler's park proposals should be implemented without delay. Like most of its rivals, Dallas had not done an adequate job of providing places of public leisure during the early-twentieth-century building boom.[44] The greenbelt along Turtle Creek, north of downtown, and Kessler Park in Oak Cliff were direct results of the 1911 plan. Yet, because of the cafeteria-style manner in which Dallas civic leaders implemented the plan, Kessler's vision of a larger network of parkways and boulevards connecting major parks and urban neighborhoods never materialized. A prominent advocate of the greenbelt and parkway along Mill Creek south of downtown and through Oak Cliff complained, "If Dallas had had the vision and courage . . . to carry out in greater measure the far reaching plans he [Kessler] submitted for her problems, our city would today be richer by millions,—and what is better still, it would be a happier and better place in which men, women, and little children might live and love and work."[45]

The conflict stimulated by Kessler's city plan is a prime example of the limits of consensus among the Dallas elite. The projects of clubwomen, demands of the city's first Left-liberal coalitions (led by Populists and trade unionists in the 1880s and 1890s and by local socialists and unionists from 1904 to 1917), and the social reforms of the Progressive Era stimulated debate and established an urban politics characterized by competition and cooperation. While most businessmen retained their faith in loosely regulated expansion, conservative fiscal policies, and civic boosterism to create a favorable business climate, municipal spending on social and cultural programs, parks, and adult education divided Dallas leaders.

Factions of the elite formed coalitions held together only by agreement on a single issue or set of issues. It was not uncommon for individuals who had opposed each other in past elections to find themselves aligned at a later date in support of new candidates and projects. Disputes were aired publicly through a wide assortment of daily and weekly newspapers (shortly after the turn of the century, Dallas possessed sixty periodicals, most of them newspapers).[46] Campaigns for city and county offices were often bitter, characterized by namecalling and political rhetoric. John Cochran, a six-term state representative who twice served as speaker of the Texas House, recalled, "Intellect clashed with intellect and the sparks flew."[47]

The 1919 campaign for mayor between independent incumbent Joe E. Lawther and Democrat Frank W. Wozencraft illustrates the contentious nature of municipal politics in early Dallas and the lack of harmony among business leaders. Lawther served one two-year term after defeating Citizens Association candidate Henry Lindsley in 1917. Lawther's administration was responsible for the elimination of grade-level railroad crossings in Oak Lawn, just north of downtown, and the construction of a scenic road around the city's White Rock Lake—built by prisoners from the Dallas jail.[48] Lawther maintained close professional ties to downtown bankers Nathan Adams and Fred Florence and theater magnate Karl Hoblitzelle. He was also associated with utility executives C. W. Hobson and J. F. Strickland, leading to frequent charges that his administration was a utility "machine."[49]

Joe Lawther represented the view held by the city's early commercial-civic elite that with the exception of public schools, municipal monies should be spent almost exclusively on physical amenities in the downtown area—and especially on street improvements. After almost four decades during which local radicals, trade unionists, and prominent women encouraged the city to take responsibility for the welfare of all of its residents, however, some elite businessmen began to advocate social as well as structural reform measures. Members of the Citizens Association, a group of businessmen organized by Lindsley to promote the commission form of government and maintained to draft reform-oriented candidates for local elections, were "anxious to dislodge what they considered an administration that was not good for Dallas."[50]

Lawther infuriated the Citizens Association by shelving most of the reform measures initiated by the city's first welfare department under his progressive predecessor. The vision of growth articulated by members of the Citizens Association—reflecting the influence of clubwomen, the city's social-work community, and the socialist-labor coalition—included free textbooks for schoolchildren and more parks, playgrounds, and public swimming pools.[51] Lindsley and his followers also responded to warnings that Dallas's slums, with high rates of tuberculosis, juvenile delinquency, and illiteracy, could no longer be ignored without jeopardizing the city's future.

The Citizens Association drafted as their mayoral candidate Capt. Frank Wozencraft, a young veteran of World War I. He was chosen for his ability as an orator and stature as a war hero, not for his experience. His only civilian job had been working for the telephone company, but Wozencraft's inexperience did not concern the Citizens Association. The group was more intent on defeating Lawther and re-establishing Lindsley's reform platform than on promoting new programs or ideas. Because Lindsley's group feared another defeat if the costs of social programs became an issue, Wozencraft ignored the rift within the business community over municipal spending and focused on Lawther's awarding of electric and interurban franchises to close political associates. Wozencraft's slogan, "No Man Can Serve Two Masters," suggested that Lawther's ties to utility magnates represented a conflict of interest.[52]

The city's newspapers were as divided in their support as was the elite. The *Dallas Dispatch* and *Dallas Democrat* supported the challenger Wozencraft, while the *Morning News* and *Times Herald* favored Lawther.[53] When asked whether his father was considered the "people's" candidate as opposed to that of the Establishment, Wozencraft's son recalled the elite's tendency to break into short-lived factions, diluting its political strength and requiring allies among the "people." The younger Wozencraft explained, "I'm not sure in those days that one drew a line between those two [the people and the Establishment] in exactly the way that one refers to it now, so the terms are apt to be misleading. . . . There were certainly some city leaders who were active in the coalition group and they asked him [the elder Wozencraft] to run." Wozencraft and those businessmen who supported his candidacy in 1919 were not radicals in the sense that they were "trying to upset the entire community," but rather a moderate faction of the commercial-civic elite, influenced by reform goals and opposed to the incumbent mayor's appropriation of utility franchises.[54]

Lawther lost the 1919 election despite receiving the support of the powerful banking contingent and the city's two daily newspapers. As had occurred six years earlier when reform-minded members of the Citizens Association joined the bankers in a successful campaign for a coveted branch of the Federal Reserve Bank, future projects would reunite the developers and merchants supporting Wozencraft and the financial and utility interests favoring Lawther.[55] Such was the nature of the variable and often fragile political coalitions formed by Dallas businessmen.

Between 1880 and 1920, the commercial-civic elite of Dallas was similar to that in many southern cities. While without a doubt the most influential group in town, business leaders did not agree on all matters of public policy and "did not have anything resembling absolute control over public opinion and the electorate."[56] Competing groups were able to force compromises and in many instances win significant concessions from those wielding political and economic power.

II

In 1904, Sarah P. Decker told women assembled at a national assembly of the General Federation of Women's Clubs, "Dante is dead. He has been dead for several centuries, and I think it is time that we dropped the study of his *Inferno* and turned our attention to our own."[57] Dallas women heard Mrs. Decker's message. Clubwomen appropriated speaking and organizational skills learned in benevolent societies, literary clubs, and choral groups and extended municipal beneficence with a vision of growth that included both dreams of urban grandeur and genuine concern for the poor. At the same time, Dallas women stretched convention by manipulating Victorian notions of elite women's traditional roles as homemakers and "ladies." Although few local women challenged the notion of instinctive female traits, they used traditional beliefs about women's talents and interests to address family issues and aspects of the urban environment associated with juvenile delinquency, poverty, and illiteracy. Through their advocacy of expanded social services and major municipal public health and sanitation programs, federated women's clubs became efficient reform vehicles in Dallas.

The "projects" sponsored by the city's elite women mirrored those of federated women's clubs in older urban areas and, although altruistic, were intended to hasten Dallas's maturation from frontier town to city. Early clubs like the Chautauqua Literary and Scientific Circle were local responses to well-known eastern organizations (the Chautauqua Club in New York spawned many such imitations across the country). Dallas women continued to depend on national organizations headquartered in older American cities to provide an ideological basis and goals for local club projects even after they turned their attention from the intellectual improvement of club members to major reform efforts.[58] The female members of Dallas's elite believed that programs established by women's clubs and expanded city services would remedy the social problems associated with urban capitalism. Club leaders viewed their accomplishments as concrete signs of the city's urbanity. Since their vision of growth was based on the local implementation of programs originated elsewhere, clubwomen valued efficient organizing and the ability to conduct effective publicity campaigns above creativity. In the process of developing these skills, club members made Dallas residents more aware of the uneven nature of urban growth, proposed solutions to social and civic problems, and gained unprecedented respect and influence while expanding public roles for women.[59]

Organized women's groups appeared in Dallas as early as 1870, when the Presbyterian Church established a Woman's Aid Society to institutionalize the nursing and undertaking services that women of all denominations provided on the frontier. The Ladies Hebrew Benevolent Association and the Methodist Woman's Missionary Society formed within the next five years for similar purposes.[60]

Women's literary clubs in Dallas date from the 1886 founding of the Shakespeare Club. Groups such as the Shakespeare Club, the Standard Club, the Chautauqua Literary and Scientific Circle, the Mathian Club, and the Schubert Choral Club were vital components in the education of women in early Dallas.[61] Clubs have been described as "colleges" for mature women. In Dallas before 1915, the year Southern Methodist University opened, clubs often provided the only post-secondary education even the most capable daughters of prominent families could secure. As leading members began to steer club activity away from exclusively cultural pursuits and toward reform efforts, the familiar structure of the clubs gave women "the self-assurance they needed to move beyond the narrow limits of the home, . . . encouraging them to pool their resources to found and fund new institutions."[62]

As early as 1898, May Dickson Exall and Isadore Minor Callaway united members of the city's five literary clubs to form the Dallas Federation of Women's Clubs. Reflecting its origin among literary club members, the federation chose as its first project the acquisition of a public library. Dallas women raised $12,000 by subscription from over 1,000 different donors. Andrew Carnegie offered $50,000 for a library building on the conditions that the city agree to provide a site and at least $5,000 yearly for maintenance. The first Dallas Public Library opened on Harwood Street in 1901.[63]

Emboldened by the success of the library campaign, leaders of Dallas's women's clubs reassessed their goals and determined to take a more active role in shaping the city. Isadore Minor Callaway often provided leadership. Born Isadore Sutherland in Michigan, Callaway wrote for the *Dallas Morning News* between 1893 and 1916 under the name "Pauline Periwinkle." In her capacity as the paper's first "woman's" editor, she coordinated news of club projects and sprinkled even the most innocuous columns with arguments in favor of suffrage and expanded roles for women. Her efforts were instrumental in easing the transition of elite women from exclusively home-centered roles into public extensions of woman's traditional sphere. Commenting on the gradual acceptance of local suffrage leaders, Callaway claimed in 1897 that "the rabid, unreasoning prejudice against the woman's movement has almost disappeared."[64] Noted child-welfare expert Dr. Henry S. Curtis called Callaway one of four outstanding women of her era (along with Dr. Anna Howard Shaw, Jane Addams, and Carrie Chapman Catt). Throughout her career in Dallas, Callaway maintained close contacts with national feminist leaders and in 1908 brought Dr. Shaw to the city to speak to a district meeting of the federated women's clubs.[65]

In addition to her work as a journalist, Isadore Minor Callaway was active in the Dallas Federation of Women's Clubs—serving as the organization's seventh president. With Mrs. Joseph E. Cockrell, she was a member of the Dallas City Plan and Improvement League, the group that brought George Kessler to Dallas. Both women worked for the implementation of Kessler's park proposals and were instrumental in securing support among business leaders for the greenbelt along Turtle Creek in North Dallas and Kessler Park in Oak Cliff. Callaway also organized a free-kindergarten movement before her death in 1916.[66]

Social reform began early in Dallas. In 1903, elite women led a campaign to establish juvenile courts and "a home for juvenile offenders not a reform school."[67] The Chicago Women's Club had been the force behind the nation's first juvenile courts in 1899.[68] Dallas clubwomen shared Chicago Judge Julian Mack's and Denver Judge Ben Lindsey's conviction that economic misery explained juvenile delinquency. The Federation of Women's Clubs proposed courts based on Lindsey's Denver model that "avoided the concept of punishment and set up a system to bring child offenders into an environment of good care and educational opportunities."[69] In addition, Dallas women concerned about the rough treatment and crude conditions facing female prisoners and children at the local jail persuaded authorities to hire a police matron in 1904.[70] Women's rights issues such as jail matrons, scholarships, and coeducation were among the primary interests of federated women's clubs in eastern cities at the turn of the century.[71]

Elite women were highly successful city builders. Many services now considered essential components of municipal government began as privately sponsored projects of women's clubs. A program's success usually led to quick incorporation by the city—often obscuring its origins with clubwomen. Local affiliates of national organizations and expanded services reassured clubwomen that Dallas was indeed a "civilized" place and not simply an overgrown frontier town. Local implementation of reform projects initiated in New York, Boston, Philadelphia, and Chicago gave comfort in much the same way as did traditional architectural forms. Despite the psychological benefits of reform work, the extension of city services was at times a painful process. Club members' goals and priorities often placed them in direct opposition to male members of their own families.

The refusal of civic leaders to pay for Dallas's first probation officer led the Federation of Women's Clubs to assume the expenses of office rent and a first year's salary for W. G. Leeman. In 1909, after a public campaign in which clubwomen were ridiculed for advocating municipal playgrounds, the federation used its own resources to support the city's first playground supervisor and two assistants. After two years of successful operation and the work of propagandist Charles Martin (hired to help offset the city's initial condemnation of the project), city officials assumed responsibility for playground maintenance and paid the salaries of playground personnel. The efforts of the Dallas Federation of Women's Clubs to ensure citizen safety during the first two decades of this century led to the city's enactment of a pure-food ordinance and the establishment of a Board of Health and a Fire Prevention Committee.[72]

In 1908, the year of the record flooding of the Trinity River and the ensuing epidemics of malaria and typhoid fever, the Federation of Women's Clubs initiated a pure-water movement. Two years later, an acute shortage led the city to impound the waters of White Rock Creek to provide Dallas, still dependent on the Trinity River, with a reserve water supply. Dallas residents had suffered polluted water for decades. During the 1890s, the Turtle Creek Pumping Station had switched from the West Fork of the Trinity to the Elm Fork because the city water supply was already contaminated. Dallas's early leaders had encouraged manufacturers of leather goods, mills processing buffalo hides, and manufacturers of cotton-ginning equipment to locate along the often sluggish river.[73] Clubwomen demanded water purification but found specific plans stalled by city officials who "were inclined to treat the matter of filtration lightly." In 1908, most local businessmen thought purification would not be necessary after the completion of the White Rock reservoir (still six years away), and they refused to support clean-water proposals.[74] Their reluctance to invest in sanitary systems even after major epidemics was typical of commercial-civic elites throughout the South.[75]

Dallas women refused to wait for the reservoir to be completed and, the year after the water shortage, stepped up demands for chemical purification. Members of the Federation of Women's Clubs spoke in neighborhoods and schools, and Isadore Minor Callaway used her column in the *Dallas Morning News* as a forum for the clean-water campaign. Pure-water advocates paired arguments that citizens, regardless of income, were entitled to clean water with warnings that repeated epidemics would give the city a reputation for being unhealthy and also would slow growth. Despite the commercial-civic elite's reluctance to support municipal projects that would increase tax rates, city government responded to public pressure and began chlorinating city water in 1911.[76]

The reform efforts and initiative taken by women's clubs to extend city services and create a more humane urban environment drew the praise of Dallas moderates. After World War I, men impressed with the time local women devoted to social services and the war effort worried that time spent on the Victory Loan Campaign might jeopardize the passage of the suffrage amendment. One Dallas man called for an organization of men to assist "in carrying this amendment for them." He estimated 1,400 Dallas women had participated in local war efforts and claimed that area men should come out in support of suffrage to "demonstrate their appreciation of the patriotic work women have been and are doing."[77] Dallas trade unions, whose vision of urban growth also included increased municipal responsibility for the poor and social services for working-class families, joined moderate Democrats in support of the suffrage amendment—their newspaper declaring American Federation of Labor (AFL) men "uncompromisingly committed" to voting rights for women.[78]

A large majority of Dallas voters supported the nineteenth constitutional amendment. Almost immediately, Dallas women ran for seats on the Board of Education and gained political representation at the state level. In April 1920, Lenore P. Hall won her bid for one of six seats on the school board, becoming the first woman to serve the city in an elected capacity since 1908 when voters elected Mrs. E. P. Turner and Mrs P. P. Tucker to the Board of Education. Hall was reelected to a seven-member board in 1922 and again in 1924, when Mrs. H. L. Peoples also was elected. Dallas women maintained a presence on the school board throughout the 1920s with the reelection of Mrs. Peoples to a second term in 1927 and, in that same year, the election of newcomer Mrs. W. P. Zumwalt. At the state level, Edith E. Wilmans served in the legislature between 1922 and 1924 as one of five representatives from Dallas County.[79]

Dallas women gained a new measure of respect through their club work in the first two decades of the twentieth century. Their success in extending city services relaxed traditional attitudes barring women from participation in public life. Respect and tolerance were, however, limited. With the remarkable exception of State Representative Wilmans, Dallas women were active in areas perceived as logical extensions of woman's traditional sphere—education, concern for juvenile delinquents, playgrounds, etc. The prominent role of women in urban movements was made more palatable by the social character of many urban issues. Manuel Castells calls women the "organizing agents of social life" and, as such, the struggle for alternatives or a better life may be construed to be part of the female domain. According to Castells, issues remote from immediate structural change have often engendered "a predisposition among men to accept women's leading role . . . and, more importantly, makes participation appealing for women in the defense or transformation of a world whose meaning is closely connected to their daily lives."[80] Elite women in early Dallas enjoyed a great deal of influence and achieved high levels of success when their city-building efforts could be rationalized as being of "natural" interest to women. Privately, within their own families, and in public campaigns for increased city services and improved urban safety, sanitation, and education, clubwomen moderated the policies favored by Dallas business leaders. In their efforts to implement a more humane vision of growth—one that combined ambitions of grandeur with real concern for the quality of urban life—Dallas women were paradoxically shielded from accusations of "unwomanly" behavior by the same patriarchal mores that limited their activity.

RADICAL ALTERNATIVES:

POPULISM AND SOCIALISM IN DALLAS

Suppose the government were called the "Manu-facturers Association," would it make much difference in the deal workingmen are now getting from it?
—Union announce-ment in the *Dallas Laborer*[1]

IN THE FINAL DECADES OF THE nineteenth century and first decades of the twentieth, two generations of Dallas radicals challenged the local elite's faith in ostensibly laissez-faire capitalism. Like clubwomen, Dallas Populists and Socialists generally favored the city's expansion. Unlike female members of the elite, however, Dallas Populists and Socialists sought more than the modification of business leaders' vision of commercial growth and progress. They allied themselves with radical third parties in an attempt to replace capitalism with a government of and for "producers."[2]

The rapid growth of Dallas after its acquisition of railroads in the 1870s led to significant increases in the value of land surrounding the city; many county landholders amassed fortunes almost entirely on speculation. As increasing numbers of North Texas farmers fell victim to the panics that followed 1873, Populist economic policies designed to ease the repayment of debt and rhetoric emphasizing cooperation and fairness attracted Dallas County farmers and wage laborers disillusioned with the uneven nature of urban expansion. In the 1880s, the Populist movement spread first among the more than 4,000 farmers residing in Dallas County.[3] By 1890 the movement included wage laborers, middle-class reform advocates, and black trade unionists, adding an urban dimension to what was primarily a rural movement.

Local Populists concerned themselves almost exclusively with structural changes at the state and national levels. The legacy of Dallas Populism lies both in the precedent set by its constituents and in the activities of its most visible urban proponents. Populists made the first local attempt to unite county farmers, urban trade unionists, blacks, and radical members of the middle classes. Because of the contentiousness of the city's early elite and its tendency to divide into factions, successive coalitions in which Populists and then Socialists teamed with organized labor played key roles in the city's public life and in the development of local institutions between 1886 and 1917.

The formation of the Texas People's Party in Dallas in 1891 gave nineteenth-century radicals a political base distinct from that of the city's business leaders. The intense opposition activated by Dallas's first Left-liberal coalition, the coalition's financial insecurity, and the racism that precluded the full cooperation of many prospective members was the first indication of obstacles that were to be faced by coalitions of the Left throughout the city's history.

Populism posed a real challenge to the Texas Democratic party. People's party candidates gained enough votes between 1892 and 1896 to force the Democrats to include Populist-inspired reform measures in their party platforms. Dallas became the center both of Texas Populism and of conservative reaction to cooperative ventures organized by the Farmers' Alliance. The gubernatorial election of 1896, in which conservative Democratic nominee Charles A. Culberson defeated Populist attorney Jerome C. Kearby (298,528 votes to 238,692 votes) remains the only instance in which both of the leading candidates for Texas governor resided in Dallas.[4]

Dallas socialists organized shortly after the formation of the Socialist party of America in 1901. They resurrected the Populist theme of fairness and extended the Populist legacy of local radicalism into the first two decades of the twentieth century. Socialist party members in Dallas were active participants in the process of city building. They sought to influence popular opinion and stimulate social change. The socialist vision of an equitable society that rewarded producers with adequate land, job security, comfortable housing, free education, and reliable city services and sanitation appealed to the city's workers and enabled a relatively small but articulate and dedicated band of socialists to exert disproportional influence on Dallas's growing trade unions, schools, welfare institutions, and reform movements.

Both the growth and influence of socialism in Dallas and the Socialist party's decline during World War I paralleled that of the national movement. After a brief period of antiradical hysteria following the 1901 assassination of President McKinley by an "anarchist," Dallas residents accepted the presence of a new radical ideology with remarkable tolerance.[5] Residents of the city's slums and working-class neigh-borhoods responded enthusiastically to socialist demands that elected officials be accountable to their constituents. The election of a social-ist to the committee that wrote the city's 1907 charter (establishing a commission form of government) ensured the inclusion of grassroots political measures through which voters could recall elected officials with whom they were dissatisfied—a national reform goal of conse-quence. The presence of a radical on the charter committee was a sym-bolic inclusion as well. Dallas socialists organized working-class coalitions that recalled two "public-be-damned" school board officials within five years of the charter's adoption. When business interests, led by banker J. T. Trezevant and one of the mercantile Sanger brothers, tried to amend the charter to remove the popular recall provision, Dal-las socialists led the successful fight to keep the 1907 document intact.[6]

Before World War I, socialism was not a "dirty word" to most Dal-las residents. Dallas Socialist party leaders came from well-connected, native-born, middle-class families or were solid trade unionists. Although socialist pacifism during the war led to questions concerning party loyalists' patriotism, early-twentieth-century socialists were not subjected to the virulent public criticism and physical intimidation directed at party members and their associates during the 1930s.

As was the case with the Populists, the growth of socialism in Dallas was impeded by limited financial resources and the racism of many white socialists. The statewide movement did not attract significant numbers of African Americans, even though socialism's primary con-stituents in the Southwest were tenant farmers—a group containing a disproportionate number of blacks. The efforts of Dallas's socialist leadership to combat locally the racism evident in the statewide move-ment were thwarted by the persistence of racism among Dallas rank-and-file socialists—many of them union workers whose livelihoods were threatened by rural blacks brought to Dallas as scabs during peri-ods of labor unrest. To some extent, Dallas's Socialist party was also a victim of its own success. Party activity aimed at raising the class con-sciousness of the city's workers peaked around 1915, by which time Dallas unionists had heeded the call to activism and established their own newspaper, political committees, and means of negotiating with the local elite.

In addition to providing an alternative vision of urban expansion based on "fair" rewards for producers, Dallas radicals established inno-vative institutions such as the Farmers' Alliance Cotton Exchange and the city's first night school and employment service. Perhaps more importantly, Dallas radicals broadened the spectrum of acceptable social and political thought by representing the Left with intelligence, humor, and conviction.

I

Late-nineteenth-century discontent among southwestern farmers stemmed in part from unsupervised federal policies of land disposal that resulted in the acquisition of vast tracts by individual speculators, foreign syndicates, and corporate buyers. Pioneers and small farmers usually lacked money for improvements after the purchase of land and quickly found themselves in debt.[7]

On regaining control of the state government from Republicans in the early 1870s, Texas Democrats thwarted the homestead ideal by granting 32 million acres of prime Texas land from the public domain to twelve railroad corporations.[8] Increasing crop specialization, stimulated by the need to compete with larger operations, and a rise in the cost of consumer goods resulted in a loss of economic independence for many small farmers. If prices for cash crops were low or if the crop failed altogether, farmers were forced into debt. During the last quarter of the nineteenth century, the proportion of Texas farms operated by tenants increased from one-third to one-half. Between 1890 and 1900, the number of mortgaged farms increased from 7,000 to 38,000.[9]

The farmers who established local alliances in the late 1870s seeking protection from high interest rates and a cycle of debt were neither capitalist reformers nor socialists. While most retained a firm belief in the sanctity of private land ownership, southwestern farmers organized to explore alternative means to finance and market crops.[10] As the farmers' movement became emphatically political, the Farmers' Alliance replaced the Patrons of Husbandry or National Grange. In Texas alone, the Alliance eventually possessed 4,000 lodges with membership estimated at 250,000.[11]

During the mid-1880s, the Alliance hierarchy seriously underestimated the sense of comradeship many rank-and-file members felt toward the Knights of Labor.[12] With the exception of Montague County's William Lamb, Alliance officials were out of touch with grassroots sentiment that aligned the interests of farmers, as agricultural producers, with those of wage laborers against the dominant interests of corporate capitalism.[13]

The emergence of Dallas as the southwestern hub of Populist activity resulted in part from the city's central location and accessibility as a railroad center and marketplace. Farmers from throughout North-Central, East, and Northwest Texas customarily made trips to Dallas to purchase farm implements and arrange financing. After the official opening of the Oklahoma Territory in 1889, the number of regular rural pilgrims in Dallas increased. Also significant in the city's ascendance as a meeting ground for Populist leaders was the early radicalism of the Dallas County Farmers' Alliance and encouragement offered by the *Dallas Mercury*.

Farmers in Dallas County watched with growing interest as the city's skilled workers organized during the 1880s. Their proximity to the city exposed members of the Dallas County Alliance to union rhetoric emphasizing the need for class solidarity. Dallas's stature as a regional publishing center enabled both farmers and workers to find amenable forums among the city's myriad newspapers. The *Dallas Mercury* reinforced a growing perception among farm leaders, many of whom attended regular meetings of the Dallas Trades Assembly, that the city's workers and the county's farmers shared common goals. By the middle of the decade, local farmers had extended the Alliance vision of cooperation among agricultural producers to include wage laborers.[14]

The radical Dallas Alliance and those in Robertson, Palo Pinto, and Erath counties defied state officials and the Alliance's *Rural Citizen* and passed a resolution supporting the Knights of Labor in their struggle against Gould railroad interests. The "Great Southwest Strike" began on March 1, 1886. Support for organized labor grew in dozens of county Alliances, as farmers attended joint political meetings with Knights of Labor assemblies and provided direct aid to those on strike. The prolabor *Dallas Mercury* called farmers "the spinal column of this great railroad war." Dallas's Democratic establishment clearly perceived the aroused class consciousness of the region's farmers as a threat. The city's major newspapers blamed farmers for the continuation of the strike and worried that a permanent union of the Farmers' Alliance and the Knights of Labor might dislodge the Democrats in upcoming state elections. In the midst of the spring strike, H. F. Broiles, an independent candidate supported by Knights and Alliance members, exacerbated conservative fears by winning Fort Worth's mayoral race.[15]

Neither the Knights of Labor nor the Farmers' Alliance possessed the resources necessary to battle the likes of Jay Gould and his general manager, R. M. Hoxie. No formal settlement ended the Great Southwest Strike. After three months, the union was in shambles—most of its leaders jailed and members destitute. Those who returned to work did so on company terms. Ironically, the strike that destroyed the Knights of Labor (national membership dropped from a high of 700,000 in 1886 to 100,000 in 1890) legitimized the radical wing of the Texas Farmers' Alliance by demonstrating to moderates within the agrarian movement that the state Democratic party, with its close ties to speculators and railroad interests, was an inappropriate vehicle for reform. With a growing number of Alliance members convinced that change depended on an independent movement of producers, organization among farmers accelerated.[16]

The divisiveness of the Great Southwest Strike—fueled by contrasting images of Gould and impoverished workers—strengthened growing bonds between Dallas County farmers and organized labor. The two groups shared an emerging vision of a producing class that, when organized and educated, would work toward social and economic reform. The railroad strike had a polarizing effect on producers and Dallas business leaders and called into question the policies of the latter.[17]

The Dallas County Alliance's 1886 decision to cosponsor the Texas State Fair with the city's assembly of the Knights of Labor provided early evidence of the new coalition's potential. Without consulting the local farmers and farm-machinery manufacturers who provided most of the exhibits, three prominent bankers (J. B. Simpson, E. M. Reardon, and Capt. William H. Gaston), merchant Alex Sanger, developers T. L. Marsalis and John S. Armstrong, and W. J. Keller, a street-railway magnate, selected an East Dallas site on which to hold the first State Fair. Farm activists were unhappy with the swampy location of the exhibition site—on Main Street at the Texas & Pacific railroad tracks. Farm implement and machinery dealers joined Alliance members and refused to display goods on land that C. A. Keating, president of the largest agricultural equipment firm in Dallas, called "the worst kind of a hog wallow."[18]

Alliance members considered the somewhat arbitrary and impractical location of the fair another example of the local elite's lack of consideration for any but its own interests. With the Knights of Labor, farmers formed a rival fair association and announced that the Texas State Fair, on high ground in North Dallas, would open its gates one day before the East Dallas exposition.

Both fairs drew crowds but proved to be financial disappointments. In a characteristic example of the politics of competition and cooperation that typified early Dallas, the rival fairs merged the following year, but not before farmers and workers forced the commercial-civic elite to change the venue. Representatives of a combined fair association sold the two original sites and chose a new 80-acre location, farther east along the Texas & Pacific tracks but on higher ground, agreeable to both business interests and the fledgling Populist-Labor coalition.

Business leaders were quick to oppose both the changing structure of state politics and the local cooperation of farmers and organized labor. Although, in the spring of 1886, the *Dallas Morning News* had published locally for less than a year, it immediately aligned itself with the Dallas elite. The *News* condemned the railroad strike and declared the farmers' support of the Knights of Labor folly. In May 1886, the paper published a long letter from William Lang, former grand master of the Grange, critical of the Farmers' Alliance. Like the Alliance's state officials, Lang did not recognize the extent to which rank-and-file Alliance members identified with organized labor. He issued vague warnings concerning labor unions and "class organizations." From his desk in Hamburg, Germany, where he served as United States consul, Lang proposed that Texas farmers limit their organizational efforts to educational programs. He recommended that Alliance members acquire a thorough knowledge of economics, agronomy, and commercial and political ethics.[19] Outraged by the publication of Lang's letter and recent editorial criticism, Dallas's County Alliance resolved to "use its best effort to suppress the circulation of the Dallas *News*."[20]

The *Rural Citizen*'s endorsement of a *Morning News* editorial two months later exposed the widening chasm between the Alliance hierarchy and Dallas area activists. Advocating fewer regulations on business in order to free capital from all restraints, the *Morning News* condescendingly declared that alienated farmers mistakenly believed labor rhetoric and that "class legislation, more government, more paternalism, more State socialism" would not alleviate the inherent difficulties of frontier life.[21] Betrayed by their movement's official paper, many North Texas rank-and-file Alliance members dropped their subscriptions to the *Rural Citizen* and patronized Elbridge Gerry Rust's *Dallas Mercury*.

Rust's weekly paper, since its origins in the early 1880s, had received substantial community support. The *Mercury* editor's consistent advocacy of reform measures and his humorous barbs intended to deflate the blustery rhetoric of Dallas boosters appealed to discontented farmers.[22] Alliance members wrote frequent letters to the editor in which they outlined plans for cooperative economic programs and articulated a reform vision that appealed to many Dallas residents with populist sympathies.

As radicals assumed more power within the state Alliance, they acted quickly to sever ties with the *Rural Citizen* and to replace conservative movement officials. Within a year of the Great Southwest Strike, Rust sold the *Dallas Mercury* to a cooperative funded with $50,000 by the state Alliance. Robert F. Butler, president of the Dallas County Alliance and vice president of the state organization, temporarily assumed the *Mercury* editorship. Butler changed the paper's name to the *Southern Mercury*. Although it became the official organ of the state Farmers' Alliance, the *Mercury* tackled a variety of local issues and retained its prolabor stance. Rust's decision to remain as business manager into the 1890s ensured the paper's smooth transition from local reform sheet to the primary voice of Populist advocacy. The *Mercury* attained a readership of 35,000 and cemented Dallas's position at the center of southwestern populism.[23]

Although the farmers' movement had moved far beyond the educational focus of the Grange, in 1887 most members still considered themselves reform-minded Democrats. It took a concerted effort by Dallas bankers and merchants—an effort that in the end doomed one of the most innovative cooperative strategies ever designed to circumvent the American financial community—to convince the bulk of the Alliance's members that their goals could not be achieved within the Democratic party.

The limited success of the decentralized system of cooperative stores operated by county Alliances led movement leaders to contemplate a mass-marketing concept. Merchants reacted to Alliance stores with hostility—engaging in selective price cutting and the circulation of false reports. In an attempt to avoid middlemen and sell directly to East Coast and export buyers, the Alliance's executive committee established a central cotton exchange to market and sell the cotton of Texas Alliance members. In September 1887, Dr. Charles W. Macune, chairman of the executive committee, opened the "Big Store of the Alliance," or Farmers' Alliance Exchange of Texas, in downtown Dallas.

Macune shared the cooperative vision of growth articulated by Dallas County's radical Alliance leaders. In an effort to empower producers, he devised an alternative to the dominant marketing system in which Texas cotton was purchased in rural areas and then channeled through middlemen in Dallas to buyers on the East Coast and abroad. Most farmers depended on the quick sale of their crop to pay debts accrued during the year. As a result, they sold cheaply to local buyers. These rural agents turned the crop over to Dallas investors who warehoused it until prices were high.

A trip to Boston convinced Macune that a central exchange could sell directly to eastern factories if it possessed sufficient capital to underwrite its contracts. County Alliances established cotton yards where local business agents weighed, sampled, and numbered each bale. Following Macune's explicit instructions, agents wrapped the samples and ticketed them according to weight, grade, and county yard number, and expressed them in sacks to the central store in Dallas. Export buyers selected from among samples at the Dallas exchange, thus competing directly with local buyers. Mass marketing worked. In a single transaction, Alliance members shipped 1,500 bales of Texas cotton from twenty-two stations across the state to England, France, and Germany.[24]

Macune's technique of bulk shipping the 1887 cotton harvest to eastern and export buyers raised cotton prices for all Texas farmers but did little to break the cycle of debt suffered by the movement's poorest members. To address members' desires to "make a crop" without merchants or bankers, the directors of the Dallas exchange announced a joint-note plan that would provide Alliance farmers with the credit necessary to harvest their 1888 crop.

The joint-note plan was both innovative and complex.[25] The *Southern Mercury* was called into service to print explanations of the exchange's plan. Each Alliance member who wanted supplies on credit estimated individual needs for the coming year and pledged cotton worth at least three times the amount of credit requested. The farmers were to execute a collective joint note for the total estimated amount of supplies. For security, established local farmers who cosigned notes took mortgages on their neighbors' growing crops. The collective note would draw interest throughout the summer and fall and be payable after the 1888 harvest. The exchange required detailed information from each farmer whose request for credit passed before a "committee of acceptance." Macune and exchange president J. D. Fields planned to use the notes as collateral to borrow money to purchase supplies, to be shipped on a monthly basis between May and November.

Not surprisingly, Macune was unable to negotiate loans with Dallas bankers. The Alliance did not expect to be similarly rejected by bankers in Fort Worth, Galveston, and New Orleans. In Houston, Macune acquired a small loan and found a few mercantile houses willing to advance supplies, but the regional financial community's opposition to collective financing and marketing was solid. Alliance leaders underestimated the reach of the Dallas commercial-civic elite as well as its resolve to thwart any alternative to the local version of ostensibly laissez-faire capitalism. Macune found himself facing a formidable credit embargo at the very time of year that the capital assets of regional banks were most liquid. In addition to the unexpected strength of the local elite, Macune faced another perennial obstacle for those who challenged Dallas business leaders: the meager resources of his constituents. The exchange was jeopardized when it could not secure capital to meet its obligations for supplies shipped in May. A June mass rally secured pledges from farmers throughout Texas and carried the exchange through the season. It was apparent, however, that the organization of banking interests and resulting lack of available credit doomed further experimentation with collective notes.[26]

At the Alliance's August 1888 convention, an undaunted Macune proposed establishing a treasury within the state exchange. Farmers would circulate exchange treasury notes within the order by purchasing supplies at Alliance stores. The idea appealed to many. Since the Greenback movement of the 1870s, farmers had longed for inflationary measures that would allow some chance of escaping the crop lien by devaluing debts.

Again, the Dallas elite exerted its influence. As editor of a central Texas newspaper in the mid-1870s, Macune had angered the city's business leaders by opposing land incentives for railroad construction (Dallas leaders offered both land and money to the Houston & Texas

Central and Texas & Pacific railroads in the early 1870s). The radical Alliance economist also advocated a tax code structured to favor farmers and others who improved land, rather than large speculators, and he proposed government ownership of all means of public transportation.[27]

Macune's 1888 plan to reduce the debt of Texas farmers was anathema to Dallas bankers and investors who held the notes. In the midst of debate over Macune's proposed treasury plan, an article in the *Dallas Morning News* cast doubt on the Alliance business manager's integrity. The paper announced, "It is not generally known that the alliance exchange has been in the hands of a receiver for about six weeks." Asserting that a Maj. Hugh F. Ewing, not Macune, controlled Alliance money, the *Morning News* claimed that an agreement had been made between Dallas merchants and other creditors and officers of the exchange. The article continued, "Dr. Macune has made many errors—many egregious errors—and blunders."[28] The Alliance's investigative committee exonerated Macune after Ewing explained that he was merely the exchange's bookkeeper. The following day, the *Morning News* retracted its claim at the end of a long story on the Alliance convention and admitted that it should have used the word auditor instead of receiver. The paper quoted Alliance leaders as saying that allegations regarding a deal with Dallas bankers and merchants were also "without foundation."[29]

The damage to Macune's credibility was irreparable. Although the delegates stood by their business manager, they deemed his treasury-note plan too much of a risk and refused to implement it. Frustrated by his inability to acquire the financing necessary to circumvent Dallas bankers and by personal attacks, Macune resigned his position as exchange business manager two months later.[30]

After the experience of the Dallas exchange, large numbers of Texas farmers committed themselves to Greenback economic principles—calling on the government to issue paper money without specie support and coin silver in addition to gold—in an attempt to increase agricultural prices and ease the repayment of debt. Texas Governor Jim Hogg's 1890 appointment of conservatives to the state railroad commission motivated the left wing of the Democratic party, mostly farmers, to form the Jefferson Democratic Caucus. Party regulars, incensed at the lack of loyalty displayed by Jefferson Democrats, expelled them from the Farmers' Alliance. Leaders of the dissident group and their rank-and-file supporters formed the People's party in Dallas on August 17, 1891.[31]

Although radical members of the farmers' movement formed the nucleus of People's party leadership (the state Alliance met the day after the new party was formed, and delegates to both conventions stayed at the same Dallas hotel), the People's party appealed to many urban residents. The precedent for cooperation between farmers and laborers, set during the Great Southwest Strike, was reinforced by the presence and activity of union members during the organizing convention.

People's party delegates elected Patrick Golden, a union painter and officer of the Dallas assembly of the Knights of Labor, to the Committee on Permanent Organization and Platform (an executive committee of sorts) and to the speakers committee. Dallas labor delegate J. T. W. Loe, an active proponent of the eight-hour workday, coauthored the Texas State Federation of Labor's 1889 platform. Not all Populists fit the newspaper caricature of an impoverished farmer. Among the approximately two hundred delegates who convened in the city hall auditorium were prosperous middle-aged urban tradesmen, young union activists, landowners with homes in the city, and radical members of Dallas's legal community. In addition to the Dallas delegates, members of the Independent party that elected Fort Worth's antimonopoly mayor in 1886 swelled the ranks of "urban Populists." The convention publicly criticized the *Fort Worth Gazette* for reporting that inaccurately pitted the very rich against the very poor. Perhaps most noted at the time was the presence of delegates representing the Colored Farmers' Alliance and urban black trade unions.[32]

In the decades between Reconstruction and the passage of early-twentieth-century "reform" measures that effectively removed most African Americans and many poor whites from the electoral process, Texas blacks consistently opposed Democratic candidates in state elections. To be effective, Populists needed black support. Although the Texas People's party has been described as "the most radical, uncompromising Populist movement in the nation," the racial tension that haunted southern and southwestern Populism throughout the 1890s surfaced during the party's opening session.[33] People's party leaders combined an eagerness to lure blacks away from the Republican party with concern that white voters would reject an interracial political movement. With traditions of segregation and white supremacy maintained through extrajudicial actions and formal institutions that disallowed access to blacks, Dallas was a hostile environment in which to propose racial cooperation.

In 1890 Dallas blacks were segregated into shanty towns located along railroad rights-of-way and floodplains. Job prospects were limited; most African Americans in Dallas were day laborers or domestic servants. Blacks who possessed specific skills were confined to segregated union locals and often excluded from Trades Assembly functions. Similarly, the practices of black professionals were limited by the racism of white residents. Organizers of the People's party clearly intended that the convention include black delegates, yet representatives of black organizations were not uniformly welcomed. The convention's response to Melvin Wade, a militant black leader from Dallas, is telling.

Wade, a member of North Texas District 78 of the Knights of Labor, began his political career twenty-three years before the People's party convention as a member of the three-man Dallas County Board of Registrars. Established after a military district commander sent a detachment of soldiers to regulate post–Civil War affairs in Dallas, the county board reduced eligible white voters to about 390 and certified almost as many blacks.[34] Wade's leadership ability and popularity in the black community resulted in his election to the post of alderman in 1870. He served the city in that capacity until a special election in March 1872 returned control of municipal and county governments to white landowners and merchants.[35]

The president of the registration board, Jesse Asberry, had offended prominent Dallas residents with what they called "overbearing and insulting conduct," and thus Wade's participation on the board did not endear him to Dallas whites. The *Dallas Herald* described him as a "dark-skinned" press agent promoting a new Austin paper called *The Free Man's Press*—"a red-hot anti-white man's paper" that appealed to "silly blacks and radical Radicals."[36]

In 1889 Wade served on the Texas State Federation of Labor's ten-member platform committee. Calling for an eight-hour workday law, repeal of the national bank, government ownership of railroads and communications systems, and the abolition of grand juries, state senates, and the United States Senate, Wade made what the *Morning News* described as "one of his characteristic speeches, urging the necessity for loud talk by the workingman."[37]

By 1891 a political alternative to the largely ineffective Republican party led by N. Wright Cuney of Galveston was appealing to Wade and the Dallas blacks he represented. Despite genuine interest, Wade's awareness of racial tensions between black and white assemblies of the Knights of Labor and between "colored" and "regular" county Alliances tempered his enthusiasm for the new party. As the convention opened, Chairman William Lamb spotted Wade at the rear of the auditorium and asked if he was to be among them. Wade's response, "I understood the People's Party was to be organized here this morning. But I want to see a thing before I go into it," reflected his reluctance to join a coalition led by whites.[38]

Lamb's keynote address detailed the evils of capitalism and described both major parties as corrupt and dominated by corporate interests. He called for the appointment of a committee to author a formal statement of Populist principles. Lamb also mentioned the willingness of many Texas blacks to join the party and asked that delegates consider their particular claims. Wade immediately asked why Lamb's address made special reference to black issues if, as Populist rhetoric promised, all party members were to have the same privileges. Despite the naive (or patronizing) claims of convention organizers who insisted the party favored complete equality, Wade demanded further clarification. Citing segregated public transportation as an example of social inequity, Wade said he wanted to tell blacks if the People's party "proposed to work black and white horses in the great common political field."[39]

African American delegates also objected to the convention's selection of all-white committees. They warned the delegates that representation among the party's leadership was a prerequisite for black support. The assembly rejected the notion of segregated Populist clubs and a proposal that local white party leaders appoint a black spokesman for each congressional district. Delegates selected two moderate blacks for positions on the party's statewide executive committee. Conspicuously overlooked was Dallas's Melvin Wade. The exclusion of such an experienced and popular black leader revealed the party organizers' attitude toward Wade's militancy. They wanted Wade "as an ally, but they were not yet sure they wanted him as an ally in leadership."[40]

Wade's outspokenness and articulate manner also troubled area newspaper reporters. He is alternately described as one of "a couple of darkeys" and "a prominent colored Dallasite" in the course of a single article. Clearly the presence of a militant challenger who questioned

the degree to which delegates would stand by their often in-
flated rhetoric confused and disturbed convention participants and
observers.[41]

The convention experience of Melvin Wade and his Dallas followers
is significant because of the messages implicit in his exclusion from
party leadership: (1) Only moderate black leaders could expect to participate in white-led reform movements. (2) White "radicals" would
reject any sign of black militancy. (3) Blacks were not to confuse white
support for black political rights (in exchange for black votes) with
support for full social and economic parity. Long after the articulation
of the national People's party program in Omaha in 1892 and the
defeat of William Jennings Bryan and subsequent demise of Populism
after 1896, Dallas blacks received ample reinforcement of the conclusions drawn from Wade's experience. The specter of racism not only
prevented the People's party from winning the support of Melvin
Wade and his many supporters both within and outside of the labor
movement but discouraged black participation in later efforts to build
coalitions in Dallas.

The 1891 organizing convention established a political apparatus
through which Dallas's Populist-Labor coalition and farm activists
from around the state worked toward economic reform. For the
remainder of the decade, the People's party provided an ideological
framework for local radicals who sought an alternative to the civic policies of Dallas business leaders. The influence of the *Southern Mercury*,
the charisma of urban Populists such as Golden, Loe, and Jerome
Kearby, and the continued activism of the Dallas County Alliance
ensured that the Texas People's party reflected the concerns of Dallas
radicals. Indeed, it was largely a product of their vision.

Collectively, Dallas Populists gained little in the way of county or
municipal services. They emphasized restructuring the nation's financial system and reforming state policies regarding cooperative ventures, organized labor, and the regulation of railroads and land
syndicates. The tendency to seek change at the federal and state levels
reflects the rural situation of the majority of Populism's adherents.
Two prominent Dallas Populists combined their work toward national
economic reform and political change at the state level with local
visions of municipal and county governments that would be responsive
to the needs of workers and agricultural producers. Their careers
demonstrate some of the ways in which the third party's economic

agenda and radical view of society influenced Dallas's growth during the 1890s.[42]

In the summer of 1892, area Democrats selected union painter Patrick H. Golden to represent Dallas County in the Twenty-third Texas Legislature.[43] Remarkably, Golden had the support of both factions of the local Democratic party despite his defection to the People's party a year earlier.[44] The son of Irish parents who had died while he was in his teens, Golden became a painter like his father and joined the union in his native New Orleans before his twentieth birthday. He moved to Dallas in 1886 and immediately established himself in the 100-member local painters' union, the Dallas Trades Assembly, and the Knights of Labor. In addition to his appointment to two major People's party committees, Golden served four terms as president of the newly established Texas State Federation of Labor. Because of these activities, Golden had declined to run for the state House on two previous occasions and did not campaign in 1892. On his forty-sixth birthday, however, Golden accepted the nomination, as "the laboring classes would not be satisfied" otherwise.[45]

While a member of the legislature, Golden pursued a Populist-Labor agenda. He introduced an eight-hour bill during his first month in office. Golden claimed that reform-minded Democrats repeatedly placed a mechanics' lien law on the party platform but refused to approve legislation. The Populist lawmaker had initiated a campaign to pass a lien law while he was president of the Texas State Federation of Labor. Union activists and members of the Farmers' Alliance pursued the project over the next eighteen months until March 1893, when the legislature approved a compromise lien law by a vote of 59 to 46. Ironically, both Golden and Texas House Speaker John H. Cochran, a Dallas moderate, voted against the "unfair" Henderson Substitute, as the compromise bill was called, because it restricted the amount a laborer or materials supplier could collect from a delinquent owner to no more than the contracted price. Since modifications were often made during construction, trade unionists sought means by which they could be compensated for completed work not specified in the original contract. Supporters of Golden's original bill were able to add another amendment that made owners liable for all mechanics' expenses beyond the contracted price unless an owner provided a written breakdown of costs to the point that work ceased.[46] One of Golden's final acts as a legislator was to guide through the House a bill that would make it a misdemeanor to discharge an employee because of union member-ship.[47]

Golden, shortly after his return to Dallas, was appointed by the city's aldermen to the post of street superintendent. Street improvements, generally seen as a preserve of the city's business community concerned with downtown congestion, were also a priority of Golden's Populist constituents. Since Dallas had begun paving streets in the early 1880s, improvements had been made almost exclusively in the city's downtown (see Table 2).[48] By the end of the decade, very little public money had been allocated to paving or even grading outside the business district, while downtown streets had been re-Macadamized in several instances.[49]

Lacking the resources of the city's wealthier residents, who often had drives and streets in front of their homes graded and graveled at their own expense, the urban working class sought increased allocations for residential grading and flood control. County farmers wanted more attention paid to the city's outlying roads over which they transported their produce. City records and insurance maps demonstrate that during the period in which the People's party provided a viable alternative to Democratic party politics (and Patrick Golden served as street superintendent), streets in the working-class neighborhoods north of the business district were graded and other improvements were made beyond the downtown area. Masten, a major artery leading north from downtown, was Macadamized. In addition, Junius, Worth, Haskell, and Gaston (through streets east of the business district favored by county farmers) were graded and graveled even though the area was sparsely settled. Sections of Gaston even received a Macadam surface.[50]

The Populist-Labor coalition elected several sympathetic aldermen; its most vocal advocate at the municipal level was butcher Max Hahn, who served on the city council between 1898 and 1900. With the favorable exception of Golden, Dallas Populists and early trade unionists ensured the election of moderates such as six-term Representative John Cochran (who served nonconsecutive terms between 1874 and 1893) and Senator Barry Miller (1899–1901) to state posts.[51]

One of Golden's principal allies in Dallas was the state's premier trial attorney, Jerome C. Kearby. Born in Arkansas and reared in Denton, Texas, Kearby, like many of his small-town contemporaries, moved to Dallas because the city's two new railroads had spared it from most ill

TABLE 2

STATEMENT OF STREETS AND ALLEYS PAVED IN THE CITY OF DALLAS THE FISCAL YEAR 1888–89

NAME OF STREET	FROM	TO	PAVING			
			LINEAR FEET	SQUARE YARDS	UNIT PRICE	COST
Alley	Elm	Main	200.00	399.73	1.55	619.58
Commerce	Jefferson	H. & T. C.	5,478.50	32,230.70	1.59	51,212.25
Ervay	Elm	Commerce	400.00	1,677.50	1.55	2,600.90
Ervay	Commerce	Gano	—	19,630.50	—	—
Akard	—	—	—	—	—	—
Field	Main	Commerce	200.00	800.00	1.60	1,279.62
Harwood	Elm	Commerce	400.00	1,688.60	1.60	2,725.69
Main	Sycamore	H. & T. C.	3,050.00	20,373.33	1.59	32,477.61
Market	Main	Commerce	200.00	1,333.33	1.60	2,132.63
Masten	—	—	—	—	—	—
Poydras	Main	Commerce	200.00	444.49	1.60	710.88
Pearl	Main	Commerce	400.00	2,815.50	1.60	4,620.72
Martin	Main	Commerce	200.00	800.00	1.60	1,279.59
Preston	Elm	Commerce	400.00	2,142.20	1.60	3,341.22
Patterson	Masten	Sycamore	630.22	2,158.80	1.33	2,889.33
Sycamore	Elm	Pacific	—	—	—	1,374.65
Sycamore	Main	Commerce	200.00	800.00	1.60	1,279.62
St. Paul	Elm	Commerce	400.00	—	—	2,600.90
Stone	Elm	Main	200.00	605.90	1.62	980.64

Source: 1889 Annual Report, City of Dallas, Texas/Dallas History and Archives Division, Dallas Public Library

effects of the Panic of 1873. Kearby became the most renowned trial lawyer in Texas through his defense of Knights of Labor leaders after the Great Southwest Strike of 1886. Labeled "Populism's most urbane speaker," the articulate attorney retained many of his small-town ways. Folk habits such as squatting on the sidewalk in front of his office while whittling a stick endeared him to county farmers, as did his endorsement of Greenback economic principles.[52] With solid support among workers, small-business owners, and farmers, Kearby ran for the United States House of Representatives in 1894. As early-

CURBING			TOTAL COST	PAVING TYPE		
LINEAR FEET	UNIT PRICE	COST		WEARING SURFACE	FOUNDATION	
—	—	—	619.58	Bois d'arc	Gravel	
8,979.00	0.37	3,366.99	54,579.24	Bois d'arc	Gravel	
600.00	0.38	225.00	2,825.90	Bois d'arc	Gravel	
6,417.00	—	—	34,115.59	Macadam	—	
—	—	—	19,159.20	Macadam	—	
200.00	0.38	75.00	1,354.62	Bois d'arc	Gravel	
855.00	0.38	320.64	3,046.33	Bois d'arc	Gravel	
5,476.65	0.38	2,053.75	34,531.36	Bois d'arc	Gravel	
200.00	0.38	75.00	2,207.63	Bois d'arc	Gravel	
—	—	—	2,404.50	Macadam	—	
—	—	—	710.88	Bois d'arc	Gravel	
0.38	—	288.02	4,908.74	Bois d'arc	Gravel	
400.00	0.38	150.00	1,429.59	Bois d'arc	Gravel	
685.00	0.38	256.78	3,598.00	Bois d'arc	Gravel	
1,191.50	0.38	443.67	3,333.50	Macadam	—	
—	—	—	1,374.65	Macadam	—	
315.00	0.38	118.12	1,397.74	Bois d'arc	Gravel	
800.00	0.38	300.00	2,900.90	Bois d'arc	Gravel	
400.00	0.38	150.00	1,130.64	Bois d'arc	Gravel	

Total Cost = $175,628.59

twentieth-century Dallas historian L. B. Hill explained, "The very qualities, however, which made him a popular man with the masses and one of the most eminent criminal lawyers in Texas, made him weak with the cool, compromising leaders, who in the end usually control the destinies of campaigns and candidates."[53] In an election characterized by wholesale ballot stuffing, Kearby lost to an incumbent who had held the House seat since 1888. Recent research indicates that Kearby did indeed win the election, which was then stolen by the Democrats.[54]

Two years later, Kearby almost succeeded in his attempt to become governor of Texas despite a split within the ranks of Populism. Kearby and his Dallas supporters joined agrarian radicals in opposition to the National People's party when it supported Democratic presidential nominee William Jennings Bryan. Recalling the vote fraud and violence committed by Jim Hogg's Texas Democrats two years earlier, Kearby asserted, "Do you expect us to run now with the creatures who heaped these insults on us? . . . So help me God, I will never march with you into the Democratic Party."[55] Bryan's defeat in the presidential race marked the decline of the People's party, although Texas Populists still polled over 100,000 votes in 1898.

After the party's disintegration, there remained in North-Central Texas a significant number of disaffected Populists who, like Kearby, would not be reconciled to Democratic party politics. In the first decades of the twentieth century, many former Populist speakers became local organizers for the Socialist party. Most, however, dropped out of politics altogether.[56]

Apart from the banking contingent and some of the leading merchants, Dallas residents viewed Populist efforts for change as well-intended and did not denigrate those associated with the People's party. Kearby remained in Dallas and continued practicing law "with a stronger and a more honorable reputation" than before he first ran for public office. The legal work of Kearby and that of his son Jay, an 1896 graduate of the University of Texas, set a precedent for the radical Dallas attorneys who followed them in the first three decades of the twentieth century.[57]

II

After the demise of the People's party, Texas Populists who remained politically active and were unwilling to rejoin the Democratic party turned to the newly established Socialist party of America as a political and ideological alternative. A younger generation of tenant farmers joined them in their conversion to socialism. White share-tenancy in Texas increased rapidly during the depression of the 1890s. A poll tax written by reform Democrats and passed by the state legislature shortly after the turn of the century disfranchised many poor farmers. In 1903 and 1905, the Democrats passed a series of election laws that further narrowed the electorate by requiring nominating primaries. In the guise of eliminating election abuses, reform Democrats attached financial and residential stipulations to voting rights and effectively removed most blacks and Hispanics and many white tenants from the political process.[58]

The Populists who joined the Socialist party had once made up the dissident left wing of the agrarian movement. They supported Julius A. Wayland's *Appeal to Reason* and looked to the Kansas newspaper for political guidance. By 1907, the *Appeal to Reason* had a national circulation of over 300,000—making it one of the largest weekly periodicals in the country. Nearly one-sixth of the paper's subscribers were socialists in Texas, Oklahoma, Louisiana, and Arkansas.[59] The ex-Populists carried the religious fervor of the old agrarian movement into the Socialist party. Southwestern socialism often depended more on the charisma of its orators than on ideology and claimed a moral authority that distinguished it from socialism in the Northeast.

Long-time Dallas trade-union leader Louis Hicks recalled his father, Joshua (J. L.), a Populist organizer in the 1890s, joining the typographical union in 1905, the Socialist party four years later, and remaining an active socialist until his death in 1921 (the elder Hicks ran unsuccessfully for state comptroller on the Socialist ticket in 1912).[60] J. L. Hicks was typical of a generation of Populist radicals who served as early socialist candidates. With high levels of name recognition, the old Populists were logical socialist choices for statewide elections. Yet the farmers' movement did not blend directly into southwestern socialism. Most former Populists, especially those who owned their own land, returned to the Democratic party. James Green, in his study of socialism in the Southwest, found a low correlation between Populist voting in the last decade of the nineteenth century and socialist voting in the first two decades of the twentieth century due to non-Populist elements (tenant farmers, miners, railroad workers, etc.) that made up the bulk of the Socialist party in the Southwest. The tenant class increased again during the cotton boll-weevil blight and economic panic of 1907. Despite the continued activism of Hicks and his contemporaries, the new socialist organizers who traveled throughout Texas after 1907 came from trade-union struggles in cities and towns instead of from earlier agrarian campaigns.[61]

As a rule, Texas socialists faced little repression until after the first decade of the twentieth century, when they were perceived as a real political threat by the Democrats. By 1910 the Oklahoma Socialist party, with 5,482 registered members (800 more than in New York), was the largest in the nation and paid more dues to the national party than any other state. The strength and proximity of the Oklahoma party, the influence of the *Appeal to Reason* (which circulated widely in North-Central Texas), and the area's Populist legacy enabled socialist organizers to attract adherents throughout the state. As a result, the Texas Socialist party claimed 6,000 members by 1912.[62]

As the Populist movement waned in Dallas, a determined group of young professionals—primarily teachers, journalists, and attorneys—used their communications skills to unite fragments that remained from the city's first Left-liberal coalition, recent middle-class migrants, and a new generation of workers. The result was a lively radical movement that endured until the First World War.

Even before the *Southern Mercury* fell victim to the economic crisis of 1907, the Populist newspaper had lost its position at the vanguard of Dallas radicalism to George Clifton Edwards's *Laborer*.[63] Edwards, a Sewanee- and Harvard-educated Dallas native, began publishing in the spring of 1904 with the support of the Dallas Trades Assembly and thirty-three affiliated unions.[64] The paper's masthead motto, "Organization, Education, Fraternity," reflected Edwards's vision of socialism as an educational movement through which enlightened workers could wrest control of their communities from capitalist interests. Edwards campaigned against local feelings of helplessness and the common belief that capitalism was "natural" due to "innate" human tendencies toward competition. In his first edition, Edwards claimed:

> The fault is not with the frame of things—it is with perfectly human conditions which we are perfectly able to change if we organize and educate. The impelling motive of our lives should be through organization of the working class, and through their education, to realize the ideal of fraternity.[65]

While an advocate of grassroots political action, Edwards also encouraged Dallas workers to join and support the Socialist party to ensure the expansion of educational efforts by socialist organizers throughout the United States. In keeping with the goal of enlightening the masses, the *Laborer*'s price was very low—making it accessible to almost all workers. A single issue cost a nickel and yearly subscriptions to the weekly sold for one dollar.[66] Edwards was born into a prominent Dallas family. His father had moved to Dallas from Tennessee and became a pioneer member of the Dallas bar, serving as city attorney in the 1870s, as alderman from 1887 to 1890, and as an elected justice of the peace between 1898 and 1908. Despite this family background, Edwards was not a wealthy man.[67] Even after he began to practice law in 1910, the meager fees he received as a "poor man's" lawyer did not provide the financial cushion necessary to ensure the newspaper's success. The *Laborer* depended largely on the generosity of individual Dallas socialists and union members and the ongoing support of the Trades Assembly. Some of the city's Jewish merchants supported Edwards's paper and local organizing efforts while maintaining ties to European socialism through the Arbeiter Ring or Workmen's Circle.[68] Despite the limited resources of its publisher and its subscribers, the paper endured until the eve of World War I.[69]

On his first editorial page, Edwards explained the need for a public voice to carry on the radical legacy begun by local members of the People's party. He claimed that about 70 percent of Dallas residents "give up a large share of their wages" to about 30 percent "who own their homes and somebody else's." According to Edwards, the stockholders of the Dallas Fair, the members of the Commercial Club, the mayor, the aldermen, and other prominent citizens "have their views on life, on politics, and above all, on 'business,' expressed in our two dailies." The purpose of the *Laborer* was to provide a fair balance—to "set forth the news, the opinions, and the aspirations" of the rent-paying majority.[70]

In later columns, Edwards was careful to appeal to Dallas trade unionists who owned their homes—warning them that individual prosperity should not lessen their support of working-class issues. He assured prosperous tradesmen that business interests thought of all workers simply as "voters to be cajoled, or as bits of labor to be bought." When the Commercial Club, "the official noise maker of the capitalists of Dallas," needed the aid of the Trades Assembly to pass a 1904 bond issue to improve Fair Park, union members were not included in a post-election letter publicly thanking Dallas groups who supported the improvement plans. Edwards pointed to this snub as an example of how, when in need of votes, the commercial-civic elite was "not above 'recognizing' the union man who owns a little home. But as for remembering after the election—that is another story."[71]

Initial issues of the *Laborer* announced the formal organization of

Dallas socialists. Socialist Party No. 36 held meetings every Sunday afternoon in a downtown hall on Akard Street between Elm and Pacific. Ads for the meetings promised good music and promoted a familial atmosphere by welcoming women and children. The party presented a series of free lectures on economics throughout the spring and summer of 1904. Topics ranged from traditional Populist themes such as cooperation to general interpretations of Marx and W. W. Stopple's analysis of "The Lack of Political Probity in Dallas." To enhance cooperation and strengthen personal bonds, the local began a series of monthly dances in July. The eagerly awaited square dancing was always preceded by speeches and music. Dallas socialists presented a full slate of candidates for the 1904 municipal elections—signaling the political presence of a new radical alternative.[72]

The *Laborer* reviewed popular pamphlets to expose Dallas readers to socialist ideology and to national and international trends. In addition, the Laborer Publishing Company printed and sold the first socialist pamphlet written and published in Dallas. In "Shall we work or BE Worked?" H. D. Winniford, a member of Local 36, lamented the policies of local business leaders:

> The bad things our admitted good men have done and the crazy things our smart men have done, have pretty near made us slaves. Without our consent they have sold the world. Now they purpose that a few men shall own the machinery and leave us beggars for the right to live.[73]

Winniford's theme was a familiar one—that the expansionist policies of the city's commercial-civic elite rarely resulted in increased city services or improved standards of living for Dallas workers.

As the Dallas local gained strength, it became increasingly necessary to outline exactly what the party envisioned in order to counter popular fears and the accusations of the city's major newspapers.[74] J. L. Hicks wrote a regular column for the *Laborer* in which he described for Dallas readers life in a socialist state. Hicks argued that socialists were not against growth and that socialism was not "a new and untried principle" but an extension of the ideology underlying the public schools and the state's road and bridge system. At the federal level, Hicks pointed to the postal system, the Alaskan railroad, and the Panama Canal as examples of popular programs based on socialist principles. Instead of seeking to overturn the government, Hicks claimed socialists "are the only people who are trying in a practical way to keep the government from being overturned."[75]

Dallas's radicals used newspaper articles, pamphlets, lectures, and meetings to promote their vision of an ideal urban setting. They juxtaposed images of cooperation and a more equitable division of city services with competitive policies that disproportionately benefited the commercial-civic elite.

The Socialist party and the *Laborer* grew steadily throughout their first decade in Dallas. By 1911, the party had about 400 members eligible to vote in municipal elections (between 4,500 and 5,500 citizens typically participated in city elections between 1911 and 1915). Party supporters—including women and men unable to vote because of poll taxes and residency requirements—numbered close to 1,000. A central committee coordinated Dallas County socialist activities through separate branch secretaries and organizers in Central Dallas, South Dallas, and Oak Cliff. Over 11,000 copies of the *Laborer*'s city campaign special edition circulated in 1911. Two years later, Edwards and four socialist colleagues ran for mayor and the city's four commission seats respectively. Edwards campaigned against incumbent mayor William M. Holland who had the backing of the Citizens Association. Since Dallas's adoption of the commission form of government in 1907, Citizens Association candidates had captured every municipal office. In the 1913 election, Edwards received 1,809 votes to Holland's 3,164. While none of the socialist candidates won his race, the party carried seven of the city's thirty-three precincts.[76] The consciousness-raising and educational programs through which Dallas's socialists spread their radical vision of a local government responsive to the rent-paying majority brought the party political respectability.

The city-building activities of Dallas's early socialists fall into two categories—those activities that led to the formation of new institutions or changes in statutes, and those that fostered an environment in which radical ideas and ideologies could be disseminated without fear of repression. Dallas socialists initiated community services and fought legal battles to protect laborers, children, and blacks. Other activities—newspaper articles, well-publicized dances, weekly meetings, rallies in city parks, protests at city hall, and the distribution of pamphlets—advertised the lively presence of a radical alternative. These actions expanded the range of acceptable political and social thought and contributed to the competitive atmosphere that characterized the city's public life. Although supporting actors played significant and often recurring roles, socialism's leading man in early Dallas was George Clifton Edwards.

Perhaps the most far-reaching institution established by Dallas socialists was the free night school opened by Edwards and the Rev. Hudson Stuck, dean of St. Matthew's Episcopal Cathedral.[77] Upon his return to Dallas from Harvard in 1901, Edwards taught algebra and Latin at Oak Cliff High School and lived among the cotton mill workers in Dallas's worst slum, immediately south of downtown. Eleven- and twelve-year-old children regularly worked twelve-hour days alongside their parents in the cotton mill. Children as young as six worked off the payroll. Fifteen-hour days were not uncommon during peak periods. The operatives lived in squalid shotgun houses and suffered high rates of tuberculosis and other respiratory diseases caused by the fine cotton lint they inhaled at the mill. The practice of working young children severely limited the educational opportunities of mill employees.

Dean Stuck, a native of England influenced by the social gospel movement, offered Edwards the use of St. Matthew's kindergarten facilities and encouraged the twenty-three-year-old socialist to open a night school.[78] Classes began in the fall of 1901 after Edwards went door-to-door through the slum searching for interested students. Using donated materials, Edwards taught five nights a week from 7:30 to 9:00 (after completing his "regular" teaching job). Students as young as seven, along with many of their parents, learned to spell their names and read newspapers. Years later Edwards wrote, "The sight of grown men and women trying to use those abandoned kindergarten chairs and tables would have been ludicrous if it had not been both serious and pitiful." Edwards ran the night school for more than a year with the assistance of Agnes Nichols and her sister Octavia, a Dallas teacher whom he later married.

The little school at St. Matthew's was an unqualified success, and Dallas school superintendent J. L. Long, after listening to a fiery appeal by Edwards, had little difficulty convincing the school board that night school was "a useful and needed thing." After Long "saw the vision," Alice Osmond and Affie Johnson, both experienced Dallas elementary teachers, relocated the school to a vacant building near the cotton mill.[79] Under the auspices of the school board, night school remained the only educational option of many young mill workers for several decades.

While Edwards turned his after-school energies to the establishment of his newspaper, he remained interested in the plight of Dallas's poorly educated workers. He convinced Superintendent Long to appoint a colleague, J. O. Mahoney, principal of a new all-adult branch of the night school so that "all the illiterates of Dallas, working people ambitious to get on, foreigners who knew little English, might be benefited."[80]

Working conditions in South Dallas motivated Dean Stuck, Edwards, and George Hinsdale, another local socialist, to join in an effort to push a child-labor law through the Texas legislature. They secured the help of former state senator Alexander Terrell. The Dallas trio wrote a basic bill that limited the hours a child could work and established minimum working-age limits. Terrell found a sponsor who introduced the bill, to surprisingly little open opposition. The powerful textile industry found the law unworthy of a public fight, since it could be rendered impotent through amendments. George Edwards, Jr., recalls that even though the altered bill provided a basis for all future Texas laws limiting child labor, its passage gave his father little immediate pleasure. Living among the operatives in South Dallas, the elder Edwards recognized that economic privation and limited opportunities would continue to push many children into the cotton mill. Edwards's own family did not escape the harshness of the South Dallas slum. Before leaving the cotton mill district, both he and his wife contracted tuberculosis and their two infant daughters died of dysentery.

The efforts of Edwards, Hinsdale, and Stuck to pass a child-labor bill and the successful 1911 campaign to retain the city charter's recall provision were the most public legal battles in which early Dallas socialists played prominent roles. The collective legal work of Edwards and fellow socialist attorneys was less well known, although it set statewide precedents for lawsuits against loansharks.[81] Edwards's activism against illegal lenders stemmed from his representation of Dallas blacks, who often turned to loansharks after being denied legitimate credit. Earl Miller, a close friend of Edwards and active member of Local 36, represented union members similarly exploited by loansharks.[82]

James P. Simpson, Jr., a childhood friend of Edwards's son and an attorney in Dallas after World War II, described the elder Edwards as "an artist with the usury laws." The socialist's legal artistry culminated in a ruling (still a part of the state legal code) that allows borrowers to recover triple the amount of interest paid if the rates charged are found to be usurious. Since many of the city's lenders ignored the state ceiling on interest rates, Edwards earned not only the respect of his clients but also that of many middle-class residents and his peers in the Dallas bar. Edwards's reputation as a formidable attorney spread. According to Simpson, even those among the city's elite who resented his political views "secretly sent their [black] servants to Mr. Edwards when they got into trouble with the loansharks."[83]

In addition to spurring the activism of Edwards and Hinsdale, the severity of conditions at the cotton mill molded the early career of another young Dallas socialist. In 1909 Carl P. Brannin, recently graduated from Texas Agricultural and Mechanical College (now Texas A&M University) with a degree in textile engineering, joined his family in Dallas. Like many of their small-town contemporaries, the Brannins had moved to the city in search of greater financial opportunities. Carl Brannin accepted an apprenticeship at the cotton mill, which had promised him a managerial position ensuring excellent pay and a good measure of security after a year of training.

The noise, dust, and heat in the mill stunned the young apprentice, as did the presence of children, the long hours, and low pay (women received seventy-five cents a day, unskilled men received one dollar, and skilled weavers on piecework rarely earned more than two dollars daily). Over sixty years later, Brannin vividly described eight- to ten-year-old "doffer boys," already hump-shouldered from pulling bobbins of yarn off spinning machines. During his training, Brannin caught an arm in a machine and, although not seriously hurt, was made aware of the hazards mill workers faced daily. Although Brannin qualified for a position as assistant superintendent, he left the mill after a year and spent the remainder of his long life working toward expanded opportunities and improved conditions for laborers.[84]

An omnivorous reader, Brannin called himself an "alumnus" of the Dallas Public Library "in literature, history, biography, and liberal arts."[85] Henry George's *Progress and Poverty* and the concept of the Single Tax led Brannin to reject the values of an acquisitive, competitive society. Charles M. Sheldon's *In His Steps*, an imaginative account of Jesus's reactions to life in a Midwestern town, also affected Brannin's early career.[86] Like St. Matthew's Dean Stuck, Brannin was attracted by the altruism of the social gospel movement.

In 1912 Brannin went to work as a desk secretary for the YMCA in downtown Dallas. The "Y" maintained an orthodox religious stance but was quite liberal socially. Brannin and the organization's educational secretary formed reading groups in which they discussed the works of George, Upton Sinclair, Walter Rauschenbusch, and other advocates of socialism and "social" religion.[87] During his time at the "Y," Brannin met Edwards and noted that despite his radicalism, the leader of Dallas's socialists was not ostracized—he maintained social contacts and regularly played handball with a well-known pastor and one of the city's most prominent attorneys.[88]

Responding to the number of young men from small towns who arrived in Dallas looking for work, Brannin established an employment service through the YMCA (the city had no such agency in 1912). In order to avoid competition with Dallas's growing trade unions, Brannin's employment service placed only unskilled laborers. Dallas employers were extremely receptive to applicants sent by the YMCA, and Brannin was almost immediately promoted to employment secretary. His department soon incorporated the reading and discussion groups, which continued and evolved into a vocational night school that provided instruction in typing, shorthand, bookkeeping, sales techniques, and English for foreigners (although the language class was frequently attended by poorly schooled rural migrants).[89]

Although Brannin did not officially join the Socialist party for three more years, he maintained close personal and political ties to other Dallas socialists. His work to ease the transition of rural and foreign migrants led him to conclude that local advocates of socialism shared his vision of a city in which workers received a fair share of the benefits of urban growth. Members of Dallas's socialist local neither pushed a rigid "party line" nor required formal membership. This tolerance encouraged alliances with Brannin, Dean Stuck, progressive ministers, reform advocates, and the institutions they represented. Toward the end of 1914, Brannin moved to Cincinnati to work with the Rev. Herbert S. Bigelow at the People's Church, but the employment service Brannin had begun in Dallas continued to flourish. Upon his return to a very different city in 1933, Brannin renewed his interest in the plight of the unemployed and formalized his ties with Dallas's Local 36.[90]

Less tangible than achievements such as the free night school and employment service, but no less important to the city's development, was the ability of a radical Left to moderate the conservative tendencies of the local elite. The presence of respected attorneys such as Edwards and Miller and native Texan E. M. Lane—a "natural orator" and frequent speaker at both city hall protests and socialist rallies—at the forefront of Dallas socialism made warnings that radicals were dangerous and "foreign" appear hysterical.[91] Edwards's strong showing in the 1913 mayor's race motivated the Citizens Association to back a more liberal candidate in 1915 (the reform-minded Henry D. Lindsley).

Socialist activity before World War I served to broaden the local political spectrum. The *Laborer*'s radical editorials and the pro-union position of the *Dallas Craftsman* ensured that centrist stances by other papers were not interpreted as "leftist." The presence of a well-articulated radical alternative ensured the acceptance of Dallas's moderate and liberal newspaper columnists and editorial writers and spared them the venom of conservative critics. In June 1915 the *Dallas Morning News* endorsed the University of Texas Department of Political Economy's policy of teaching socialist principles and subsequently ran a letter to the editor from prominent socialist J. L. Hicks congratulating the paper on its stand. Hicks, familiar to Dallas readers as a regular columnist for the *Laborer*, asserted in his letter that since Socialist candidates had received more than 25,000 votes in each of the state's two most recent biennial elections, Texas youth should not be "guarded against finding out what this movement is and on what ground its adherents claim popular recognition and support."[92] The *Morning News*'s stance in favor of academic freedom and tolerance (not in favor of socialism) generated little controversy. Socialist advocates like Hicks defused (or absorbed) conservative criticism of moderate positions.[93]

In this environment, "loyal" Democrats advocated land reform—a regular socialist theme inherited from the Populists. The *Dallas Democrat*'s Willis Andrews mourned the scant congressional attention given recent federal land-reclamation proposals. He argued that widespread tenancy and hunger encouraged "bolshevism" and urged local moderates to support redistribution of land owned by speculators and syndicates. According to Andrews, "Land held out of use for speculative purposes, while there is hunger in the world, is a violation of the law of nature, and a travesty on the principles of justice among men."[94] No doubt many of Dallas's prominent bankers and developers recognized the similarity between Andrews's rhetoric and that of local socialist E. M. Lane.

World War I heightened suspicion of all socialists, yet local pacifists received a fair degree of understanding and little public censure. Carl Brannin's parents respected their son's pacifism. On hearing that the family might lose "friends" should Carl be jailed as a conscientious objector, Lewis Brannin declared that type of friend not worth having. The elder Brannin, a well-respected Dallas Democrat, took time away from his busy real-estate business to circulate a petition calling for Eugene Debs's release from federal prison in Atlanta.[95]

Long-time state senator and newspaper editor J. C. McNealus also campaigned on Debs's behalf, claiming, "He ought never, in my opinion, to have been sent to prison. . . . His imprisonment was not necessary for the public welfare, because he is not an advocate of fire-brand violence. He is sympathetically and altruistically opposed to war and uncompromisingly committed to free speech." The *Dallas Democrat* endorsed political amnesty for all pacifists and questioned punishing objectors for their antiwar sentiments when such beliefs were held as late as 1917 by President Wilson himself.[96] Six months after the United States declared war on Germany, only 1 in 50 (of between 1,500 and 2,000) farmers at a Dallas convention supported the war.[97] The *Democrat*, a Dallas institution since 1883, noted the wartime ambivalence of Dallas workers and North Texas farmers and reflected the opinions of its subscribers in its tolerance for socialists and war objectors.

Although dissension among Dallas socialists concerning pacifism and the ensuing rupture of the Socialist party shattered the local organization, tensions had appeared before the outbreak of war. The decline of socialism has long been attributed to factionalization during the war years and government repression—especially suppression of the socialist press after 1917, which destroyed vital lines of communication between farmers and urban wage earners. The Dallas local, however, had peaked several years earlier and, while the splintering of the national party and wartime repression certainly brought an end to socialism as a local alternative, neither explains the relative stagnation of socialism in Dallas during the years immediately preceding United States participation in World War I.

Dallas's socialists succeeded in heightening class-consciousness among the city's workers. Ironically though, the local was weakened when an autonomous working-class movement led by officers of AFL-affiliated unions began to pull away from middle-class socialist leaders and pursue a nonpartisan course. In addition, the Dallas local was plagued by racism—preventing the unification of black and white workers and tenant farmers. The egalitarian rhetoric of progressives such as Edwards and Brannin alarmed native southern workers steeped in traditions of white supremacy, while the racism of state socialist leaders dissuaded otherwise interested blacks from joining the party.

In 1913 William Reilly, an immensely popular Dallas typographer, established the weekly *Dallas Craftsman*. Reilly, a native of Tyler in East Texas, joined the union in Dallas at age sixteen and twice served as its local president.[98] While adamant on issues such as organizational freedom and the advantages of closed shops, Reilly, unlike George Clifton Edwards, stopped short of calling for an end to capitalism and massive changes in the organization of society. As a result, the *Craftsman* appealed to advertisers seeking to attract the patronage of Dallas workers but unwilling to support the *Laborer*. During the war years, each issue of the *Craftsman* consistently ran between twenty and twenty-five ads under the title "Entitled to the Patronage of Dallas Wage Earners."

Increased competition from the *Craftsman* came at a time when Edwards's attention was focused on his growing law practice and Woodrow Wilson's postmaster general began a crackdown on the socialist press. Papers such as the *Laborer* depended on the mail for distribution to rural readers. The postal system's confiscation of socialist newspapers restricted the *Laborer* to Dallas proper, where it appealed primarily to workers and competed directly with the *Craftsman*. Although the *Laborer* was doomed, Edwards's disappointment was tempered by his enthusiasm for the emergence of strong leadership within the local labor movement and his exhaustion after over a decade of juggling publishing, teaching, and law.[99]

Reilly was typical of the trade union hierarchy that emerged after 1915. He encouraged local workers to pursue a more conservative political course while maintaining close personal ties to Dallas socialists. National divisions between socialists and labor leaders and the disintegration of the Socialist party into warring sects after 1919 reinforced the decision of local unions to reject socialism as a political alternative. The significant success of Dallas unions during the war combined with the general confusion of the American Left to encourage workers to restrict their efforts to local issues and marked the mass return of Dallas's voting members of the working class to the Democratic party.

As was the case with the state organization, Dallas's socialist local was unsuccessful in its attempts to attract African American members.

Socialist leaders saw their efforts to build coalitions thwarted by racism and business practices that pitted white workers against blacks. Edwards wrote in the *Laborer*, "Every time race hatred is stirred, the Southern labor problem is made worse. And every effort to hinder Negro education, keep him down to a wretched ignorance, is but a scheme that will help pull us down by subjecting us to a sort of labor competition almost if not quite as bad as slavery."[100] But, despite the editor's warnings, evidence surfaced in the pages of his own paper that Dallas union members saw blacks as a cheap source of unskilled labor that could be used against them instead of as potential allies in a united labor movement. In space allocated to reports from the various Dallas unions, the following appeared: "Work is dull; nothing doing for the Pale Face. The dusky man seems to be in demand just at present."[101]

Despite the efforts of Edwards and Nat Hardy, who took over much of the editing of the *Laborer* in 1912, racism was not eliminated from the party's local chapter. Prospective black members were further discouraged by a state party that advocated segregated locals as opposed to Oscar Ameringer's integrated socialist organization in Oklahoma. With the election of Judge E. O. Meitzen of Lavaca County to the office of state secretary in 1911, the forces of segregation within Texas socialism triumphed, and attempts to organize blacks and Hispanics were irrecoverably crippled.[102]

In Dallas, the socialist local virtually disintegrated amid dissension over pacifism, lack of confidence in the state party apparatus, and rifts in the national organization. Toward the end of 1918, Covington Hall, a veteran of southern organizing campaigns, and Tom Hicks, former editor of the Hallettsville *Rebel*, planned a new paper to be based in Dallas and named after Hall's old Populist paper, *Voice of the People*. They were unable to revive the Populist legacy of local radicalism, however, and the paper never materialized.[103] By 1920 the Socialist party could claim only 40,000 members nationwide. As J. Louis Engdahl, editor of the party's official newspaper, toured the Midwest, he was told again and again, "We had a fine local, but the war came."[104] Dallas's socialists would have told Engdahl the same story. The turmoil of the war years overshadowed the gradual transference of worker loyalty from radicals to more conservative union leaders, much as it masked the local's inability to interest the city's blacks.

The effectiveness of early Dallas's radicals was limited by the meager resources of farmers and wage laborers and by persistent racism among whites. Nevertheless, local Populists and Socialists heightened class consciousness among workers and provided two generations of trade unionists with an alternative model of urban expansion based on fairness, cooperation, and the empowerment of producers. In addition, Dallas radicals established enduring urban institutions, organized or lent support to campaigns for new or improved city services, and moderated the political choices of a conservative local elite.

FAIRNESS REVISITED:

LABOR'S BID FOR RESPECTABILITY

If this country ever comes to grief it will never come through the efforts of laboring men.
—Dallas businessman W. C. Holland in 1898[1]

AS A CROSSROADS MARKETPLACE surrounded by small and midsized wheat and cotton farms, Dallas possessed little in its economy or society to stimulate the development of labor organizations until after the arrival of the Houston & Texas Central and Texas & Pacific railroads in the 1870s. The railroads, once again, proved to be a harbinger of change.[2] In addition to the large pool of wage laborers employed by the railroads themselves, the ensuing booms in population and construction lured building tradesmen and practitioners of a wide variety of crafts to the city.

Beginning in the 1870s, labor organizations grew quickly in Dallas. The remnant of the La Reunion colony and the city's relatively large number of migrants from the Ohio River Valley tempered the traditional southern view of unions as "Yankee abominations." While newspapers throughout Texas exhibited a growing distrust of labor unions as early as the 1880s, Dallas remained fertile ground for organizing efforts during the next forty years.[3]

Early Dallas was neither consistently supportive of organized labor nor virulently anti-union. Typically, residents were open to the idea of organization among workers and developed short-term pro-union or anti-union stances based on perceptions of events immediately preceding a particular strike or dispute. Middle-class support was linked primarily to issues of "fairness"—narrowly defined to mean faithful adherence to contractual agreements. Since the sanctity of contracts was a primary value of the local elite, a public stand in support of a legal contract involved less risk for either organized or unorganized workers than did actions protesting dangerous working conditions and low wages.

When striking workers convinced residents that an abusive employer violated a legal contract, as was the case during the 1898 streetcar workers' strike, they enjoyed widespread popular support. Conversely, Dallas workers were also expected to respect a contract. Two decades after the street railway strike, building-trades unions that demanded unscheduled raises alienated many middle-class union "supporters" who had sided with striking electrical linemen earlier that year.

Dallas's late-nineteenth-century trade unionists articulated a vision of urban growth in which merit and productivity would replace inherited social class and fortunes based on speculation as the primary determinants of an individual's standard of living. This vision emphasizing fairness and increased social and economic roles for producers blended easily with the ideologies of middle-class radicals and with the altruism of early reform advocates. Trade unionists sought protection for union-made goods and a more inclusive city government. They opposed poll taxes and the at-large election of aldermen. Their consistent advocacy of municipal ownership of street railways and utilities similarly reflected a commitment to empower the city's producers. In combination with Dallas County farmers and the middle-class, urban populists who supported Jerome Kearby, labor emerged as a vital component of the politics of competition and cooperation that characterized Dallas from the 1880s to the conservative years following World War I.

The Populists' *Southern Mercury* and four short-lived union newspapers presented labor's agenda between 1885 and 1906. Later, the socialists' *Laborer* and William Reilly's *Craftsman* became regular voices for skilled labor in Dallas.[4] Weekly meetings, the distribution of pamphlets and flyers, a cooperative store, and dances sponsored by the Trades Assembly (later the Dallas Central Labor Council) increased the level of class consciousness among the city's skilled workers and developed an esprit de corps that strengthened the bargaining positions of member unions.

The relative passivity of Dallas's unskilled workers did not stem from widespread anti-union sentiment. Instead, the city's nonunion workers often endured conditions far worse than those faced by skilled union tradesmen and concluded that the risks involved in publicly supporting labor outweighed potential benefits for workers without unions. While the carpenters won a ten-hour day in 1886 and campaigned for the next two decades for eight hours, mill workers in

South Dallas routinely worked twelve hours. County tenant farmers, employees of small shops and factories, women, and the city's beleaguered black population remained largely unresponsive to skilled labor's calls for support for shorter days. Given the trade unions' rejection of organizing industrial workers before World War I and the unions' rightward turn during the war years, it is not surprising that the voices of Dallas's lowest-paid workers were not raised in support of issues presented by relatively prosperous tradesmen.

Despite deep divisions based on skill levels and on race, Dallas's unions thrived from the early 1880s until immediately after World War I, when Dallas employers organized the Open Shop Association as a reaction to the militancy of the city's building-trades unions. Labor was most effective during or immediately after periods of radical political activity. The coalition with Populists during the 1890s elected painter Patrick Golden to the state legislature and butcher Max Hahn to the city council. As local socialists gained strength, Gilbert Irish, a union printer, was elected to the council between 1902 and 1906, and to the committee that wrote the city's 1907 charter.[5] At the socialist movement's peak, Dallas voters sent union musician John W. ("Bill") Parks, a two-time president of the Texas State Federation of Labor, to the state legislature for three terms between 1912 and 1918.[6] As was the case with the Populists and the socialists, Dallas trade unionists lacked the financial resources to consistently mount successful political campaigns against candidates chosen by Dallas business leaders. They did, however, exert enough influence to sway crucial city council votes and ensure the election of moderates to the state legislature.[7]

The primary weakness of Dallas trade unions as a means of grassroots organization was the racism of white union members. Although African Americans organized early, they remained segregated into smaller, less powerful locals. Viewed as a reserve labor pool by employers and as a threat to job security by white workers, Dallas blacks remained on the periphery of working-class activism and were justifiably reluctant to join either Populist- or socialist-led coalitions of white workers and county farmers.

As union strength reached its peak at the end of World War I, another crucial weakness became apparent—a gulf between the city's struggling rank-and-file and prosperous union leaders that allowed for the co-optation of much of the union hierarchy by local business leaders. Ideological arguments also divided Dallas unions. In their zeal to discredit militant building-trades officials, conservative delegates to the Central Labor Council helped undermine the city's largest and most powerful unions.

I

In the spring of 1882, a small group of Dallas craftsmen established a local assembly of the Knights of Labor.[8] Its rapid growth inspired organization among the various trades. Local typographers became the first Dallas group to apply for a national or international union charter in October 1885. Almost three-quarters of the just over one hundred printers in the city joined the union.[9]

Not quite a year later, a roomful of Dallas carpenters met surreptitiously—under the pretense of a card game—at the Swiss Avenue home of J. J. Johnson and unrolled the new charter they had received from the five-year-old United Brotherhood of Carpenters and Joiners of America. Founders of Dallas Local 198 organized cautiously lest news of their efforts cost them their jobs. Affiliation with the national organization must have inspired confidence, however, because almost immediately, union members struck for a ten-hour day. (In 1886, Dallas carpenters routinely worked from sunrise to sunset for two dollars a day.) Work stopped throughout the city, and four days later, local contractors agreed to the carpenters' demands. The new union had won Dallas's first strike.[10]

The success of the carpenters and the initial growth of the Knights of Labor encouraged Dallas musicians, tailors, painters, saddle and harness makers, horse-collar makers, stone cutters, and stenographers to organize within the next four years.[11] The city's early trade unions grew alongside the Knights of Labor; throughout the last two decades of the nineteenth century, many skilled workers were members of both a local trade union and an assembly of the Knights of Labor. The national rivalry between the Knights and AFL-affiliated trade unions resulted in little acrimony in Dallas but did ensure that the development of organized labor in the Southwest followed the national pattern in which relatively conservative trade unions triumphed over more overtly political groups such as the Knights.

In addition to the wage increases and shorter days sought by most of the early unions, the stenographers added a controversial demand

TABLE 3
DALLAS LABOR ORGANIZATIONS IN 1892

Organization	Local Established*	Members*
Knights of Labor, Assembly No. 1931	1882	—
Knights of Labor, Assembly No. 4125 (Black)	c. 1885	—
Dallas Typographical Union, No. 173	1885	75
Cigarmakers' Union, No. 262	1882	24
United Brotherhood of Carpenters and Joiners of America, No. 198	1886	300
Brotherhood of Painters and Decorators of America, No. 46	1887	100
Dallas Saddle and Harness Makers' Union, No. 18	1889	110
United Brotherhood of Carpenters and Joiners of America, No. 622	1890	120
Dallas Eight Hour League	c. 1889	—
Horse Collar Makers' Union, No. 8	—	—
Musicians' Protective Union, No. 48	—	—
Stone Cutters' Association	—	—
Tailors' Union, No. 78	—	—
Building Laborers' International Protective Union, No. 1, Texas (Black)	—	—
Dallas Branch of the American Federation of Labor	—	—

* Many early figures are not available.

Sources: *Memorial and Biographical History of Dallas County, Texas*; and AFL Minutes, Labor Archives, University of Texas at Arlington

for equal compensation for women "providing the same service" as men.[12] By 1892 Dallas's fifteen labor organizations ranged in size from the cigarmakers with 24 members to the typographers, saddle and harness makers, and painters—all with at least 100 members—to the carpenters, who maintained two Dallas locals totaling 420 members (see Table 3).[13]

Dallas's earliest black labor organizations, Local Assembly No. 4125 of the Knights of Labor and the first Texas chapter of the Building Laborers' International Protective Union, also date from the years between 1882 and 1890. Both groups met weekly and shared space in the downtown Labor Hall on Elm Street with several of the white unions.[14] Black waiters also organized early—the *Dallas Morning News* quoting a "very smart looking" member of the new union who announced that organization was necessary because "the waiters of Dallas, as a whole, were used worse than dogs."[15]

Throughout the 1890s, Dallas unionists sought to promote an aura of respectability. Organizers eschewed the secret tactics employed by the early carpenters' union. Announcements for meetings and social events became commonplace in the city's major newspapers as did follow-up stories on proceedings. Delegates met as a quasi-official body known as the Trades Assembly (or Trades Council) to coordinate organizing and public relations efforts. The umbrella group not only determined labor's local agenda but also pursued a strategy designed to encourage relationships with Dallas County farmers. Officers of the Dallas County Farmers' Alliance sat alongside delegates representing AFL-affiliated unions in the Trades Assembly. County farmers helped Dallas union leaders move a mechanics' lien law through the state legislature, and the city's tradesmen routinely attended Alliance conventions and meetings of the Jefferson Democrats (the dissident left wing of the Alliance that founded the Texas People's party in Dallas in 1891). The coalition of farmers, AFL-affiliated trade unionists, and the Knights of Labor persisted even after Samuel Gompers issued a ruling demanding the Knights' expulsion. Two years after Gompers's mandate, delegates representing the Knights of Labor still attended meetings of the Dallas Trades Assembly.[16]

Local union members vigorously supported the cigarmakers in their national boycott of Liggett & Myers. Dallas cigarmakers commended the city's tradesmen for the "zeal" they displayed in demanding that local retailers carry alternatives to the eight brands of tobacco affected by the boycott. In an attempt to guide working-class consumption, the

Trades Assembly made arrangements with *The Liberator* to publish a list of union "requests" concerning which local businesses to patronize and which to avoid. "Requests," such as an 1892 announcement asking that John A. Fisher Clothing Club, representing Kohler & Co., "be given the cold sholder [*sic*]," were tangible results of union efforts to empower skilled workers and create an urban environment that emphasized fairness.[17]

The Populist-Labor coalition of "producers" was given a boost in March 1893 when the last of the city's large trade unions, the typographers, affiliated with the Trades Assembly. Two months later, a downtown Dallas street parade during the typographers' state convention turned into a celebration of solidarity among the city's trade unionists, area farmers, urban populists, and the Knights of Labor. The Trades Assembly encouraged the organization of as many of the city's skilled workers as possible and sent experienced representatives to assist printing pressmen, cooks, and waiters in forming or stabilizing their unions. Attempts to include railroad workers (boilermakers and switchmen) in an urban labor movement were less successful. Some of the railway unions had recovered from the Great Southwest Strike, but the organization of railroad work kept union members out of town or on call for extended periods and chronically prevented regular attendance at Trades Assembly meetings by railway delegates.[18]

The leadership abilities of union officers such as Patrick Golden and James Scott and their prominent positions within the Populist-Labor coalition attracted the attention of other Dallas groups that were competing for influence and seeking to change civic policies. Dallas police officers asked union members to sign petitions protesting police salary reductions. The Dallas elite recognized labor's vitality and appealed to union leaders to orchestrate support for a wide variety of urban issues during the 1890s. Business leaders sponsoring efforts to navigate the Trinity River called on the Trades Assembly to help organize a public celebration of the arrival of the first commercial boat and official "opening" of the river. After hearing the report of a committee that met with the manager of the navigation company to ascertain the nature of the celebration and parade, Dallas unionists determined that such events could enhance the image of organized labor and decided that all local unions would turn out under the banner of the AFL.[19]

Inherent in early unionists' decisions to cultivate a positive and respectable local image was the threat of manipulation by those who owned the city's major newspapers. The commercial-civic elite encouraged organized labor to support growth-oriented policies by promising job security and increased wages. As prominent businessmen recognized labor as a viable competitor, union leaders increasingly found themselves opposing those who controlled the public opinion so vital to early union successes. Throughout the 1890s, however, and well into the twentieth century, Dallas leaders needed labor's support. Navigation of the Trinity, downtown street improvements, land reclamation, and the extension of services to newly annexed areas were controversial projects requiring allies among the city's skilled workers.

While labor emerged as a political force with a coherent urban agenda during the 1890s, union leaders remained accountable to rank-and-file members. Even the most popular leaders learned to avoid public implications that they controlled a bloc of voters. Trades Assembly president James Scott, a veteran of the Texas State Federation of Labor and the Eight-Hour League, was stripped of his office after he told a reporter from the *Dallas Times Herald* that his "people" voted his way. Scott's own union, the carpenters, initiated his removal. The Assembly exonerated its former president when he agreed to correct his statement to the *Times Herald* and made him secretary of the Trades Assembly the next year, but the experience served to remind the union hierarchy that it led a popular movement.[20]

The city's early trade unionists gained credibility through the struggle for an eight-hour workday. The eight-hour movement developed as a central working-class issue in the early 1890s, as the coalition of populist farmers and workers gained momentum. Despite high levels of activity and much public debate, workers could claim only partial victory after a decade of struggle. While working hours continued to be determined primarily by the city's employers, early calls for shorter work days influenced public opinion and enabled a later generation of reformers to reduce the hours of many Dallas workers.

In 1889 Dallas union leaders dominated a state convention called to organize the Texas Federation of Labor. Designed to unite labor councils across the state, the Federation platform initially called for an eight-hour law to be passed by the state legislature. Dallas's Patrick Golden, J. T. W. Loe, James Scott, and black union leader Melvin Wade figured prominently in the development of the 1889 platform, which also called for a single tax on land value; a repeal of all other taxes, calling them fines "placed upon intelligence, energy and labor"; dissolution of the national bank; government ownership of railroads, telegraphs, and telephones; and the abolition of the grand jury system, the United States Senate, and all state senates. The State Federation also called for the Australian ballot and a state lien law for mechanics.[21]

Some of the delegates wanted to separate the eight-hour issue from the rest of labor's controversial political platform in order to gain broader support. Acknowledging the choke-hold that business interests had on city councils throughout the state and divisions based on race and skill levels that could thwart strikes and boycotts, Dallas delegate Loe argued that any move to shorten workdays was inherently political and could be successful only if a grassroots movement elected legislators willing to pass a state law. Loe's position carried by a large majority. Dallas carpenter James Scott urged every delegate to return home and organize Eight-Hour Leagues and "agitate this movement."[22]

By February 1890, Eight-Hour Leagues had been established in Dallas, Houston, and San Antonio, and organizational efforts were underway in Fort Worth, Waco, and Austin. While the Dallas group remained convinced that only a state law could reduce the hours of most of the city's workers, members initiated a local campaign to restrict hours worked on municipal projects. Scott, Loe, and James Boggs, representing the Eight-Hour League, presented Dallas aldermen with a petition bearing 1,731 signatures that called for eight-hour workdays on all municipal jobs.[23]

The eight-hour ordinance, which would go into effect the first day of May, 1890, passed unanimously at an emotional city council meeting in early March. In a rare example of unity, white workers packed city hall alongside Melvin Wade and the black unionists he represented. Almost immediately, however, efforts to sabotage the new ordinance began. One council member agreed to vote in favor of the measure because of its obvious popularity but warned that such an ordinance would flood the city with excess labor from around the state. To whites in the council chambers he proclaimed, "Yes, every negro will rush here."[24]

Opponents of the eight-hour ordinance found an ally in acting city attorney R. E. Cowart, an Oak Cliff resident with strong ties to prominent investors and contractors and ambitions for a permanent appointment. Because the Dallas city charter mandated that municipal projects costing more than $500 be awarded to contractors, virtually all laborers employed on city jobs worked for area construction companies. Charging that the city could not exert authority over workers it did not directly employ, Cowart deemed the eight-hour measure in violation of the city charter. The ordinance was dead by mid-April.[25]

After this defeat, the city's trade unionists returned their attention to efforts to pass an eight-hour law in the Texas Legislature. In 1892 the Trades Assembly voted to present to all state senators a resolution supporting a state law and demanded that local candidates for the legislature support an eight-hour bill.[26] Not surprisingly, Patrick Golden, a veteran of the eight-hour movement running as a Populist for state representative, won the endorsement of the Trades Assembly. He became the first member of the local Populist-Labor coalition to serve at the state level. One of Golden's initial actions in Austin was to sponsor a broad labor bill that included an eight-hour law and other elements of the 1889 State Federation of Labor platform. The Dallas Trades Assembly, recalling the failed attempt to restrict working hours on municipal projects, asked Golden to add a provision to his bill that would strike from Dallas's city charter the section relating to "letting by contract all city work over . . . $500.00 as now exist [*sic*] in the charter, it being apparent that this clause in the charter was against the interest of the city of Dallas and particularly the laboring people."[27] Although measures sponsored by early labor legislators such as Golden generally died in committee or, when passed by the House, failed in the Senate, the resulting public debate altered common notions of what a "typical" workday entailed.[28]

Many Dallas employers ostensibly responded to organized labor's calls for an eight-hour workday but paid their employees so poorly that most had little choice but to work longer. Since workers generally received no more than the usual rates for "overtime," employers could bow to public sentiment favoring eight hours and still rely on an ample supply of workers "willing" to work longer. Beginning in 1893, the Trades Assembly set up "watch-dog" committees to investigate working conditions throughout the city. Initial committee reports described what became a common scenario: a contractor building an addition to the Federal Building accurately claimed not to require crews to work more than eight hours daily. Crews routinely worked longer, however, because he did not consistently pay the "established rate." Another Trades Assembly committee expressed concern over similar conditions affecting painters at the courthouse.[29]

Typographers and building tradesmen, who maintained the city's largest unions, continued to work more than eight hours a day throughout the 1890s. Labor remained firm in its support of shorter workdays but the flood of migrants pouring into the city and white workers' limited perception of blacks—as a reserve labor pool ready to take the jobs of strikers—effectively deterred attempts to achieve an eight-hour workday through direct action. Although the Trades Assembly consistently pursued an agenda geared toward the empowerment of the city's skilled workers, labor's dependence on public opinion discounted the possibility of rapid social change.

A decade after initial organizational efforts, the city's trade unions reached a plateau. The Dallas elite recognized labor as both a political competitor and a potential ally, and leaders of the Populist-Labor coalition, such as Jerome Kearby and Patrick Golden, received the support of many middle-class voters. Yet the barriers of race, gender, and class restricted the coalition's growth. Labor's right to organize was generally acknowledged, but support for elements of the unions' agenda that would empower producers (the elimination of poll taxes and at-large council elections and the municipal ownership of utilities and street railways) was limited to skilled workers, farmers, and a few middle-class radicals. The city's first major strike converted the passive tolerance of union activity that characterized the attitudes of most middle-class Dallas residents to widespread support for union workers. The pastor of the First Methodist Church, a local judge, a moderate newspaper editor, politicians, representatives of the commercial-civic elite, and the president of the city's Freethinkers Association took public stands in the union's favor during the course of a month-long strike.

On November 10, 1898, 107 members of the Amalgamated Association of Street Railway Employees of America No. 93 left their jobs to protest treatment accorded two union members by management of the Dallas Consolidated Electric Railway Company. Motormen and mule drivers, who had obtained a closed-shop contract during the previous summer, went on strike to protest contract violations resulting from the discharge of Frank Hildreth and the demotion of William Traw. Barn and shop workers and those engaged in track repair immediately struck in solidarity with the motormen and drivers. (Despite the contract's provision that non-union workers could be hired in the barn and shop as long as union members were given preference, every employee of the streetcar company except two day foremen had joined the union.)[30]

The company's new superintendent discharged Hildreth after the union man made a remark expressing his preference for the old boss. The union believed that the superintendent had over-reacted and invoked its contractual right to binding arbitration to settle the dispute. The Hildreth case was to be decided by three arbitrators: one chosen by the company, one by the union, and a neutral arbitrator agreed upon by both parties. Near the conclusion of the investigation, the neutral arbitrator mysteriously left town during an evening recess. The union demanded the reinstatement of Hildreth, whose family depended on his income, pending a new investigation. The superintendent's removal of Traw, a senior mechanic, from the streetcar shop exacerbated the situation; he was reassigned to a repair crew on the tracks—work usually given junior employees. When the company refused to investigate either case further, the union called a strike.[31]

Initially the strike limited streetcar service in Dallas to a few main routes covered by company foremen and managers. Calls for strikebreakers were met with caution. Several potential strikebreakers, lured to the company barn by the promise of steady work, expressed sympathy for the strikers. One told a reporter for the *Dallas Morning News*, "I want to find out just what the grievances of the men are before I agree to take a car out on the line."[32] On the third day of the strike, citizens attending a mass meeting at city hall urged the company to abide by the arbitration clause in its contract. Residents concerned about the lack of public transportation appointed a committee headed by popular Judge W. S. Simkins to help settle the dispute. Railway company president C. H. Alexander infuriated the populace by declaring Simkins an unfit representative and by refusing to meet with the citizens' committee. Alexander dismissed the possibility of further arbitration. He announced that he would not be bound by the terms of the contract, since signing an agreement with the union had been a mistake on his part.[33]

The street railway president's flippant attitude toward a legal contract and refusal to deal with the citizens' committee drew condemnation from diverse elements of the community. Alexander's accusations that union members were packing the lines with rocks and boarding cars to threaten passengers did not dilute support for the strikers. Rev.

G. C. Rankin of the First Methodist Church charged that the "dignity of [the] superintendent" had been wounded by a "harmless" remark. Declaring that workers were not "slaves to be driven by the company," Rankin added, "It is not necessary for them to take off their hats . . . when the superintendent of the road comes around."[34]

Two days after the first mass meeting, another large crowd packed the city hall auditorium. Col. W. C. Holland, a prominent civic leader, told the crowd that the actions of the strikers were "justified" and praised union members for their honesty and intelligence. Senator-elect Barry Miller joined Holland in support of the strikers and added that workers needed to organize to ensure fair treatment. Alderman Max Hahn was cheered by his working-class constituents when he approached the podium and announced, "I say for the boys to keep cool; don't violate the law. You will not go hungry as long as I run a butcher shop."[35] Perhaps the most unusual source of support for the streetcar workers came from O. Paget, president of the decidedly middle-class Dallas Freethinkers Association and a proponent of the ideas of R. G. Ingersoll. Paget spoke before three hundred strike supporters at the Union depot on November 17 and four days later addressed the Trades Assembly.[36]

Public ownership of the streetcar lines, a national issue, became a subject of debate throughout the city from the first days of the strike. Like Rev. G. C. Rankin, many Dallas residents were recent migrants from rural areas. They responded to Populist-inspired union rhetoric advocating cooperation as a means of bypassing big-business interests. Commuters complained about their inability to transfer between lines even though the street railway system had been consolidated and was operated by a single company. Others, such as *Dallas Democrat* editor J. C. McNealus, favored an end to franchised public transit because the street-railway owners refused to install fenders and employ conductors despite accidents and violent incidents. Sensing widespread discontent with the company's policies and support for the union's position, McNealus established a public fund to help needy strikers and replaced Judge Simkins as the de facto head of the citizens' committee.[37]

The mass meetings continued into the strike's second week. On November 20, over a thousand people turned out for a rally in front of city hall. John J. Dumont told the crowd that an organized group of employers had chosen to exploit one of the city's weakest unions. He noted that the contracts of building tradesmen, who maintained the strongest of Dallas's early unions, had not been violated. McNealus agreed, contending that "Mr. Alexander and his associates have started in to crush organized labor; they say it must die. No man has taken so radical [a] step as this in the past twenty years."[38]

Dallas unionists recognized that the results of the streetcar strike had repercussions beyond the fate of an individual union and its members. The street-railway company challenged the right of all workers to organize by flagrantly violating a contract and then declaring it void. In addition to donations made by individual union members to the citizens' fund for strikers, the Trades Assembly allocated part of its budget to strike relief and sent a committee to the city council to protest private ownership of a public franchise.[39] A supportive telegram from Eugene Debs and the presence in Dallas of the union's international president, W. D. Mahon, buoyed the strikers' morale, as did continued expressions of public support.[40]

As the dispute entered its fourth week, the union faced total defeat despite overwhelming popular support for the strike. Many unmarried strikers with little seniority left the city to seek work elsewhere. About sixty workers remained on strike, but streetcar service was approaching normal levels through the use of strikebreakers. The total dependence of many of the city's workers on public transportation thwarted efforts to organize an effective boycott. The union had won the battle for public support but could not force the company to the bargaining table.

On the night of December 2, an explosion in the western part of the city ended the stalemate. Dynamite strategically laid on the track along Elm Street blew up a streetcar carrying only a strikebreaking motorman, who was able to jump to safety. As a crowd of about two hundred onlookers began to disperse, another explosion was heard in East Dallas. A second streetcar had run over dynamite on the tracks; again the explosion was well timed and caused no injuries. During the night, police found another stick of dynamite on the tracks near the Sanger brothers' department store and four dynamite caps that damaged a Main Street bridge over the Texas Trunk Railroad. An investigation yielded no clues as to who was responsible for the explosions and the police made no arrests. Almost immediately, however, the street railway offered to rehire the striking workers.[41]

Although the union rejected the initial offer, negotiations continued and the strike ended on December 7. In an apparent attempt to save face, Alexander left the city on a "business trip" to New Orleans. Less than eighteen hours after his departure, the union reached an agreement with company representative Edward Moore. The strikers were rehired or put on the extra list pending vacancies. The company agreed to hire no new workers until after the last of the strikers on the extra list was reassigned. The union, whose original contract expired January 1, 1899, won an extension until June of that year and a two and one-half cent per hour pay increase after January 1, 1899. Given the desperate situation strikers found themselves in before the explosions, the union gave up little. Unlike the old contract, however, the new agreement did not contain an arbitration clause; future disputes were to be settled in court. Details regarding Hildreth and Traw were not made public except that, as with the other strikers, they would be rehired according to their levels of seniority.[42]

No new information regarding the explosions was forthcoming after the resolution of the strike. Union members credited McNealus with the settlement, but members of the local elite Dr. C. M. Rosser and George A. Carden both enlisted as negotiators, and the weight of public opinion clearly applied enough pressure to force Alexander and his associates to sign the new contract.[43] No doubt the violence popularly attributed to the strikers—whose actions members of the local elite had previously deemed justifiable—increased the desire of many business leaders to end the strike. Others sought to sidetrack calls for municipal ownership of the street-railway system. Few Dallas business leaders found it difficult to offer public support to a popular union whose strike affirmed one of the basic tenets of capitalism—faithful adherence to the terms of a contract.

The 1898 streetcar-workers' strike established Dallas's early union leaders as credible political players. During a kind of "honeymoon" period after the strike, Dallas daily newspapers covered even the most controversial activities sponsored by the city's unions without pejorative commentary.[44] The *Morning News* actually gushed in a May 1899 account of a visit to Dallas by Eugene Debs, "the apostle of modern socialism." Describing Debs as "a noted labor leader" with "plenty of personal magnetism," the *News* seemed particularly pleased at the presence of a national luminary in Dallas. The paper included a sketch of Debs alongside a summary of his "remarkable" career. Debs's introduction to an audience of five hundred by the president of the Dallas School Board indicates the local prestige accorded organized labor by the end of the nineteenth century.[45]

From their origins in the early 1880s, Dallas's frontier trade unions built an impressive labor movement in a decidedly hostile region. In tandem with supporters of the People's party, Dallas's skilled workers provided an alternative vision of growth to that of the city's elite—one that promised to empower producers and sought to protect workers from the vicissitudes of the marketplace. As the Populist movement waned, union leaders worried that exploitation of skilled workers would increase. Local employers withheld wages, imported scabs from out-of-state, and relocated factories to employ convict labor even in the best of times.[46] Fear that they would lose ground on their own motivated Dallas's organized workers to seek new allies and build a new coalition.

II

During the first two decades of the twentieth century, Dallas's trade unionists joined forces with local socialists to consolidate union gains, improve working conditions, and reestablish an alternative to the policies of Dallas business leaders. While the leadership of Socialist Local No. 36 and that of the Dallas Trades Assembly remained separate, many rank-and-file union members joined the Socialist party, and a large percentage of union voters in municipal elections between 1904 and 1915 supported socialist candidates.

Socialism provided an ideological framework within which union leaders developed strategies and set goals. Few of the city's early trade unionists were inclined toward revolution; they were committed instead to increasing wages, improving local conditions, and gaining for skilled workers a greater degree of control over the work environment. The coalition of trade unionists and Dallas socialists rested on a shared vision of an equitable society and suspicion of civic policies that disproportionately benefited business interests. It did not reject the notion of growth as an urban ideal but wanted to extend the benefits of new development into working-class neighborhoods and schools and protect workers from fluctuations in the business cycle.

The educational efforts of Dallas's middle-class socialists, most of whom were social democrats, raised levels of class consciousness among workers and helped local unions attract many new members. The number of unions affiliated with the Trades Assembly grew from thirty-three to fifty-six in the first two decades of the twentieth century.[47] From its beginnings, the Socialist-Labor coalition played an active role in Dallas's development. The city's Commercial Club sought the coalition's support for bond issues as early as 1904.[48] In the highly competitive atmosphere that characterized civic life in Dallas before the First World War, such short-term alliances were not unusual.

George Clifton Edwards's *Laborer* played a "watch-dog" role as well as serving as a forum for announcing union victories. Edwards and his staff criticized union members who demonstrated a lack of allegiance to their class. In an article about the city's typographers, the *Laborer* declared, "There is a remarkable lack of fraternal feeling among the members of No. 173. Dallas's union is getting the well-earned reputation of being one of the coldest, most selfish, and greedy organizations." At issue was the practice of senior printers' working full time without offering occasional half days of work to unemployed union members. The socialist editor warned, "Men who hold their situations at a high wage by virtue of the self-denial and heroic unionism of former printers in this city, should not be so greedy and selfish."[49]

The typographers apparently took such criticism seriously and initiated measures to enforce class solidarity. Members caught with any literature not bearing the union label were fined. Since many of the city's typographers worked only part time as printers, the union demanded that they carry union cards in their secondary trades as well.[50] Through the *Laborer*, socialists such as Edwards, Nat Hardy, and J. L. Hicks reinforced the vision of social justice and improved conditions for producers that was the legacy of an earlier generation of local populists and union organizers.

While the city's workers continued to support the *Laborer* until its suppression during World War I, they also acquired other voices. Alfred Andersson's *Dallas Dispatch* and William Reilly's weekly *Craftsman* were neither affiliated with a specific political party nor controlled by the local elite. Andersson began his daily in 1906 as part of Edward W. Scripps's United Press organization. A native of England and a Princeton graduate who also had attended Heidelburg University, Andersson possessed a lively, sensational style. Scripps told his editor to publish the *Dispatch* for the masses; until World War I, the paper sold for a penny. The *Dispatch* remained independent of party but consistently sided with labor and publicized utility abuses. Scripps insisted that Andersson never yield to pressure from the city's powerful downtown merchants. As a result, the *Dispatch* could not depend on department-store patronage. Instead, Scripps's organization backed the paper long enough for it to develop a following among the city's workers. As circulation figures approached thirty thousand, small-business owners eagerly purchased Andersson's advertising space.[51]

The *Dispatch* also proved to be a safe haven for labor organizers. Andersson established a work environment in which union activity, however visible, did not jeopardize one's job. R. H. Campbell, a *Dispatch* printer, was the principal organizer and one of the first officers of the Dallas Central Labor Council—a formal confederation of Trades Assembly unions that received an AFL charter signed by Samuel Gompers and Frank Morrison in 1910. A year after its formation, forty-seven affiliated unions sent delegates to the Central Labor Council.[52]

By 1915 Dallas's union leadership had begun to develop local strategies independently from radical third parties. A new generation of union leaders matured, more influenced by the AFL than by socialism. Exhortations by George Clifton Edwards and Nat Hardy to include blacks in a united movement of workers alarmed the city's skilled tradesmen as did internal divisions within the Socialist party. Local trade unionists adamantly rejected industrial organization and "waged a successful fight" against organizing efforts of the Industrial Workers of the World.[53] By the end of the 1910s, union rhetoric echoed that of liberal reformers.[54] The vision of radical social change and empowerment articulated by local socialists on behalf of all producers was transformed by a more conservative generation of labor leaders into a greater share of capitalist pie for skilled tradesmen.

World War I accelerated a rightward shift in the thinking of Dallas trade-union leaders. Changes in ideology and the prosperity of the union hierarchy resulted in a widening gulf between Dallas Central Labor Council officials and the rank-and-file of the city's most powerful unions. While receptive to the hierarchy's claim that socialism was no longer a viable political or economic alternative, the city's skilled workers—especially those in the building trades—refused to disavow strikes and limit their activities to public relations campaigns and electoral action. On the contrary, as was the case across the country, Dallas experienced a flurry of labor unrest, strikes, and militant collective actions during the war.

Fearing a loss of local prestige after the suppression of socialist newspapers and the arrests of several prominent officials of the state

Socialist party, Dallas's new generation of union leaders disassociated themselves from the city's faltering socialist local (many, however, remained on friendly terms with individual socialists for the rest of their lives). Within the powerful typographers' union, L. L. Daniels, the last of the nineteenth-century printers to hold a major union office, completed his final term as president in 1913. A significant number of the new generation of union printers who held office after that time were sons of the local's organizers and charter members.[55] These second-generation unionists remembered their fathers' disappointment after the factionalization of the People's party. As internal divisions grew among socialists, the new leadership of the typographers' local dismissed radical social change in favor of reform. The national strength of the typographical union and the local's close ties to the *Craftsman* (published by William Reilly, a former president of the Dallas union) enlarged the scope of the printers' influence. With the exception of the building-trades hierarchy, officers of the unions affiliated with the Dallas Central Labor Council followed the lead of the typographers and rejected both radical politics and militant tactics after 1917.

The Dallas Central Labor Council articulated a new, nonpartisan program based on education, organization, cooperation, and "intelligent political action." While retaining the traditional Populist theme of cooperation among producers and the socialist emphasis on education, union leaders rejected strikes in favor of an electoral strategy. As explained in "Trade Unions: Past, Present, Future," a Central Labor Council pamphlet distributed during the war, "It may not take much [*sic*] brains to go on a strike, but it takes genuine thinking and wise planning to learn how to win a victory politically." In addition to higher wages and reduced hours, the new union hierarchy sought the respect of the city's commercial-civic elite. Conservative union officials envisioned labor organizations not only as vehicles for political and economic power but also as a means to enhance the social status of skilled workers. The Central Labor Council determined association to be "the distinguishing feature of the age" and noted that, for workers, trade unions take the place of the "debating society and the professor's lecture."[56] The new generation of union leaders tried to balance the needs and demands of the workers they represented and their own ambitions for enhanced local prestige.

Because Dallas's elite and many middle-class residents supported the war, union leaders were quick to point to examples of patriotism among the city's workers. The trade union hierarchy convinced the rank-and-file that labor demands must not be perceived as interfering with the war effort. Attempts to replace strikes with political strategies were less successful. Particularly troublesome to Central Labor Council officers was the militancy of the city's huge carpenters' union. With the cost of living on the increase, Dallas carpenters rejected the notion that the War Labor Board's proscribed wage represented a fair assessment of the value of an average work day. On July 1, 1918, carpenters meeting at the Labor Temple rejected an offer from the Builders' Association that would have raised union workers' daily wages from five (the War Labor Board rate) to six dollars. With many of its almost 1,000 members already receiving the union's demand of $6.40 per day, 300 carpenters denied the full wage increase halted work on the American Exchange National Bank and the Texas & Pacific and Goldsmith buildings. R. E. Roberts, secretary of the carpenters' union, announced that the work stoppage would not affect construction of the aviation repair depot, as carpenters working on government projects and paid five dollars daily "would remain in good standing in the union and stay on their government jobs."[57]

The willingness of carpenters "in the service of the country" to stay on the job, general awareness that basic costs were indeed rising, the high demand for skilled workers, and public opinion favoring the union forced the Builders' Association to acquiesce. Within nine days, every union carpenter in Dallas returned to work at a daily wage of $6.40. The *Dallas Morning News* reported that while no formal agreement had been made, "the carpenters, in effect, have had their demands acceded to."[58]

Despite the Central Labor Council's warnings that aggressive tactics would destroy popular support for union gains, carpenters and other building tradesmen used their own umbrella organization, the Building Trades Council, to seek wage increases and shorter workdays. Less than a year after receiving their 1918 wage increase, Dallas carpenters led the building trades in a sympathy strike supporting Texas Power & Light (sometimes called Dallas Power & Light) linemen. In March 1919, about thirty union linemen and several nonunion sympathizers quit their jobs after the light company rejected demands for wage increases, an eight-hour workday, and a closed shop. The strikers asked the city's Board of Arbitration to hear the case and offered to return to work during the investigation. The light company, however, refused arbitration.[59]

After a fourteen-week stalemate, almost half of the strikers had left town for new jobs. The Building Trades Council concluded that a light-company victory, which appeared inevitable by the end of May, would set off a chain reaction of union-busting activities in which closed-shop construction sites would be the next targets. Led by the carpenters' M. A. Holland, the Building Trades Council instigated a sympathy strike involving twelve affiliated unions representing five thousand tradesmen. Many rank-and-file members of craft unions represented by the more conservative Central Labor Council voiced their desire to join the strike but were restrained by what union officials called "inviolate agreement with their employers" and contract clauses disallowing sympathy strikes.[60]

Building tradesmen combined these bold new tactics with Dallas unions' long-standing sensitivity to public opinion. The striking workers emphasized the company's unwillingness to present its case to the arbitration board and declared that, as a municipal utility ostensibly managed in the service of the people, Texas Power & Light should submit to the decision of the people's representatives. Holland even denied that the walkout could be accurately termed a sympathy strike. He explained that the building-trades delegates had determined that "they could not in fairness to the linemen continue to perform duties which put them in the position not only of working with non-union men, but with strikebreakers."[61]

The electrical workers also appealed to the public's sense of fairness. They admitted that the union could not force the light company— whose management read like a roll call of Dallas's commercial-civic elite and included John Carpenter, William H. Gaston, Harry Seay, Edward Titche, Charles L. Sanger, J. F. Strickland, and Steve Munger—into arbitration but added that "arbitration can be brought about if public sentiment in its favor can be crystallized."[62] In a statement to the arbitration board, reprinted in the *Dallas Morning News*, Local 69 of the International Brotherhood of Electrical Workers challenged the light company's claim that wages, hours, and hiring practices were company business. The union asserted, "we know that the business of a public service corporation is the people's business."[63]

Immediately after the building trades' June 1 walkout, the eighthour issue resurfaced as a galvanizing force in favor of the strike. Since the eight-hour drive initiated by the Populist-Labor coalition of the 1890s, one Dallas union after another had either officially or unofficially won the eight-hour workday.[64] The passage of an eight-hour law for federal workers, as well as the typographers' widespread use of a study attributing an increased life span of ten years for printers between 1900 and 1919 to the eight-hour day, altered many Dallas residents' definitions of a full workday.[65] As was the case during the 1898 street-railway workers' strike, the city's nonaligned workers and middle-class residents responded to union calls for fairness. Union rallies in city parks and along downtown streets drew large crowds. While altercations between unionists and strikebreakers remained under control during the first week after building tradesmen joined the strike, crowds protesting the light company's intransigence forced the police commissioner to order the disruption of "unlawful" assemblies and cut short Mayor Frank Wozencraft's trip to Buffalo, New York, for a conference on city planning.[66]

Acting on the mayor's request and despite Texas Power & Light's continued refusal to abide by an arbitrated decision, the city's arbitration board investigated circumstances leading to the linemen's strike and issued a public report of its findings. Members of the board displayed a lack of strong sentiment either in support of or in opposition to organized labor. Again paralleling the 1898 streetcar-workers' strike, board members and middle-class residents responded to issues of fairness and took the union's side against an exploitative employer while ignoring or rejecting demands that would substantially change the structure of the workplace.

The arbitration board's report declared that the five-dollar daily wage received by linemen at the time of the strike was insufficient and that "on account of the hazard and danger to which linemen are constantly exposed in the performance of their duty, coming into contact as they do with wires charged with high power and deadly currents of electricity," they should receive no less than $6.50 per day. The board also strongly recommended that the linemen's workday be shortened from nine to eight hours. Its unequivocal support for a shorter workday reveals the extent to which organized labor's vision of fairness and an improved standard of living for skilled workers affected the attitudes of Dallas residents, regardless of class. Nevertheless, the city's trade unionists were unable to garner widespread support for policies that would increase employee control over the workplace. The electrical union's demand for a closed shop was rejected by the board. The report stated that an employer's right to hire any qualified employee was "irrevocably fixed in both the Federal and State Constitutions."[67]

Thousands of striking workers shut down construction sites until a violent incident changed the tenor of the dispute. On the morning of June 11, 1919, one man was killed and four injured in a clash between union linemen and strikebreakers. The incident occurred north of downtown and attracted a crowd of several hundred people before police arrived. Responding to reports that strikebreakers were mistreating pickets, two union leaders and their driver approached the intersection of Routh Street and Cedar Springs in a red roadster. Between twelve and fifteen employees of the light company were working at the site. Reports conflict as to how many more union men appeared in other vehicles, but in the fighting that ensued, Al Shrum, a twenty-two-year-old apprentice electrician and the driver of the union leaders' car, exchanged shotgun blasts with a company guard. The guard was killed and Shrum, another union man, and two bystanders injured. Within a week, Dallas police issued arrest warrants for eight union members in connection with the shootings.[68]

John W. Carpenter, vice president of Texas Power & Light, issued a report stating that the guard had been seated in one of the company's trucks with his shotgun in a box and was shot before he could reach the gun and fire at his assailants. According to Carpenter, a nonunion lineman then jumped from a pole and returned fire with the guard's gun. The strikers and a neutral eyewitness insisted that the shotgun was positioned across the guard's lap when they arrived and that he had fired the first shot. A strikebreaker agreed that the gun was in the guard's hands but testified that the union man fired first. The presence of well-known union leaders in an easily identifiable red car did not support Carpenter's assertion that the guard's killing was premeditated. The participation of several uniformed soldiers in the fistfighting that led to the shooting further complicated the investigation. The soldiers' identities or loyalties were not made public.[69]

By the end of June, four union men were indicted for murder, three were released, and one remained at large. By October, charges were dropped against all of the strikers except Shrum. The doctor who performed the autopsy on the company guard announced that the shot from the victim's head was the size used by the company's guards and that the shotgun used by Shrum had been loaded with shot of a different size.[70] Faced with unanswered questions and growing sympathy for Shrum, who was raised in Dallas County and presented several character witnesses, the prosecution relied solely on testimony of strikebreaking linemen. Shrum insisted that he had fired into the truck only after receiving a leg wound from the guard's second shotgun blast. The jury convicted Shrum of manslaughter instead of murder and sentenced him to three years in prison. The young electrician's attorney immediately filed an appeal, and Shrum was released on $3,000 bond.[71]

The investigation into the "strike riot," as the press labeled the June 11 incident, and Shrum's subsequent trial dominated local news coverage during the summer of 1919. The strike itself remained in the background. Newspaper articles referred time and again to the violent events of a single day and neglected the issues that led to the dispute. Fear engendered by predictions of further "union" violence evaporated the support that linemen and their allies among the building trades had received during the first two weeks of June. On the Fourth of July, the *Craftsman* announced that the Building Trades Council had called off its sympathy strike.[72] Union linemen were not allowed to return to their light-company jobs and either found work elsewhere or left the city. The strikebreakers hired by the company continued to work nine-hour days for wages the city arbitration board considered substandard.

The linemen's failure emboldened conservative leaders who had refused to participate in the sympathy strike—especially leaders of the typographers', pressmen's, and stereotypers' unions. Although the typographers donated $250 to the strike fund, the donation represented support for the linemen among the union's rank-and-file and not that of its leaders.[73] The union hierarchy concurred with *Craftsman* editor William Reilly, still an active member of the printers' union, who advised against the strike. Reilly declared that the militancy of the building trades "cost union labor much prestige that it had been years in attaining."[74] Motivated by the *Craftsman*'s rigid stance against strikes and other "destructive tactics," a grassroots movement of building-trades activists and moderates within the Central Labor Council proposed the establishment of a new labor newspaper. In support of Reilly, the city's more than 250 typographers withdrew from the Central Labor Council for three months until the Labor Temple Association dropped plans for the new paper.[75]

During the fall of 1919, a construction boom stimulated by the war continued to fuel the local economy and generated an unprecedented need for skilled laborers. Virtually all of the city's established unions won wage increases and experienced rapid growth. Strategic arguments between moderate and conservative elements of the Central Labor Council and the more militant Building Trades Council were suspended while union demands met with little resistance. Dallas's union plumbers, who numbered just over a hundred, received nine dollars a day, compared to the six dollars paid their Austin counterparts. Despite their participation in the unsuccessful Texas Power & Light sympathy strike, the city's painters' union acquired a hundred new members between March and November.[76]

Union rhetoric continued to emphasize fairness and an improved standard of living for skilled workers. The rank-and-file, however, used its new prosperity to benefit a broader spectrum of the working class, indicating that the nineteenth-century vision of cooperation among all producers influenced Dallas unionists long after the Central Labor Council hierarchy narrowed its focus. The local carpenters' union donated $5,000 to the Greater Medical Center fund. Plumbers sent contributions to aid storm victims in Galveston.[77] The Central Labor Council established a cooperative grocery store next to the downtown Labor Temple. Union resources also enhanced the social lives of working-class families. The Labor Temple Association resurrected the socialist tradition of casual weekend dances and occasionally sponsored fancy-dress balls.[78]

Even organized workers in the service sector saw wages and conditions improve during the 1919 postwar boom. Despite the recent failure of the linemen, Dallas waiters threatened to strike until counter workers won a 33 percent weekly increase and table waiters received a 20 percent wage hike. Union waitresses, although their scale remained below that of waiters, received an increase as well. The pay of Dallas's almost 400 union waiters compared favorably with that of organized waiters throughout the Southwest except in oil-boom towns.[79] The *Craftsman* attributed the union's rapid growth during October and November to recent migrants attracted to Dallas by the Texas State Fair. Waiters told the paper that they had remained in the city because of the local union's strength.[80] The 150-member butchers' union also reported rapid growth and steady work, with weekly wages of $35 to $40.[81]

Toward the end of 1919, the militancy of the building trades resurfaced. Organized labor's steady growth and local traditions convinced leaders of Dallas's Bridge and Structural Iron Workers' Union that middle-class residents would once again respond to issues of fairness and support union demands for an unscheduled wage increase. Under the contracted wage scale of seven dollars per day, young journeymen (who comprised about one quarter of the local union) left the city for oil-field jobs that paid eight dollars daily. The cost of living in Dallas greatly exceeded that in rural areas near the oil deposits, magnifying the dollar-a-day wage disparity. George W. Livingston, business manager for the ironworkers, delivered an ultimatum in which he gave contractors three months to meet union demands. The day after the deadline, 62 iron workers (out of a 250-member union) still not receiving the eight-dollar wage walked off their jobs.[82]

The ironworkers' aggressive move, following three months of relative quiet during which tactical arguments within the local labor movement virtually ceased, surprised both Dallas business leaders and conservatives within the Central Labor Council. Perhaps more astonishing to employers was the fact that 75 percent of the union men received the unscheduled wage increase—although placed in the context of labor gains during the war years and immediately afterward, the ironworkers' demand for an unscheduled increase was a logical "next step" in the process of strengthening the union and not an entirely new development. Emboldened by the success of the ironworkers and outraged when contractors hired unskilled laborers to erect steel building frames, the city's carpenters, electricians, painters, and plasterers refused to work until the remaining ironworkers were back on the job. In the second week of their strike in support of the ironworkers, Dallas carpenters presented their own demands for an eight-dollar daily wage.[83]

On November 18, 1919, between three and four hundred business leaders—alarmed at what they labeled the influence of "illiterates, foreign agitators, IWWs, [and] bolshevist elements" within Dallas unions—organized the Dallas Open Shop Association.[84] Only ten or twelve of those present at the organizational meeting in the roof garden of the posh Adolphus Hotel heeded the warnings of Tom Bell, a representative of the Texas Bureau of Labor Statistics, and voted against a resolution declaring Dallas an "open shop town." Bell urged business leaders to avoid open-shop organizing, warning that in San Antonio, Beaumont, and Austin it had "aggravated the very conditions it sought to palliate." Dallas employers dismissed Bell's objections as well as those of M. A. Holland, the Dallas carpenter who had organized the sympathy strike the previous summer. In his new capacity with the United States Department of Labor, Holland challenged what he called false perceptions of labor spread by inaccurate newspaper reports. He explained that union wage scales were supposed to provide minimum wage requirements, with experienced or especially talented workers earning more. According to Holland, Dallas employers, as a rule, "seek to keep their men down to the minimum wage, releasing those least efficient." As a result, the building trades sought an increase in the wage scale to ensure fair wages for the majority of union members. George W. Livingston of the ironworkers' union also spoke to the assembly, presenting an offer from the ironworkers to return to work if the decision regarding a new scale was left to an arbitration board.[85]

Despite Holland's and Livingston's assurances that the city's building tradesmen were not randomly violating contracts, members of the Open Shop Association elected as president W. S. Mosher, notorious for his anti-union activities at Mosher Manufacturing. The new organization set up offices in the Chamber of Commerce building. Its general manager, T. P. Roberts, initiated a publicity campaign that netted 250 business and 3,000 individual members. The Open Shop Association established a free employment service to replace strikers and brought over 1,500 scabs to Dallas—some from as far away as California and New England.[86]

The formation of the Open Shop Association was a reaction by the city's commercial-civic elite to a vital, locally led labor movement and the increasing militancy of the building trades. Roberts designed the Open Shop publicity campaign with the aim of replacing Dallas residents' situationally dependent support for labor with hostility toward all union activity. Toward this end, Open Shop proponents made much of labor's defectors. In an article heralding the formation of the Open Shop Association, the *Dallas Morning News* featured former union printer Gilbert Irish's declaration that "union labor has become too strong."[87] Irish, a contractor in 1919, rejected aggressive building-trades tactics that directly affected his company. Other small business owners who had emerged from the prosperous sector of the working class during the war years found themselves bargaining uncomfortably with union representatives and, like Irish, publicly stated their dissatisfaction with labor's growing militancy.

Dallas's conservative union leaders underestimated the danger posed by the Open Shop Association and refused to view its formation as a full-blown assault on labor. Calling Dallas businessmen "wise and fair," the conservative editor of the *Craftsman* wrote that the Open Shop movement revealed "more of the 'defensive action' than one of affront" and confidently predicted "there will be no harm come from the declaration of the Chamber of Commerce." The *Craftsman* complained that the ironworkers' evasion of a contract, which was not set to expire until the spring of 1920, was an act of "bad faith" and not representative of the manner in which labor organizations usually behave.[88] Conservative union officials sought to discredit building-trades leaders such as Livingston by blaming them for the appearance of the Open Shop Association and anti-union articles in area newspapers.

Delegates to the Central Labor Council downplayed both the rift within organized labor and the Open Shop Association's obvious intentions to crush the power of the building trades. While out-of-state strikebreakers undermined the ironworkers and their allies and union leaders publicly condemned their rivals, the *Craftsman* proclaimed Labor Council delegates to be on "better terms than in years past." According to the paper, grievances within the Central Labor Council had been resolved and "the old spirit of brotherly kinship" renewed.[89]

There were signs, however, that rank-and-file unionists recognized the danger presented by a quasi-public organization of employers. Several hundred workers staged a rally at the Labor Temple to protest the Open Shop movement. In a letter to the editor of the *Craftsman*, Oscar Calvert scoffed at four hundred "self-delegated guardians of all the people" and warned of their danger.[90] Calvert and the protesters recognized that the Open Shop Association, with its Chamber of Commerce backing and close ties to the publishers of Dallas's newspapers, could manipulate public opinion and radically alter the climate in which local unions had flourished for forty years.

The building trades responded to the Open Shop Association with another aggressive move. Three days after employers declared Dallas an "open shop town," the painters' union, already on strike in support of the ironworkers, joined in the demand for an eight-dollar daily wage. Since painters were contracted to work at seven dollars per day until March 1920, their action—mirroring that of the ironworkers and carpenters—further polarized the city's working class.[91] Without the support of a united labor movement, the building-trades unions could not withstand the strikebreaking tactics of the Open Shop Association. Younger members drifted off to the oil fields. Since contractors imported nonunion workers from rural Texas counties and from out of state, many experienced union workers found themselves without jobs and were forced to leave Dallas as well. By the middle of 1920, building-trades leaders, who lost two sympathy strikes in the course of a year, were completely discredited. Virtually all Dallas construction sites operated as open shops.

Because the prospect of militant trade unions presented a threat to the politics of boosterism and loosely regulated growth and was perceived as incongruous with Dallas's reputation as a low-cost location for businesses and investments, the Open Shop Association united the city's elite. Generously funded by a system of voluntary dues, the organization grew steadily. By the time typographers called a selective strike for reduced hours in May 1921, twenty-five of sixty-six printing shops in Dallas were affiliated with the Open Shop Association. Since the majority of the union shops accepted demands for a forty-four-hour week, the typographers' walkout involved only thirty workers in seven shops.[92] Union leaders who had opposed the building-trades sympathy strikes in 1919 found it difficult to convince rank-and-file printers to support a walkout of their own. Three years of antistrike rhetoric had left the rank-and-file confused and unprepared to make financial sacrifices for a minority of members. The selective action standardized the forty-four-hour week for almost all union printers, but a 10 percent assessment to benefit strikers led to resentment and cost the union many members.[93]

Poor relations between the rank-and-file and union officials plagued No. 671 of the Brotherhood of Railroad Trainmen as well. A grassroots movement emerged among members of the Dallas local seeking an alliance between engineers, firemen, conductors, and trainmen and closer ties to the shop crafts. When shopmen staged a nationwide strike during the summer of 1922, Dallas's union activists prepared to seize the opportunity to unite all local railway workers in a work stoppage protesting dangerous conditions. Activists' plans were thwarted when W. G. Lee, national president of the Brotherhood of Railroad Trainmen, telegraphed the Dallas lodge and ordered all members to carry out their normal duties during the Federated Shop Crafts strike. Faced with continuing rebellion among the Dallas rank-and-file, many of whom were not reporting to work, Lee announced, "Illegal action will not be tolerated," and threatened the Dallas local with expulsion.[94] Lee's opposition to an amalgamated railroad union was described in the (Chicago) *Labor Herald* as "a prime cause of defeat and despair."[95] His ultimatum to the Dallas lodge and its strict enforcement by local union officers served to defuse the last significant challenge to conservative union policies until the economic upheavals of the 1930s.

The Central Labor Council hierarchy began to encourage craft unions to include arbitration clauses, intended to lessen the probability of strikes, in new contracts. When arbitration failed, conservative labor leaders supported the selection of an "umpire" to decide the case. Between 1919 and 1925, Elmer Scott, the city's most visible reform advocate, served as umpire in separate disputes involving painters, stereotypers, and pressmen. In the first two instances, Scott ruled in favor of the unions. Delegates to the Central Labor Council began to think in terms of a possible coalition with reform-oriented patrons of Scott's Civic Federation. Because Dallas's reformers supported moderate local candidates and the state Democratic party, union officials intensified efforts to disassociate organized labor from radical politics.[96]

Throughout the 1920s, Dallas labor organizations were unable to counter the well-orchestrated anti-union propaganda of the Open Shop Association. Without innovative leaders such as Holland of the carpenters and Livingston of the ironworkers, the policies of the Central Labor Council did not appeal to younger workers and recent migrants. For the first time since their origins in the 1880s, Dallas's major unions declined in size. Perhaps most importantly, labor leaders no longer spoke in terms of empowerment but emphasized the need to restore credibility and stability to their organizations through nonpartisan politics and low-risk tactics. Labor leaders' increasing emphasis on respectability and white workers' growing alarm at the number of black migrants competing for local jobs combined to restrain union demands. Disowning its roots in radical politics and revising its traditional vision of empowerment to include only a narrow spectrum of the working class, Dallas's labor movement lay dormant until the Great Depression.

Nevertheless, the militancy of the building trades during and immediately after World War I convinced Dallas business leaders that unions threatened future growth, and they were motivated to undertake campaigns to publicly discredit organized labor. After forty years during which trade unionists were accepted as rivals and potential allies in the local politics of competition and cooperation, the relationship between the city's commercial-civic elite and organized labor became stridently adversarial. Although local unions declined during the 1920s, the anxieties of Dallas business leaders grew as reform proposals and a renewal of sectional rivalries among downtown merchants divided the elite. Amid a revival of the Ku Klux Klan, prominent civic leaders began to question the wisdom of the elite's contentiousness.

The decision of the Central Labor Council hierarchy to align itself with the city's reform community was a fateful one. The surprising local strength of reactionary politics stymied a promising reform movement and further diminished trade union influence by forcing reformers and union members to support the elite's candidates in an effort to thwart the Klan. Although hallmark events in the city's history—the adoption of the council-manager form of government, the violent repression of local factory workers, the Texas Centennial Exposition, and the formation of the Dallas Citizens Council—occurred in the 1930s, it was the instability that began with the militancy of the building trades and continued during the 1920s that convinced key members of the Dallas elite that the politics of competition and cooperation had become unmanageable.

Part Two

Reform, Reaction, and Downtown Rivalries as Threats to Growth

White supremacy is not imperiled. Vice is not rampant. The constituted agencies are still regnant and if freedom is endangered it is by the redivius of the mob spirit in the disguising garb of the Ku Klux Klan.

— Dallas Morning News, 1921[1]

Even though early-twentieth-century Dallas businessmen were in the vanguard of initiators of Progressive-era changes in the structure of city government, the institutionalization of social reforms associated with Progressivism came late to Dallas. The willingness (and ability) of clubwomen to sponsor social services and nonsectarian charities, the activities of benevolent societies, and the local commercial-civic elite's reluctance to expend municipal resources on any but the most basic and least controversial social services combined to create a strong tradition of private charity. Citizens Association mayor Henry Lindsley, a municipal reformer along the lines of Cleveland's Tom Johnson, established the city's welfare department in 1915, but it foundered under a series of directors until the early 1920s.[2] The Dallas Civic Federation, a private agency founded in 1917 by middle-class professionals and male and female members of the elite, also matured during the 1920s.[3]

Dallas professionals interested in social reform, primarily white, middle-class teachers, social workers, and members of the clergy, acquired influence through their dominance of the new fields of social welfare and professional social work. Like clubwomen, social reformers believed that city government and private organizations could work together to mitigate the results of poverty and environmental degradation. Both groups sought increased public spending on social-welfare programs and linked prospects for Dallas's continued growth to the well-being of workers, recent migrants, and residents of the city's slums and shantytowns. Social reformers did not reject the elite's predisposition toward growth; like businessmen and clubwomen, middle-class reform advocates relished their roles as city builders. They did, however, challenge the business community's vision of largely unregulated urban expansion and the prevailing attitude that poverty was the "natural" condition of the socially and mentally inferior.

Significantly, Dallas's social reformers were able to secure consistent financial support among the elite. The presence of prominent business leaders and their wives among the patrons of the Civic Federation reflects the flexible nature of boundaries that separated various segments of the city's middle and upper classes. A keen observer of Dallas in 1920 might have predicted that the growing popularity of environmental reform would precipitate another clash between business leaders, middle-class reformers, and clubwomen who favored increased municipal spending on social services and those who were committed to conservative fiscal policies. Indeed, the mayoral election of 1919 pitted a reform advocate chosen by Lindsley's Citizens Association against a representative of the old guard.[4]

But the institutions that promoted social reform in Dallas grew in the midst of a particularly strong revival of the Ku Klux Klan. Faced with the prospect of Klan-controlled city and county governments, Dallas's middle-class reform community and its well-heeled backers rejected the urban politics of competition and cooperation favored by the elite's challengers between 1880 and 1920. Instead, reformers joined union leaders and veterans of the defunct Socialist party in support of moderate businessmen, who also received the backing of fiscal conservatives anxious to present a united front against the Klan. In a context of declining union militancy and the demise of the local Left, moderate members of an essentially conservative commercial-civic elite provided the only practical alternative to Klan control. Many supporters of the Civic Federation began to perceive controversial social-reform programs as threats to civic stability because of their tendency to divide the elite. The decision of prominent businessmen to publicly oppose the Ku Klux Klan enhanced the status and leadership role of the business community, while reformers' reluctance to forcefully present the case for improved social services forestalled significant changes in the urban environment and perpetuated local traditions of private charity.

After 1926 G. B. Dealey, John Surratt, and others who opposed

Klan incursions into civic affairs and supported city planning efforts became Dallas's most visible reform advocates, while social-work professionals became more and more absorbed in casework. Moderates within the business community turned their attention from agencies addressing social and environmental conditions to structural reforms that would ensure their continued control of city government. By the end of the decade, some civic leaders, including Dealey and Surratt, began to question the wisdom of downtown merchants' recurring sectional rivalries. The specter of future challenges from either organized labor or the Klan elicited new concerns about the divisive nature of civic affairs. Dallas leaders began to consider measures to improve the urban environment, the reactionary politics of the Klan, and their own internecine squabbles as threats to the city's continued growth.

I

The history of social reform in Dallas parallels the early career of its most visible social worker, Elmer Scott.[5] Scott, a former executive with Sears Roebuck and Co., had opened the department store's Dallas branch—its first major expansion project. Along with his reputation as a manager, Scott was well known in national reform circles. Among Richard Sears's considerations when he chose Scott to head the Dallas distribution center were his protégé's reform activities in Chicago, which angered business partner Julius Rosenwald. Scott immediately immersed himself in local reform efforts. Within three years of his 1906 arrival, Scott became president of the Dallas Recreation Association, overseeing the establishment of the city's first six playgrounds at public schools.[6] Disagreements between Rosenwald and Scott continued, however, and even intensified after Sears moved to Europe. Despite the success of the Dallas expansion, Scott retired in 1913 at the age of 47.[7]

Mayor Henry Lindsley, after his election in 1915, asked Scott to organize and head the city's first municipal welfare department. Scott studied welfare departments in major American cities and recommended the establishment of a Department of Public Welfare, a Department of Health, and a Department of Parks and Playgrounds. The Department of Public Welfare was divided into an employment bureau designed to provide vocational guidance and employment for the handicapped, a legal aid bureau, a board responsible for the censorship of "Commercialized Amusements," and the office of a court sergeant who would serve as a "friendly counselor" in the courts. The organization of a censorship board reveals Dallas's close social kinship to the urban South. Censorship boards, focusing on motion pictures, also were appointed in Fort Worth (1911), Nashville (1914), and Memphis (1920). A New Orleans ordinance prohibiting "indecent" movies dated from 1909.[8]

Encouraging a blend of public and private cooperation typical of older American cities throughout the nineteenth century, the new municipal welfare department established close ties with Dallas's private United Charities. Flora Saylor headed that group and directed one of the first programs in Texas to train social workers. The Department of Public Welfare assumed sponsorship of a social-work institute whose instructors included Rabbi George Fox of Fort Worth, then president of the Texas State Conference of Charities and Corrections; professors from Southern Methodist University and the state normal school that later became Texas Woman's University; and Raymond Robins of Chicago.[9] Reform efforts in Dallas were linked to the national movement by well-known speakers, including Mrs. Frederick K. Schoff of Philadelphia, president of the National Congress of Mothers; lecturer Charles E. Zeublin; Mary McDowell of the University of Chicago and settlement-house work; David Latshaw, international secretary of the YMCA; Judge William H. Wadhams from New York's Court of General Sessions; Samuel A. Greeley, Chicago sanitary engineer and sanitary specialist; and C. J. Atkinson, executive secretary of the Boys' Club Federation of New York. The welfare department engaged five economics students from newly established Southern Methodist University to conduct the first study of living costs in Dallas. Their report, based on data collected from fifty families, provided city commissioners with guidelines for revising the wage scale of municipal employees.[10]

Scott organized an umbrella group to unify the efforts of Dallas's eight nonsectarian charities (United Charities, Infants' Welfare and Milk Association, Dallas Baby Camp, Dallas Free Kindergarten Association, Dallas County Humane Society, Empty Stocking Crusade, Mission Lodging House, and National Newsboys Association). The city granted the Welfare Council, as the coordinating body was officially known, a first-year budget of over $50,000.[11]

Emboldened by the apparent acceptance of reform ideals by influential business leaders, Scott advocated city allowances to dependent mothers and provision for the "feeble-minded" (the state had no program for mothers, and Scott considered Texas's appropriations for mental health inadequate). He also proposed an organization similar to the Big Brothers and Big Sisters.[12] Scott discovered, however, that it was far easier to secure municipal funding for existing charities, many of which had been the projects of women's clubs for several decades, than to fund new programs.

According to Scott, reforms initiated by the Department of Public Welfare were not received favorably in Dallas "except by a faithful few who understood and believed in its objectives." Workers often resented the centralization efforts of middle-class professionals employed by the welfare department, since centralization caused interruptions in the customary patterns of obtaining assistance and reassigned familiar personnel. The censorship of motion pictures also proved to be unpopular among some workers. Stronger opposition came from conservative members of the commercial-civic elite who held hard-line views against public spending on social programs. Several city commissioners and the *Dallas Times Herald* were openly hostile toward Lindsley and any program associated with his administration. The free-legal-aid bureau, the city employment office, the reorganization of Parkland Hospital, and the establishment of an overnight shelter for the homeless—precisely the social programs that appealed most to the city's workers—cost Lindsley vital support among business leaders.[13]

Kathleen McCarthy notes that social services in Chicago also were "carried into practice . . . by a small coterie of committed reformers." She adds that even when "participation at the fringes of the [Chicago] movement was large, a tiny nucleus of dedicated adherents appeared behind every good cause, whether cultural, scientific, charitable, or reform."[14] The same may be said of Dallas.

Scott lost his job in 1917 when Joe E. Lawther defeated Lindsley in the mayoral election. Although the Citizens Association regained control of city government two years later, Scott's experience convinced him that reform efforts should not depend on the whims of politicians and that something must be done "to maintain the social and cultural values of the community."[15] He envisioned a forum within which reform-minded professionals could act without interference and restrictions. Scott attended the convention of the National Conference of Social Work, which reinforced his commitment to reform. Scott's vision of urban expansion guided by "an elite of well-trained social analysts and practitioners, standing above class, above special interest, impartial and objective, serving only the general good" appealed to a variety of middle-class residents, businessmen, and clubwomen interested in social reform.[16] While Scott's education and business acumen—and his status as a member of the Idlewild Club and founder of the Texas Lawn Tennis Association—placed him solidly within the middle class and among the city's social elite, he determined not to return to the business world and dedicated the rest of his long life to softening the rough edges of growth in Dallas.

Scott and Jules K. Hexter established the Civic Federation as a permanent institution through which social awareness could be increased and the pool of social workers expanded. Nearly 150 men and women attended the organizational meeting in 1917. Founding members elected Judge Joseph E. Cockrell president; Hexter, La Monte Daniels, Mrs. C. H. Huvelle, and Mrs. A. A. Cocke, vice presidents; and J. Dabney Day, treasurer. Scott was named executive secretary. One hundred attendees volunteered support. They included G. B. Dealey of the *Morning News*, merchants, physicians, professors, attorneys, club leaders, and professional women. Two brothers involved in downtown development offered the group a real-estate office in the heart of the business district on Commerce Street at a nominal rental fee, and the Civic Federation opened its doors shortly afterward.[17]

The stated objectives of the new organization were vague:

• To unite all social forces and movements in effective effort without in any way affecting the initiative and independence of existing organizations.

• To arouse public opinion and keep the people awakened and informed on matters of common welfare, through lectures, schools, demonstrations, literature and other means.

• To maintain research of the best thought and activities of other communities.

• To maintain a central office as a common meeting place and to accumulate a library and exhibits.[18]

The new organization's statement of purpose was intended to defuse fears that the Civic Federation would "take over" projects and charities operated for many years by women's clubs and benevolent societies. It was also designed to appeal to business leaders who placed a high value on efficiency and to elements of the city's elite likely to support programs and reforms that had been enacted in New York and Chicago.

Despite (or because of) its failure (or refusal) to articulate a specific plan, the Civic Federation survived the war years. It continued the Dallas School of Social Work's training of social workers—formerly sponsored by the city welfare department—and organized Home Service instruction with the assistance of the American Red Cross. The Social Service Institute (as the Civic Federation renamed the Dallas School of Social Work) flourished in the 1920s under the direction of Gaynell Hawkins, one of the university students who conducted the original cost-of-living survey. Hawkins engaged Dr. Edward T. Devine, considered by many the "Dean of Social Work in America," to conduct a five-day institute in 1923 and an extended program three years later. Contacts made during a year at the New York School of Social Work enabled Hawkins to draw upon the talents of both national figures and local professionals and academics. By the mid 1920s, the Civic Federation was firmly established in Dallas and occupied its own building on Maple Avenue, north of downtown.[19]

The reform community extended its influence through more than three hundred sessions of the Dallas Open Forum, sponsored by the Civic Federation and held in the City Hall Auditorium between 1919 and 1937. Dr. Owen Lovejoy, the first Forum speaker, had a national reputation in the field of children's services and later served as president of the National Conference of Social Work. Organized to conform with the objectives of the Open Forum National Council and with the aid of the National Council's founder and president, the success of the Dallas Open Forum placed the city on the lecture circuit. The formal structure of the sessions was established immediately. After the initial address, Elmer Scott moderated a public discussion in which the speaker fielded questions and allowed the audience to make comments. Occasionally an especially controversial topic, "Closed Shop vs. Open Shop" for example, would be given two succeeding sessions in which speakers presented opposing viewpoints.

Some Forum sessions were used to disseminate information, as was the case when an academic explained various aspects of census taking. Most of the earlier sessions, however, featured either prominent lecturers (including John Dewey; James J. Mallon, warden of Toynbee Hall, London; Judge Eleanor Wembridge; Bertrand Russell; Sherwood Eddy; and Norman Thomas) or experts on foreign affairs and cultures (Japanese Liberal leader, Yusuke Tsurumi; member of the American Peace Commission in Europe, Dr. Robert J. Kerner; Dr. Samuel Guy Inman on intervention in Mexico; and Professor Richard Burton on theater as a social force).[20]

Reactions to the Open Forum ranged from that of the city commissioner who declared that the sessions were a "menace to civilization" and should be suppressed, to that of a local socialist who considered the Forum "opiated salve." At the height of Ku Klux Klan activity, anonymous writers of letters to editors occasionally claimed that "their organization" would see to it that the Forum was "closed up," but no attempt was made to carry out the threat. Forum sessions drew crowds. Discussion periods following a speaker's address provided local reformers and activists with both a platform and an audience. In his autobiography, Scott recalls a local radical who regularly attended the Forum sessions and, regardless of the subject, raised a question about the Single Tax. "Soap-box orators," "crackpots," and hecklers were tolerated, unless "they became abusively personal."[21] For Dallas residents such as Ed Tankus, who had emigrated from Europe in the early 1920s, Forum sessions also provided an opportunity to perfect language skills. Later an accomplished regional actor, Tankus began attending the Open Forum while a student at Bryan High Night School. In a 1926 letter to Scott, Tankus acknowledged the importance of the Open Forum as an adjunct to formal adult education.[22]

Dallas's middle-class champions of reform, confident that the changes they advocated were inevitable and somewhat naively assuming they were irrevocable, emphasized adult education and the extension of aid to the needy. Their attempts to improve the urban environment did not include a radical transformation of capitalism or its dissolution. As a private organization, the Civic Federation depended on members and contributors for financial support. Its reform agenda attracted three main groups: professionals and academics, women's club members with an interest in social work and the extension of city services, and moderate business leaders. Dallas's Jewish community, with a population of over eight thousand during the

1920s, was well represented in each group. The ongoing generosity of Civic Federation donors indicates the extent to which a vision of urban expansion guided by "experts" appealed to groups within Dallas's commercial-civic elite.[23]

Some businessmen considered philanthropy, like advertising, to be good business. Others were influenced by their wives for whom social work seemed a "natural" extension of club projects. A few considered reform necessary to retain social stability and dilute the appeal of organized labor. Many Dallas business leaders associated public agencies with the patronage systems of eastern cities and supported the Civic Federation as a private alternative. Almost all of the city's wealthy residents preferred giving donations to local organizations, over which they could exert a degree of control, to paying higher taxes.[24] In addition to these motivations, the local implementation of reform measures and the presence in Dallas of prominent lecturers from New York and Chicago made Dallas's business and social elites feel part of a national network of cities, an important psychological consideration for people barely two generations from the frontier. Supporting the Civic Federation's reform goals did not jeopardize one's commitment to capitalism and publicly demonstrated that Dallas patrons were no less enlightened than their peers in other American cities.

Although social reformers introduced locally the concept of government as an active agent of social improvement and founded their own organization, their concern was limited almost exclusively to the white poor. The Civic Federation sponsored a black theatrical troupe and concerts by Fannie Gibson's Jubilaire Singers in the late 1920s and into the 1930s, but Scott's organization ignored the hard issues of irregular and limited employment, inferior educational facilities, pervasive epidemics, and an ongoing housing shortage that affected the daily lives of most Dallas blacks and Hispanics.[25]

While Dallas reformers succeeded in obtaining for white workers many municipal and privately sponsored social services, their efforts were limited as well by Scott's commitment to a private organization (he continued to direct the Civic Federation until his death in 1954) and by the often pseudoscientific practices and class biases of most middle-class social workers. Self-righteousness often accompanied altruism. Christmas parties for the homeless sponsored by the Civic Federation in 1925 and 1926 are especially revealing. In his autobiography, Elmer Scott claims that he organized the parties "not out of a philanthropic impulse but to satisfy my curiosity as to the character of the transient hobo." Scott sent a car for six of the "sorriest of the lot" who had sought lodging with the Salvation Army and "actually gave them cocktails to start off with and break down their reserve." A turkey dinner was served in the Civic Federation's coffee room and included "sandwiches" with silver dollars inside. Scott describes the "hobos" as happy with their holiday fare, then adds, "I must confess a grievous disappointment. I never found an interesting character in the lot."[26]

Since their organizations developed during the revival of the Ku Klux Klan, Dallas reformers allied themselves closely with the elite. Although often discouraged by the reluctance of business leaders to fund social services, they preferred moderate businessmen to members of the Klan and never challenged the elite as had members of earlier Left-liberal coalitions. As professionals within both the municipal welfare department and the Civic Federation assumed greater responsibility for the management and implementation of social-service programs and social workers placed an increasing emphasis on casework, members of the elite who raised funds and interpreted agency goals to the rest of the community became the city's most visible proponents of reform.[27]

II

The Ku Klux Klan revival in Dallas coincided with the rising racist and nativist sentiment that swept the country in the years after World War I. In contrast to its Reconstruction Era antecedent, the Klan of the 1920s was primarily an urban phenomenon—appealing to white professionals, middle-class clerical workers, and the proprietors of small businesses in county-seat towns and major cities.[28] Nor was the Klan exclusively a product of the South—Chicago and Indianapolis klaverns claimed more members than those of any southern city.[29] In Dallas the revived Klan eventually had close to 13,000 members (this estimate gives Dallas the largest per capita Klan membership in the nation).[30] Locally, Ku Klux Klan membership represented an active attempt to implement the nativist agenda accepted or at least tolerated by a cross section of the city's white residents. Even political moderates not associated with the Klan adopted extreme nativist positions. J. C.

McNealus, Dallas's state senator from 1911 to 1921, known for his support for labor issues and amnesty for socialist pacifists, opined:

> See how Greek and Dago and Slav is crowding out the American white man from the restaurant and the fruit trade and dethroning the American negro from his shoe-shining stand. They are insolent! They are filthy! They are un-American! Every one of them ought to be deported! And then no true American should grieve if the deporting ship never got across the Atlantic.[31]

The revived Klan announced its presence in Dallas in March 1921 by flogging a black man and burning KKK into his forehead with acid. In May eight hundred men clad in white robes and hoods paraded down Main Street.[32] Members of the local Klan's executive committee included police and fire commissioner Louis Turley, Homer Fisher of the Dallas Street Railway Co., four attorneys, a real-estate developer, a physician, a minister, and the owners of three small businesses. Dr. Hiram W. Evans, a Dallas dentist, became the nation's Imperial Wizard, and Z. E. Marvin, a drugstore magnate and owner of the twenty-nine-story Magnolia Building (which became the public symbol of Dallas almost immediately after its completion in 1922), was the local Grand Dragon. By 1923 the Klan controlled both city and county governments. The Magnolia and Oriental oil companies, R. L. Thornton's Dallas County State Bank, the drugstores and soda fountains of Skillern & Sons, and the Cullum Co. grocery, whose executive officers or proprietors later became fixtures of the Dallas elite, appeared on a Klan membership roster distributed in the mid-1920s as "KKK Business Firms 100%." At the height of the Klan revival, the State Fair Association designated October 24, 1923, "Ku Klux Klan Day" and welcomed an estimated 75,000 hooded members to the city.[33]

A revived Klan threatened Dallas's image as a forward-thinking, cosmopolitan city—ripe for eastern investment capital—and alarmed many of the moderate business leaders who supported the Citizens Association. The Klan also threatened the established civic order. Dallas's aging U.S. senator Charles A. Culberson and former lieutenant governor and state attorney general Martin M. Crane attacked the divisive character of the Klan in 1921. During the next year, as sixty-eight people were flogged by Klan members in the Trinity River bottoms, twenty-five Dallas businessmen and professionals organized the Dallas County Citizens League to oppose the Klan. Led by Crane,

League members combatted the law and order appeal of the KKK by organizing educational rallies and sponsoring anti-Klan propaganda. Police Chief Tanner publicly resigned from the Klan after the outbreak of whippings, claiming that the organization was an impediment to law officers and enforcement.[34]

When Klan-controlled city commissioners fired Helman Rosenthal, a Jewish engineer recruited in 1918 by the Citizens Association and reform advocates to manage the city's water department, a faction of the elite led by G. B. Dealey and Julius Schepps committed itself to both public and private campaigns against the Klan. Schepps and Rabbi David Lefkowitz continued to attend meetings of the Masonic order, despite the presence of many Klansmen. Schepps and Rabbi Lefkowitz used every incidence of KKK violence and intimidation to convince fellow Masons that the Klan's presence deterred growth. Schepps paid membership fees for almost fifty of his bakery employees and encouraged them to infiltrate the Klan and inform on its activities.[35]

Dealey used the *Morning News* to portray Klan members as backward and unsophisticated. The paper argued that vigilante activity undermined civic boosterism and served no useful purpose. By running a syndicated exposé commissioned by the *New York World* that itemized every known instance of Klan lawlessness, the *News* countered Hiram Evans's contention that the "new" Klan was a political organization and not the least bit interested in terrorism. Ironically, Dealey's anti-Klan stance was precipitated by a column penned by editorial page editor Alonzo Wasson without the knowledge of the paper's general manager. Wasson recalled that, although surprised, Dealey wholeheartedly supported his position. Dealey did, however, advise his editor to call a conference when breaking new ground in the future. The *Morning News* escalated its anti-Klan campaign between 1922 and 1924. The risks were considerable. Dealey later admitted that many of his employees were Klan members during the secret organization's heyday.[36]

One of the paper's traveling agents implored Dealey to tone down the criticism because it was hurting circulation in Dallas's hinterland. Dealey responded curtly, ordering the salesman to "buck up" and never make apologies for the *Dallas News*.[37]

The controversy engendered by Wasson's editorial and the ensuing criticism of Klan activities led two members of the board of the newspaper's parent company to urge Dealey to make changes in his editorial staff. In response to inquiries from throughout Texas, Arkansas, and Oklahoma, Dealey explained that none of the paper's major stockholders were Catholics or Jews and that the circulation manager was the highest ranking Catholic on the staff. An employee suggested that the paper distribute company biographies to make the lack of a Catholic presence clear to subscribers. Dealey's senior staff condemned the idea as exploitative and turned him against the plan.[38]

Editor Glenn Pricer of the *Dallas Dispatch* joined Dealey in the local campaign against the Klan. In a series of editorials dubbed an "appeal to horse sense," Pricer reinforced the *News*'s assertions that no possible benefit could come from Klan activity. With far fewer resources than Dealey, Pricer risked financial ruin as well as personal attack. Nevertheless, his message reached the lower-level clerical workers and the owners of small businesses who made up the Klan's base. A contemporary newspaper analyst considered Pricer's the "most telling blows" against the Dallas Klan.[39]

As Klan strength peaked in Dallas, remnants of the city's early Left-liberal coalitions formed an organization intended to stem the political gains of Dallas County klaverns. Organized in early 1923 as the Dallas County Farm-Labor Political Conference with long-time labor leader William Reilly as chairman, the group appealed to county farmers, trade unionists, socialists, and middle-class reformers.[40] A name change to the Municipal Non Partisan Political Association (MNPPA) more accurately reflected the group's purpose—to elect a mayor and commissioners favorable to labor and opposed to the Ku Klux Klan—and Dallas unionists' preference for nonpartisan politics after World War I. Socialist George Clifton Edwards and J. W. Parks, a labor leader and three-term state legislator between 1913 and 1918, were prominent MNPPA delegates. Included for the first time in a coalition of the Dallas Left were middle-class women from neighborhood groups, the Dallas Women's Voters League (the MNPPA's first treasurer was a woman), and social reformers.

The MNPPA sent questionnaires to local candidates, who were then interviewed and evaluated. Since the organization did not have the financial resources to field its own slate, it endorsed candidates chosen by moderates among the city's commercial elite who stood in opposition to the Ku Klux Klan. Reilly used the *Craftsman* to publicize MNPPA endorsements and in June 1924 printed 10,000 posters containing the names of candidates supported by the city's organized Left. For the three-year life of the MNPPA, Reilly continued to print candidate lists and promotional materials, including 2,000 pamphlets that articulated the organization's platform. To maximize voter turnout, the MNPPA emphasized the paying of poll taxes (although Dallas socialists and trade unionists had opposed poll taxes since their turn-of-the-century origins) and required all delegates to produce receipts. The anti-Klan editors of the *Morning News*, the *Times Herald*, and the *Dispatch* gave MNPPA activities favorable coverage despite the fact that its organizers were often the commercial elite's and the daily newspapers' most vociferous critics.

Dallas residents Thomas B. Love, who assailed the KKK as a bastion of "parochialness and bigotry," and former senator Barry Miller (a favorite of the Populist-Labor coalition in the late 1890s) joined Dealey in an attack on Ku Klux Klan candidates at the state level. They considered public Klan activity an embarrassment that threatened Dallas and Texas with the economic stagnation that afflicted the Deep South. With its extensive distribution network, the *Morning News* was an effective weapon against the Klan's ambitions to control the government in Austin. The *News* consistently supported candidates who opposed the Klan, even when it found its choice distasteful, as in 1924 when the paper backed Miriam A. ("Ma") Ferguson in the governor's race. The endorsement of the *Morning News* augmented with urban voters Ferguson's strong base in rural counties and helped her to defeat Klan-backed Dallas district judge Felix Robertson in the Democratic primary. In the general election, "Ma" and her husband "Farmer Jim" (a former Texas governor impeached in 1917 for misuse of state funds and anathema to the *Morning News*) campaigned as "two governors for the price of one" and defeated Republican George C. Butte of the University of Texas law faculty. Butte was no Klansman but was supported by the Klan in an attempt to defeat the Fergusons.[41]

The 1924 election marked a turning point in the campaign against the Klan. In the 1926 primary, the *Morning News* backed the successful campaign of Dan Moody, the candidate of Texas businessmen, landholders, and railroad interests. With its major candidates, Moody and Miriam Ferguson, staunchly anti-KKK, the Texas Democratic party ended its open association with the Klan.[42]

Night-riding and nativism, however, did not disappear in Dallas. A homecoming celebration for Hiram Evans in 1925 allegedly attracted tens and perhaps hundreds of thousands of Klan members.[43] Although windows of the Magnolia building were lighted to form a fiery cross during an Oak Cliff parade in Evans's honor, James P. Simpson, a Dallas attorney who witnessed the event as a youth, recalls that the Klan's actions generated little public controversy.[44]

Evans's "welcome home" marked the end of the revived Klan's mass appeal. After its 1926 electoral defeats, the Klan returned to the subterranean activities for which it has been best known and most feared. Its efforts to achieve respectability through political office-holding thwarted and the continued violence of its members exposed, the Dallas Klan lost much of its support among business owners and professionals. The KKK never articulated an alternative to the combination of fiscal conservatism and civic aggressiveness that Dallas business owners found so attractive. In addition, the local chapter and Hope Cottage, an orphan's home financed and built by the Dallas Klan, suffered from financial difficulties and mismanagement by the end of the decade.[45]

Unlike the low-level, white-collar workers and civil servants who kept the secret organization alive, more affluent members quickly dropped their Klan affiliations and joined the city's growth-oriented commercial elite.[46] Successful former Klansmen were welcome among the city's business leaders by the end of the decade. Since there was overwhelming agreement among the elite on issues of white supremacy and segregation, Dallas business leaders tolerated extreme nativist positions.

The immediate political result of Klan activity during the 1920s was the recognition by the reform community, organized labor, and remnants of the local Left that their support of candidates who advocated policies of municipal spending that would further divide the elite risked the election of Klan-backed candidates or Klan members themselves; the local options of reform advocates, unionists, and a few remaining socialists were effectively reduced to choosing among the more moderate of the elite's candidates. Veterans of the MNPPA generally supported the business community's efforts to revive city planning in 1927 and install a professional city manager in 1930 (although most still opposed at-large elections). With the city's trade unions paralyzed by conservative policies imposed by the Labor Council hierarchy and growing professionalization within the reform community, business leaders found themselves without real opposition from the

Left for the first time since the 1880s. This did not, in itself, mitigate the business community's long-standing tendency to split into short-lived factions but strengthened the position of moderates within the elite.

III

Although the challenge to conservative fiscal policies posed by Dallas reformers was quelled by fears of Klan incursions into municipal affairs, the 1920s did not pass without Dallas businessmen warring once again over the issue of city planning. George Kessler returned to the city in 1920 and did not hide his disgust with the piecemeal implementation of his decade-old plan. Ironically, after Kessler's death in 1923, a faction of the elite led by G. B. Dealey formed the Kessler Plan Association and invoked the planner's name "to discipline those who would stray" from its interpretation of Kessler's urban vision.[47] The local tradition of city planning directed by members of the commercial-civic elite continued until the Second World War.

In 1927 a committee headed by C. E. Ulrickson, general manager of Trinity Portland Cement, proposed a $23,900,000 bond issue that would finance street improvements and the removal of remaining grade rail crossings, construct a triple railroad underpass and reclaim part of the Trinity River floodplain at the western edge of the business district, convert Love Field into a regional airport, and construct a downtown auditorium, schools, parks, and a central boulevard leading north from the business district.[48] Despite the committee's close ties to the Kessler Plan Association and the Chamber of Commerce and its emphasis on downtown projects, the removal of street-level tracks along Turtle Creek and in South Dallas and Oak Cliff appealed to residents of those areas and plans for a central expressway drew praise from citizens who lived in new neighborhoods north of the business district. The bond proposal passed easily in every section of the city.[49]

The Ulrickson Plan was not without its critics, however. Environmental reformers such as attorney and arts patron Rhodes S. Baker considered the bond proposal too modest in scope and urged Dallas leaders to incorporate greenbelt boulevards, restrictions on advertising and land use, and other controversial elements of Kessler's plan. As was the case with most Dallas reformers, Baker was reluctant to publicly criticize moderate businessmen who initiated the bond proposal—and who at least supported the principle of city planning—so soon after the revival of the Klan. Baker expressed his doubts about the Ulrickson Plan only to members of the elite Critic Club.[50]

In contrast, Oak Cliff businessmen led by J. M. White, J. Waddy Tate, and Frank Harmon complained during public rallies that although Oak Cliff would receive some street improvements and a library for the city's black residents (which they opposed), the bond issue would disproportionately benefit downtown and North Dallas. In Tate's estimation, "Oak Cliff with one-third of the population gets one-ninth of the money."[51] Especially vilified were North Dallas proposals to expand Love Field and construct a central thoroughfare. According to Harmon, "They want us to spend our money to give Highland Park people a racetrack into the business district."[52]

Merchants who owned property in the eastern portion of the business district opposed plans for the triple underpass and land reclamation that would enhance property values to the west. Much was made of four of the five committee members' west-end ties and residence in affluent Highland Park.[53] In addition to disagreements on appropriate levels of municipal spending on social services, sectional animosity had divided Dallas businessmen since the 1880s. John E. Surratt, secretary of the Kessler Plan Association, cautioned against a renewal of the "old fight" and asserted that the elite's lack of unity "handicapped" his organization's planning efforts. Surratt contended that because of infighting among Dallas business leaders, the Kessler Plan Association found it necessary to "win the confidence of the people of Dallas as a whole before we dared approach the question of a city or a county bond program."[54] Ultimately, the Chamber of Commerce spent $10,000 on a promotional slide show to ensure the bond proposal's passage.[55]

Two years after the Ulrickson Plan received the approval of Dallas voters, Surratt and G. B. Dealey still worried that the revival of sectional animosity could threaten civic stability and undermine their efforts to make Dallas a great city. "Such a revival," Surratt suggested, "would be as bad as an epidemic of smallpox."[56] At the close of a decade that began with labor militancy and the formation of the Open Shop Association and included demands for municipal spending on social services and the revival of the Ku Klux Klan, renewed sectional divisions within the business community—indeed any divisions—increasingly concerned key members of the Dallas elite.

THE ORIGINS OF

SINGLE-OPTION GOVERNMENT

I'm getting goddam tired of dealing with "maybe" men. We need a group of "yes" men, because I don't have time to keep calling these guys.

— Four-term mayor of Dallas, R. L. Thornton[1]

Following a dramatic increase in civic insecurity during the 1920s, the decade of the 1930s was a watershed for Dallas politics and Dallas society. Somewhat deceptively for the first half of the decade, short-lived coalitions continued to form around individual issues or sets of issues, and the feuding within the business community intensified.[2] By 1936, however, a new generation of Dallas business leaders, composed primarily of Dallas County natives and migrants from small Texas towns, emerged. Unlike their more heterogeneous and cosmopolitan predecessors, the business leaders who matured in the 1920s and received national attention for their promotion of the 1936 Texas Centennial Exposition placed a premium on unity. Instead of airing disagreements in local newspapers, the new elite presented only one option to the public. Internal disputes were settled in advance and always behind closed doors.

Business leaders concerned with the elimination of intraclass feuds were given an almost incalculable boost by the Centennial Exposition, which in the midst of the Depression attracted over six million visitors to Dallas. The fair elevated banker Robert L. Thornton, its director and most effective cheerleader, to a position of unprecedented local influence. Thornton parlayed his fundraising expertise, ability to motivate others, and personal popularity into de facto leadership of the new elite.

While publicly extolling the virtues of rugged individualism and nurturing his image as a "self-made" man, Thornton formed the Dallas Citizens Council—a private agency within which competition was minimized so that a small cadre of business leaders could amass unprecedented civic power. Folksy speech and a predilection for frontier aphorisms masked Thornton's business acumen and his determination that Dallas be ruled by consensus and by businessmen.

Thornton's single-option form of municipal government reduced the roles of lawyers, educators, ministers, and health professionals, all of whom had been active in Dallas politics. Although professionals, especially attorneys, continued to seek public office after the founding of the Citizens Council in 1937, they succeeded only when supported by Dallas's business leaders. By the end of the decade, real civic power rested with a self-appointed and self-perpetuating group of chief executive officers and company presidents, and sectional disputes between downtown merchants no longer provided headlines for the daily newspapers.

As the business community united behind the Citizens Council, it rarely sought the support of the city's organized workers. Union leaders and African Americans were either co-opted or violently repressed, and many local radicals were literally forced to leave town. The Depression destroyed Dallas's lively alternative press as the new elite consolidated power through a virtual monopoly of local newspapers and radio stations.[3] Following a wave of anti-union violence in response to organizing attempts at the Dallas Ford plant, Dallas residents remained uncharacteristically passive. Repression put an end to a long tradition of city hall protests and rallies in city parks.

The new elite's use of local newspapers to distort labor's agenda and the resignation and fear instilled by the Ford Terror (orchestrated by Ford managers and sanctioned by the police and powerful members of the business community) will be examined in Chapter 6. The pages that follow here provide an analysis of how civic insecurity engendered by labor militancy, social reform, the revival of the Klan, and the elite's own lack of unity led prominent Dallas businessmen to conclude that the politics of competition and cooperation threatened future growth. As the elite "disciplined" itself and convinced most middle-class voters that an ostensibly nonpartisan mayor and city council chosen by the business community was not only palatable but also desirable, Dallas began to resemble the "empire of consensus" that most contemporary residents remember as existing into the 1970s. The generation of conservative Dallas leaders that emerged in the years before World War II dominated local elections for the next thirty-five years and effectively closed the door on dissent.[4]

I

Visible changes in the nature of the Dallas elite began in the mid-1920s with a renewed interest in the efficiency of municipal government. The commercial-civic elite, concerned that many of its members could not serve as full-time city commissioners, supported the national trend toward professional city management. Veterans of Henry Lindsley's Citizens Association and younger businessmen formed the Citizens Charter Association in 1930 to pass amendments that would establish a council-manager system of municipal government.[5]

The commission form of government, despite its regional popularity, had long been considered a transitional stage by G. B. Dealey of the *Dallas Morning News*.[6] According to Dealey, a professional city manager with a full-time staff could manage a city far more efficiently than "amateurs" elected to the city commission. Dealey and other businessmen enamored with the council-manager plan reiterated the goals of early commission advocates; they believed a professional city manager, removed from immediate political accountability, and an at-large, "non-partisan" city council could more fully and easily implement the elite's vision of urban growth. Proponents of the council-manager structure envisioned a city that was "stable and orderly as well as growing and prosperous."[7]

The *Morning News* began its campaign for the council-manager form in 1916 but was distracted in the early 1920s by the revival of the Ku Klux Klan. One result of the News's campaign against the Klan was that by the time charter changes were formally proposed, the council-manager plan not only bore the considerable prestige of Dealey and the endorsement of his paper but was also perceived as a method through which future Klan incursions into city government could be stymied. Indeed, the charter changes were proposed by the administration of Mayor R. E. Burt (1927–1929) immediately after moderate business leaders regained control of the city commission from the Ku Klux Klan. Dallas voters approved the city manager system by a two-to-one margin in October 1930. The professional manager was appointed by a nine-member council, three of whom were elected at-large while the remaining six were required to live in their districts.[8]

The city's first two mayors under the council-manager form of government reflected the changes taking place within Dallas's business community. Thomas L. Bradford, who took office in 1931, was typical of a generation of southerners born in the 1850s and 1860s who migrated to Dallas as young men after the arrival of the railroads. Like G. B. Dealey, Bradford turned a fledgling enterprise—in his case, Southwestern Life Insurance Company—into a major Dallas institution. Bradford died after a year in office. His successor was Charles E. Turner. Born in Richardson in 1885 and raised in Oak Cliff, Turner represented a new generation of Dallas leaders. Turner rose as a traveling salesman and was only in his forties when elected to the city council and chosen to succeed Bradford.[9] Members of the new generation who, like Turner, became civic leaders during the 1920s and early 1930s included bankers R. L. Thornton (b. 1880) and Fred Florence (b. 1891), and attorney Woodall Rodgers (b. 1891). Although slightly younger than his peers, Ben E. Cabell, Jr. (b. 1899), whose father and grandfather were both Dallas mayors, won a seat on the city council at the age of forty. Most of the new leaders were in their forties and fifties during the 1930s and were native to Dallas or from the city's hinterlands. Theater magnate and banker Karl Hoblitzelle, who was born in St. Louis in 1879, was a notable exception. Although only a year older than Thornton, Hoblitzelle had amassed great wealth at an early age with the success of the Interstate Theatre chain. He became an important civic leader in the 1920s when he was named to the board of Republic Bank. Hoblitzelle's influence spanned both generations because of his early success and his longevity.[10]

By 1930 Dealey and his contemporaries were well into their seventies. Bradford was younger than most of his peers, but his death resulted in a transferal of influence to younger members of the Citizens Charter Association. The organization's members of both generations agreed on two main points: first, that the council-manager form of municipal government best ensured growth and efficiency; and second, that fiscal restraint was necessary to keep taxes low, bond ratings high, and the city attractive for new businesses. The autonomy of Dallas's first city manager, John N. Edy, existed within these boundaries.[11] Almost immediately, Edy generated controversy by firing 10 percent of all city workers and instituting tighter departmental supervision (see Figures 2 and 3).[12] Dallas teachers suffered pay cuts and the school board reduced costs even further by demanding the immediate resignation of married women.[13] The cost-cutting measures and rigid enforcement of liquor and gambling laws enraged municipal employees, restaurant and club owners, and other business owners who

FIGURE 2

**COMPARISON OF RECEIPTS AND EXPENDITURES, CITY OF
DALLAS, OPERATING FUNDS 1926–1934**

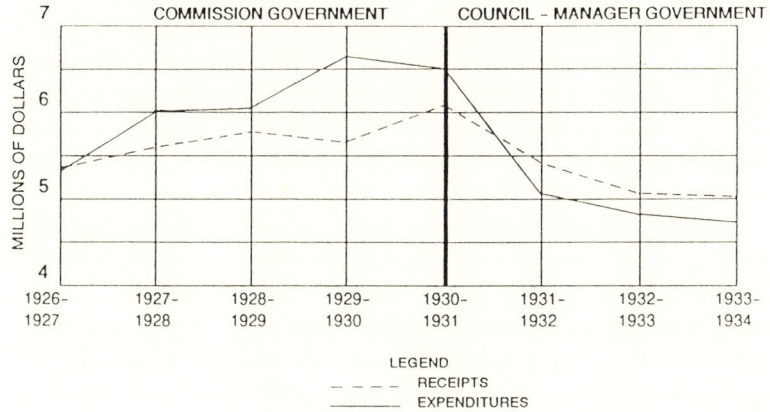

FIGURE 3

**PER CAPITA EXPENDITURES FOR OPERATION AND MAINTENANCE
OF GENERAL DEPARTMENTS, CITY OF DALLAS 1918–1933**

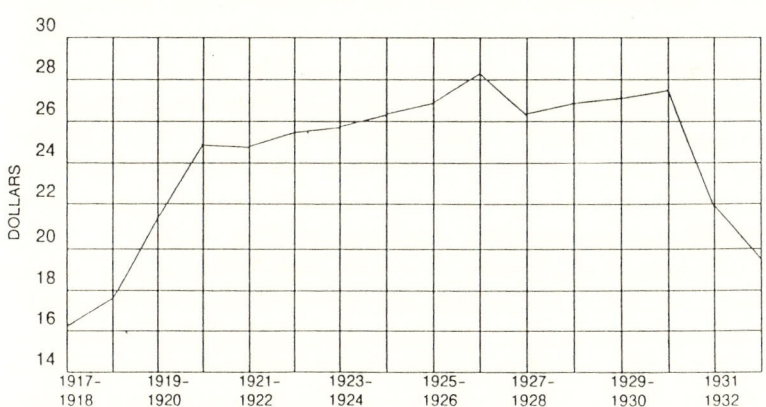

FIGURES 2 AND 3: City receipts and expenditures during the final years of
commission government compared with those under Dallas's first city manager. Such a comparison demonstrates the fiscal restraint imposed by the
Citizens Charter Association. Reproduced courtesy of the Texas/Dallas
History and Archives Division, Dallas Public Library.

depended on convention revenues. In the 1933 election, Charter Association candidates faced two full slates of opposition candidates sponsored by the newly established Home Government Association and Progressive Voters League. The rift within the business community was so pronounced that the *Dallas Morning News* refused to endorse candidates backed by the Charter Association (despite the fact that Dealey was a cofounder of the association) and remained neutral. The presence of two opposition slates neutralized opposition to Edy, and all nine Charter Association candidates, including Mayor Turner, were returned to the council.[14]

Former city employees, businessmen who wanted to oust Edy, gambling interests, and several working-class leaders formed the Catfish Club—or, more formally, the Citizens Civic Association—to unite opposition to the Charter Association in the 1935 election. The Catfish Club employed secret rituals and the grassroots organizing techniques of ward-based city government. Although club members charged that Charter Association leaders (and especially Edy, an "outsider" from Berkeley, California) were "over-educated fools," club candidates, almost exclusively businessmen and lawyers, closely resembled their opponents.[15] In spite of its failure to present a substantive alternative to the Charter Association, the Catfish Club's vitality and irreverent style attracted many working-class voters. When Mayor Turner's Charter Association–backed council and City Manager Edy established an eighty-cent-per-month sanitary sewer tax to offset municipal expenditures for the 1936 Texas Centennial Exposition, the city's workers, already suffering from low wages and irregular employment, deserted the Charter Association. After a bitter campaign during which the *Morning News* again remained neutral, Dallas residents elected all nine Catfish Club candidates to the city council.[16]

The new council replaced Edy with former Dallas street commissioner Hal Moseley and relaxed enforcement of gambling laws during the centennial year but did not change city government in any significant way. Developer John Stemmons sued the city in 1935 because it continued to delay spending on the construction of a levee sewer along the Trinity River and held up his plans to build an industrial park on the floodplain.[17] The new council had pledged to repeal the sewer tax but, instead, merely transformed the tax into a service charge and included it in water rates that were raised to make up the difference.[18]

The Catfish Club controlled Dallas's city council for four years. Council members fought among themselves, however, and in 1939, the club split into two factions—the Non-partisan Citizens Association and the Progressive Civic Association. Petty graft within the Parks Department (one park board member was impeached, another resigned) lent credibility to Charter Association charges that Catfish Club officials were corrupt and that both new parties represented "the same old gang of politicians."[19]

During the 1939 campaign, the *Morning News* again endorsed Charter Association candidates after the group agreed to promote reclamation of flood-prone land near the *News's* west-end headquarters. Association president and insurance executive Roscoe L. Thomas revitalized the organization by enlisting community leaders to broaden its appeal. Rabbi David Lefkowitz, Baptist leader Earl Smyth, and Mrs. Kirk Hall carried to church groups and women's clubs the association's promise to reinstate city government based on sound business practices. The association also secured the endorsement of the Progressive Voters League, an African American organization that had previously favored the Catfish Club. It is significant that the Charter Association benefited from the assistance of a cross section of community leaders without diluting the power of its core group of businessmen.

Dallas's diverse local economy, position as a rail hub, cheap labor supply, and the discovery of oil in its East Texas hinterlands had shielded the city from the worst of the Depression.[20] The city's relative prosperity and patterns of residential segregation masked the uneven nature of its growth. Since continued expansion appeared inevitable (between 1930 and 1940, Dallas's population grew from 260,475 to 294,734), all that many business leaders and middle-class residents required of city government was the efficient provision of adequate facilities at a reasonable cost.[21] In an effective if distorted public-relations campaign, Thomas contrasted municipal politics of the mid-1930s with an idyllic past in which benevolent business leaders—the city's "best men"—had presided over Dallas's rapid growth without concern for personal interest. During the campaign, the Charter Association promised voters that Catfish Club bickering would be replaced by harmony and efficiency if all nine association candidates were elected. The themes of harmony and unity, never before particularly important in local politics, completely overshadowed airport and highway improvements, the continued expansion and renovation of Fair Park, and other specific Charter Association programs.

The Charter Association's contention that its candidates represented

"Dallas as a whole" attracted widespread support in 1939. In a field of thirty-five, all nine association candidates won without a runoff election. The new council designated forty-eight-year-old Woodall Rodgers, formerly president of the Dallas Bar Association and a planning enthusiast, and forty-year-old Ben E. Cabell mayor and mayor pro tem, respectively. Rodgers remained mayor for the next eight years. John Edy's former assistant, James Aston, replaced Moseley as city manager. In many respects it appeared that despite the Charter Association's revitalization and the scale of its victory, its goals might be hard to achieve. The cost-cutting measures proposed by the new council might have been as controversial as similar measures earlier in the decade (when fiscal restraint and the sewer tax cost the association-backed council and the city manager his job). The Charter Association, however, managed to dominate local politics for the next thirty-five years until a federal court ordered single-member city council districts in the 1970s. The vitality and resources of a new organization, the Dallas Citizens Council, and its peculiar relationship to the Charter Association made the difference.

II

The Dallas Citizens Council and the ascendancy of a new local elite are byproducts of the civic insecurity that had been building since the period of labor militancy following World War I and are linked inextricably to the 1936 Texas Centennial Exposition. Despite the political upheavals that divided the business community during the mid-1930s, the campaign to bring the centennial celebration to Dallas attracted widespread support. The men who organized the exposition drive and later managed the fair came primarily from the younger generation of company presidents and chief executive officers—men in their forties and early fifties—who had supported the charter changes of 1930. The group most responsible for bringing the Centennial Exposition to Dallas possessed remarkably similar backgrounds. All were home grown and "self made." Few Dallas business leaders of the 1930s were college educated. Those who were had attended, almost exclusively, Texas institutions; Dallas was the only city with which they had any real familiarity.

In spite (or perhaps because) of their limited urban experience, Dallas's new generation of leaders (and its peers throughout the Midwest and the West) looked to New York, Boston, Philadelphia, and Chicago for signs of urbanity—museums, art galleries, the symphony, legitimate theater, and architectural styles—that could be re-created or transformed in Dallas. Local businessmen noted with pride Dallas's continued growth and relative prosperity during the Depression. When the city's boosters spoke about Dallas's promise, their combination of sincerity and a self-assuredness that bordered on braggadocio was infectious. Dallas was easy for Charles Turner, R. L. Thornton, and Fred Florence to sell, because Dallas was what they knew best. Unfortunately, the men who brought the Centennial Exposition to Dallas and dominated civic life for the next thirty years rarely looked far beyond the city they loved, except to note the latest urban trends and outward manifestations of culture that were accepted elsewhere. With the passing of an earlier generation lured to Dallas in the 1870s and 1880s by the railroads, the city's business community lost a wealth of urban experiences brought by migrants from the Gulf Coast, the Midwest, and Europe. As the city grew, its leadership became more, not less, homogeneous.

In 1934 the Texas Legislature appointed a Centennial Commission to accept bids for the 1936 exposition. The Charter Association's Mayor Turner and banker Fred Florence drew up a formal brief outlining Dallas's offer of almost $10 million—the state fair grounds (worth $4 million), $3.5 million from a municipal bond issue, and $2 million through the sale of exposition corporation bonds. Turner and Florence drew upon the talents and expertise of elder members of the elite. Nelson Phillips, a former chief justice of the Texas Supreme Court with political contacts across the state, assisted the younger men, as did banker Nathan Adams.[22] Many civic leaders from the southern and central portions of Texas wanted Dallas excluded from the bidding process as an inappropriate site for the fair. Dallas did not exist when Texas won its independence from Mexico in 1836. Indeed, John Neely Bryan's original settlement dated from 1841, and the city received its charter a full two decades after the Battle of San Jacinto. R. L. Thornton, another Dallas banker and president of the Chamber of Commerce, orchestrated a publicity campaign to ensure that Dallas's bid was considered by the Centennial Commission.[23] Thornton's lobbying efforts convinced the Centennial Commission, not incidentally chaired by a Dallas businessman, that the city's prosperity was reason enough to allow it to bid for the exposition. In the midst of the Depression, Dallas's high bid of almost $10 million proved to be more persuasive than San Antonio's historic Alamo or Houston's proximity to the San Jacinto battlefield. Significantly, none of the businessmen involved in preparing or generating support for the city's bid polled either their colleagues in the business community or Dallas voters regarding their willingness to contribute the promised monies.[24]

The City of Dallas donated an additional twenty-five acres of land to Fair Park for the exposition. Most of the exhibition buildings (the city's first Museum of Fine Arts, a natural history museum, an aquarium, a health and science museum, and a bandshell) blended classicism, Art Deco, and Texas motifs and were constructed specifically for the centennial. Texas spent close to $1 million on the Hall of State and allocated an additional $500,000 to advertise centennial events. In addition to funding more than fifty Dallas mural projects as part of the Public Works of Art Project in 1933 and 1934, the federal government sent $1.5 million to aid the exposition directly.[25]

The Texas Centennial Exposition brought Dallas unprecedented media attention. Much was made of the opening-day attendance of 117,000, greater than that of Chicago's 1933 Century of Progress Exhibition—to which the Texas Centennial was routinely compared. Days later, a crowd of over 50,000 heard Franklin Roosevelt speak at the Cotton Bowl, and pictures of the "Texas-sized" birthday celebration filled the pages of newspapers and magazines across the country.[26] The juxtaposition of positive images from Dallas and the grim daily lives of many Americans during the Depression created an indelible impression in the minds of a generation of Texans. "Big D" promised showy new homes, shiny cars, and fast money—if one worked hard enough. Publicist Bill Langley sent red-white-and-blue-clad "Rangerettes" across the nation to promote the fair. A newspaper photograph of J. Edgar Hoover lassoed in his Washington office by attractive young women from Texas appeared throughout the country.[27]

The centennial prompted many rural southwesterners to visit a large city for the first time. Countless others listened to friends' and relatives' accounts of the fair. The relative health of Dallas's ten state and national banks, forty-two insurance-company home offices, and seven hundred factories seemed to belie the existence of an economic crisis. By 1936 Dallas ranked third in the nation in the distribution of farm equipment and was the country's fourth largest distributor of dry goods. Dallas made more cotton gins and processing equipment than any city in the world and was among the leaders in the manufacture of saddlery, harnesses, and leather goods. Henry Ford located a final-assembly plant in Dallas and other car manufacturers established parts warehouses. With rail connections to the Northeast and throughout Texas, Dallas became the Southwest's primary automobile distributor. The city's parks, 39 theaters, 130 hotels, performing arts groups, and the new museums at Fair Park similarly impressed rural visitors.[28] To most of them, Dallas appeared quite cosmopolitan. The city's geographic isolation magnified cultural achievements, as did the rural nature of its immense hinterland.

Despite attracting more than 6,400,000 visitors between June 6 and November 30 of 1936, the Texas Centennial Exposition, like most grand celebrations in American history, lost money.[29] The fair also generated controversy. In addition to the notorious sewer tax that brought down the city council in 1935, the city was criticized for failing to install air conditioners or large fans in the exhibition buildings. The *Dispatch* scoffed that the facilities would be "nice Turkish baths" during a Dallas summer.[30] Long-time city attorney Henry Kucera recalls that acquisition of the 150 feet of right-of-way necessary to enlarge the fairgrounds involved "worlds of controversial stuff."[31] Almost immediately after the state commission awarded the fair to Dallas, boosters found it more difficult to raise money for the exposition than they had anticipated. According to the *Dispatch*, resentment in Texas cities that had lost the exposition to Dallas and corporate "niggardliness" threatened to kill the centennial.[32]

Labor disputes and architectural conflicts resulted in additional expenses. The general contractor of the Hall of State, the state-funded centerpiece of the exposition, outraged Dallas building tradesmen by hiring both union and nonunion crews. A work stoppage by union electricians, sheet-metal workers, painters, and plumbers put the project hopelessly behind schedule. A separate strike by union bricklayers over wages for weekend overtime spread to five other unions. Problems with the building's original design caused further delays, as did friction between the chief centennial architect and the local project coordinator for the Hall of State. Dallas business leaders offered a $50,000 bonus to speed up construction; although the money settled the bricklayers' strike, the Hall of State was not completed until three months after the exposition's June opening.[33]

The buildings leading east from downtown to the fairgrounds entrance were small and nondescript. Dallas civic leaders were unwilling to engage in a large-scale planning effort that would connect the city's business district with its primary recreational facility. According to a recent analyst of Dallas architecture, "Fair Park remained detached from its surroundings, never becoming the nucleus for urban growth that its promoters had predicted."[34]

Dallas business leaders could not settle the disputes that arose at the state level or stem the urban rivalries that made fundraising almost impossible outside Dallas County. Fort Worth leaders accused Dallas of trying to deny their city $250,000 in state funds for a centennial stock show and rodeo.[35] A dispute regarding allocations for public works of art divided Texas historians and, subsequently, the state legislature. Writing for the minority of the Advisory Board of Texas Historians, Dallas's J. Frank Dobie chastised the board's majority for recommending the distribution of monies by state senatorial districts without regard for historical validity. According to Dobie, the majority's recommendations also called for too many "heroic figures." He claimed that "literal statues will not kindle interest" and should be reserved for truly interesting subjects. Dobie advised legislators to honor naturalists, writers, historians, episodes, cotton, cattle, and groups such as the Texas Rangers, as well as military men and officeholders. Dobie and the other two historians who signed the minority report urged legislators to consider the "temper of the people" and reject such pedestrian proposals as a $14,000 statue of Anson Jones (an obscure president of the Republic of Texas unknown to most residents even of Jones County, in the western part of the state). The minority suggested that plans for the traditional statue be scrapped in favor of a $2,500 memorial depicting range traditions described by Larry Chittenden, the popular "cowboy poet" of Jones County. Dobie concluded, "If you wish human beings, whether young or old, to regard history, then touch their imaginations."[36]

A Dallas statue also generated controversy. As a special centennial project, the Southern Memorial Association commissioned a $50,000 equestrian statue of Robert E. Lee and a young man representing the youth of Texas who followed Lee into battle for the Confederacy. Dallas leaders displayed a gaping insensitivity by asking President Roosevelt to dedicate the statue, prominently displayed on a hilltop at the entrance to a park named in Lee's honor. Roosevelt "unveiled" the statue without leaving his car—an act attributed to his medical condition by some but interpreted as a snub by many southerners.[37]

As the fair continued to lose money during the summer of 1936, Thornton, now chairman of the Exposition Management Committee, began calling on what Stanley Marcus has described as "a natural group . . . the utility people, the heads of the insurance companies, the merchants, the heads of the banks" to keep the exposition open. Thornton, who rose to civic prominence through his indefatigable work for the Chamber of Commerce during the 1920s, witnessed the ongoing sectional conflict among downtown interests and was convinced that G. B. Dealey, Karl Hoblitzelle, and other long-time members of the city's commercial-civic elite were correct in their contention that a fractured business community could undermine Dallas's bid for greatness. In his fundraising efforts he stressed the opportunity presented by the fair and its ability to unite various factions. Before the exposition's fall closing date, Dallas business leaders had given Thornton an additional $2 million. In spite of his gross underestimation of the fair's costs, neither Thornton nor the exposition received significant negative publicity. The year 1936 was the year "the world discovered Texas."[38] Residents of "Big D" quickly forgot the Texas Centennial Exposition's attendant controversies, and few were openly critical of the centennial celebration's "manager." On the contrary, the Chamber of Commerce blamed Dallas citizens who "have been laggards in attendance" for the exposition's financial shortcomings. The chamber asserted, "The fair has been well sold to America. Out-of-state tourists have come by the tens of thousands. Texans have poured into Dallas to see the focal celebration of the Centennial year. But there have been many days when one saw only strange faces on the Exposition grounds," and urged Dallas residents to "make a point of going [to the fair] once a week."[39]

A banquet for President Roosevelt hosted by R. L. Thornton of Mercantile Bank, Fred Florence of Republic National Bank, and Nathan Adams of First National Bank symbolized the banking triumvirate's ascendancy. Catfish Club–backed Mayor George Sergeant attended the event but his presence was overshadowed by the men given credit for the fair's success.[40] Thornton was praised by his peers for his ability to convince other businessmen to cooperate, present a united front, and take on community work as a "team."[41] Thornton's personal style and ability to "get the dirt flying" appealed to other segments of the community as well. Even recent migrants and county farmers, many of whose suspicions of bankers dated back to the 1890s when Dallas financiers defeated the Populists' plans to mass market cotton, responded positively to the exposition manager's "cotton-pickin' talk."[42]

As the Texas Centennial Exposition closed, Thornton, Florence, Adams, and others who had provided "emergency" funds determined to institutionalize their efforts and hold regular meetings. In an attempt to maintain the consensus engendered during the fair, Thornton insisted that the organization remain a self-selected group of bosses—"yes and no men" who could commit money and time (their own and that of their employees) without seeking another's approval. The Dallas Citizens Council was chartered in 1937 "to study, confer and act upon any matter, civic or economic in character, which may be deemed to affect the welfare of the city of Dallas."[43]

Fittingly, Thornton wanted to call the group the "Yes and No Council." Although members chose a more conciliatory name, Thornton's criterion for admission remained intact for almost fifty years.[44] No journalists, educators, or ministers are invited to join the organization. The heads of the city's major law and accounting firms were excluded until the mid-1980s. Robert Cullum, a former Citizens Council president, cited four-term Dallas mayor and attorney Woodall Rodgers as an example of how the organization excluded even the most influential civic leaders in order to maintain the undiluted hegemony of local business leaders. Cullum explained, "Lawyers are not eligible. I don't care how prominent an attorney might be, he doesn't head a corporation."[45] Significantly, Cullum was unable to name even one civic leader besides Rodgers who had been able to become an influential city leader without Citizens Council membership. As the organization gained momentum during the 1940s, its members monopolized civic power. Several other attorneys amassed a great deal of local influence during the 1950s, as did Southern Methodist University president Willis Tate and W. A. Criswell of the First Baptist Church. Despite their prominence, these men lacked the measure of control and autonomy over human and material resources that was from the beginning a prerequisite for Citizens Council membership.

Until quite recently, the Citizens Council also excluded women, blacks, and Hispanics.[46] From its origins, the organization has represented Dallas business institutions. Along with the three big bankers, the inner circle was dominated by the heads of the major insurance companies, the publishers of the *Morning News* and the *Times Herald*, and the general managers of Dallas Power & Light (now Texas Utilities), Lone Star Gas, and Southwestern Bell. There was room for charismatic individuals such as Cullum, of the Tom Thumb food stores, and Stanley Marcus (the group's only liberal), provided they met the dual requirements of autonomous power and a ready supply of both financial and human resources. Although the early Citizens Council courted the regional managers of Sears and Ford Motors, local executives of other corporate giants and most Dallas oil men, including H. L. Hunt, either never sought or were never offered membership.[47] Until the consolidation of major banks in the 1970s, the organization remained the exclusive vehicle of those dependent on a local government that provided regular downtown improvements, kept tax rates low, and did not discourage development through "excessive" regulations. Oil executives, like the regional heads of multinational corporations, found national and international economic policies more crucial to their welfare than the actions of the Dallas city council.[48]

From its origins, the Citizens Council's modus operandi was to table any proposal that engendered even minor disagreement. In an attempt to harness the elite's tendency to split into factions, and to end sectional bickering, the organization took action only when there was a virtual consensus among business leaders. The group's scope of activity was, therefore, often quite narrow, while its thrust was very powerful. The apparent consensus gave the illusion of a small group of men who could do whatever they wanted in Dallas. The organization expanded and maintained its influence through a network of interlocking directorates. Its members actively sought and served as board members of area churches, hospitals, the art museum, the symphony, and Southern Methodist University. The Citizens Council quickly dominated the Chamber of Commerce and the Committee for Good Schools. Although the Citizens Council never explicitly endorses candidates, a large cross-membership with the Citizens Charter Association led to the misconception (albeit only a technical one) that the now-defunct association was the political arm of the Citizens Council.

The origins of the extraordinarily close relationship between the two organizations can be traced directly to Citizens Council founder R. L.

Thornton. After its two successive defeats at the hands of the Catfish Club, the Charter Association determined to prevail in the 1939 city council elections. In a meeting with business leaders, the association's president, Roscoe Thomas, appealed for cash. Thornton declared that he was inclined to support the association but first wanted to know who its candidates would be, "as he was not accustomed to backing undisclosed entries in a horse race." Thomas secured the funding and satisfied Thornton's curiosity by naming the banker to the association's nominating committee.[49]

The Charter Association proved to be a convenient political tool for members of the Citizens Council. According to former mayor and bank president Wallace Savage, a Charter Association-backed city councilman in the 1940s, the association selected candidates on the basis of their business acumen and the knowledge that they shared the Dallas elite's traditional equation of fiscal restraint and continued growth as well as younger members' concern for unity. The association sprang into public action before elections, raising funds and managing the campaign. So complete was Charter Association domination of municipal elections that some of the candidates it backed in the 1940s and 1950s never made a campaign speech. The major newspapers did not criticize the association's methods. The Dealeys of the *Morning News* and Edwin J. Kiest of the *Times Herald* were prominent members of both the Charter Association and the Citizens Council (the city's other daily newspaper, the *Dispatch*, did not survive the 1930s).

Once in office, however, Charter Association–backed council members were not directly influenced by the organization responsible for their election. Rather, class interests and a shared vision of the city and the role of municipal government determined their actions. Savage describes himself as "a young man who didn't come up with a silver spoon in my mouth, who obviously was doing reasonably well under the economic system as it then existed, and who could be expected, . . . by reason of his background and his experience to not be, . . . a wild-eyed liberal."[50] Thornton's son agrees that the "whole purpose" of the Charter Association was "to select a mayor and councilmen to run the City of Dallas."[51] After elections, the association maintained a low profile.

In stark contrast, the Citizens Council, through its regular luncheons at the Baker and Adolphus hotels, proved true to its mission "to study, confer and act upon any matter" affecting Dallas. Particularly active in support of bond issues, the group displayed what political economist Stephen Elkin calls "virtuoso political talent . . . in keeping control of the public agenda."[52] Early projects of the Citizens Council included a downtown auditorium, Fair Park and airport improvements, and a new comprehensive city plan.[53] By electing officials through the Charter Association, the efforts of the new elite manifested themselves as a civic campaign on behalf of Dallas "as a whole."[54] Its members' hands apparently unsullied by the political infighting that characterized Dallas public life until the mid-1930s, the Citizens Council convinced a majority of Dallas voters to view the business agenda as a local version of Manifest Destiny rather than as the product of vested interests. Through its insistence that the business community present only a single option to the public, its silence on issues that divided the elite, its control of the local media, and its co-optation of the Charter Association, the Dallas Citizens Council amassed unprecedented civic power in the 1940s.

Modern Dallas is a creation of interwar economic forces, tensions, and fears. The Great Depression accentuated a civic insecurity that convinced business leaders of the need for unity and enhanced class consciousness among members of the elite. Many middle-class Dallas residents remained fearful about the city's continued prosperity even as they escaped the worst of the national economic crisis. Unlike residents of New York and Chicago, people in Dallas did not easily assume that their city would remain vital and dynamic after the Depression. The generation of business leaders who matured in the 1920s and rose to prominence with the Texas Centennial Exposition benefited from both the aspirations and the insecurity of the people of Dallas. The men who orchestrated the centennial gave Dallas residents something to cheer about and, in the midst of uncertainty, promised a bright future. With the consolidation of the city's most powerful business leaders on the Citizens Council, voters were presented with a single "reasonable" agenda and guarantees of harmony and continued success.

Although the new generation shared the vision of growth articulated by the city's early leaders, its style and methods bore little resemblance to those of its predecessors. The political rivalry between business leaders who supported the Citizens Charter Association and those who formed the Catfish Club only added to the anxiety the Dallas elite felt as a result of challenges from labor, reform advocates, and the Ku Klux Klan. These challenges and the historic contentiousness of Dallas business leaders convinced the three big bankers and their associates on the Citizens Council that the capacity to work cooperatively with their peers was essential for the group's success.[55] As a result, Dallas's new business leaders rejected the politics of competition and cooperation and molded themselves into a much tighter group than the earlier elite.

In contrast to the division between public-political and private-social friends that Lynn Lawther described as typical among his father's generation, Thornton, Florence, and Adams encouraged political associates to join their social clubs and fraternal organizations and chose their protégés from among their sons' and daughters' friends. A generation of Texans, the new elite supported The University of Texas at Austin, Texas A&M University, and, especially, Dallas's own Southern Methodist University. Indeed, by the late 1940s, an SMU connection was often a young man's ticket to positions on the Citizens Council and the boards of other urban institutions.[56]

The insular nature of the new elite had significant effects on public life in the decades after the Second World War. The founders of the Citizens Council were not connoisseurs, and the city's veteran arts enthusiasts found the new elite much less eager than early Dallas merchants to support cultural institutions. A much-repeated anecdote has R. L. Thornton throwing up his hands in exasperation and promising a symphony backer a sizable donation if he could be assured that it would not obligate him to attend a performance.[57] Elmer Scott recalls another of the major bankers admitting that he had read nothing save financial news for ten years.[58]

The elite that came to power in the 1930s ran Dallas like an efficient corporation in which the authority of the board of directors was not questioned. The management of Dallas concerned itself with the wealth and prosperity of the business community. The city's African American and Latino populations continued to suffer from severely limited employment opportunities and an ongoing shortage of decent housing. Migrants from rural areas who came to the city with few skills received some of the lowest wages of any urban workers in the country. The conservatism of local union leaders and the state's right-to-work laws diminished the influence of skilled workers. The city

continued to grow but, like its Art Deco fairgrounds, repeated familiar patterns and copied accepted styles. Dallas did not innovate but
relied instead on transmitted cultural forms and temporarily imported
talent. Absolute unity allowed little else.

DALLAS'S WAR ON LABOR, 1935–1940

For workers I hold no malice,
Said Henry Ford to innocent Alice.
When my thugs beat up a man,
You must understand It's just for the good of Dallas.
— Quoted in *Southern News Almanac*[1]

IN AN ESSAY PREPARED FOR THE 1934–1935 *City Directory*, R. L. Thornton's Chamber of Commerce described Dallas as *the* marketplace of the Southwest and attributed the city's growth to the acumen of the local business community. According to the chamber, the Dallas businessman "conducts his large enterprise in impressive, modern office buildings, goes home to his attractive residence, with a landscaped lawn that enhances the beauty of a wide, tree lined street; takes his exercise on the sweeping, sporty golf courses, the hard, smooth tennis courts, or the sandy beaches that his own public spirit has created; pays his homage to God and educates his children in magnificent churches and schools that are second to none in beauty and facilities."[2]

This account of the Dallas lifestyle ignored the realities of urban life for the city's working class during the Depression. Throughout the 1930s, only white building tradesmen routinely worked fewer than fifty-four hours per week. Nonunion laborers and blacks often worked longer hours—many for weekly wages of seven dollars or less.[3] Beyond the tree-lined streets and manicured lawns of the city's business leaders lay the boardinghouse districts, slums, and shantytowns of Dallas's poor. Inadequate housing and sanitation in these areas (immediately north and south of downtown, in West Dallas, and on the city's fringes) contributed to an annual loss of more than one hundred lives to tuberculosis and over four hundred to pneumonia.[4]

Many of Dallas's poorly paid workers were women. Working conditions in the local apparel industry shocked Jack Spry, a veteran labor

organizer from Iowa. Spry declared women employed in the millinery-
and hat-manufacturing industries in Dallas during the Depression
"worse off than former negro slaves."[5] Like the millinery workers, the
city's skilled dressmakers endured long hours in poorly ventilated factories. Although their work required coordination and concentration,
garment workers were exposed to extreme temperatures and paid an
average of $9.50 per week.[6] Millinery Workers' Union organizer Car-
men Lucia recalled that "prostitution was rife" in Dallas because of the
low wages paid factory operatives and dime-store clerks.[7] One local
dress manufacturer told an employee who complained about her wages
in 1935 that five dollars a week was enough for a "girl" to live on and
that "she could make more on the outside if she needed it."[8]

Popular attitudes toward working women contributed to the
maintenance of sweatshop conditions. Dallas clothing manufacturers
argued that women's wages merely augmented those of husbands and
fathers and dismissed employee protests as the results of union agita-
tion. Middle-class social mores perpetuated a cult of "ladydom" (an
extension of nineteenth-century ideals of "true womanhood") among
women who could afford to remain at home and linked factory work
with "coarseness."[9] Women who worked to support their children or
underemployed husbands were perceived as "unladylike" by many
clubwomen whose traditional interest in reform made them potential
allies. Popular attitudes toward women and work combined with fifteen years of well-funded Open Shop Association propaganda to alien-
ate female factory operatives from much of the city's middle class.
When Dallas garment workers formed a union and organized a year-
long strike in 1935, they received little popular support. Appeals to the
public's sense of fairness, reminiscent of those of Dallas street-railway
workers in 1898 and building tradesmen in 1919, proved ineffective
against popular gender distinctions and an increasing tendency to associate labor unions with subversives.

Before the organization of the garment workers, very few of Dallas's
approximately fifty trade unions represented women.[10] Ironically, it was
the militancy of Dallas dressmakers that revived the city's labor movement and stimulated the local organization of industrial workers. The
garment workers' challenge to the elite's commitment to low wages
(as a means of attracting new businesses to Dallas) was quickly followed by organizing efforts among auto workers at the local Ford
plant and the renewed activity of the Socialist party.

By the mid-1930s, Dallas employers were clearly committed to nonunion workplaces—in order to minimize costs and "avoid trouble." Dallas's new business elite, intent on consolidating its power, countered vigorous union organizing efforts with both propaganda and repression. Newspapers presented distorted images of strikers and union leaders during the garment workers' walkout in 1935. The editors of the city's major daily newspapers condoned brutal tactics used by Dallas police against female pickets and frequently stirred racial antagonisms and anti-Semitism.

In 1937 the management of Ford Motor Company, in collusion with local police and business leaders, recruited a strong-arm squad that terrorized the city until the end of the decade. In contrast to the distorted and unsympathetic treatment accorded the garment workers two years earlier, Dallas's daily newspapers ignored violence associated with local efforts to organize industrial workers. Because of its opposition to the Congress of Industrial Organizations (CIO), even the city's AFL-affiliated labor weekly remained silent. In the midst of repression, union organizers were unable to overcome the obstacles of a working class divided by race and skill level. Dallas's relative lack of large factories especially hurt the CIO's local efforts. Few Dallas shops employed more than fifty people. As a result of the elite's five-year war on labor, anti-union sentiment was institutionalized in Dallas and the last significant challenge to business hegemony until the civil rights movement of the 1960s was suppressed.

The National Labor Relations Board (NLRB) vindicated the women fired and blacklisted by Dallas dress manufacturers and, in 1940, convicted Ford Motor Company of "indiscriminate ruthlessness and organized gangsterism" aimed at "maintaining the status quo of non-organization" in Dallas.[11] The federal government's cease and desist order and punitive actions did little, however, to offset repression's chilling effect on dissent in Dallas. The ritualistic beatings that maimed dozens of actual and suspected union organizers and sympathetic auto workers in 1937 drove the city's younger generation of radicals out of town and frightened local workers into submission.

Dallas business leaders, despite their vehement opposition to an organized work force, recognized the significance of class- and interest-based organizations. They poured both human and material resources into local institutions such as the Open Shop Association, the Chamber of Commerce, and the Texas Dress Manufacturers' Association. With those who presented alternatives to its version of urban development effectively silenced, the new Dallas elite found itself virtually unopposed in the decades after 1940.

This chapter presents an analysis of organized labor's last local attempt to implement early Dallas unionists' vision of a society that provides equitable rewards for producers. It highlights first the activities of the working women who conducted the longest strike in Dallas history. Garment workers took to the streets not solely to demand higher wages but also to protest the social and economic consequences of Dallas business leaders' preoccupation with growth. The focus then shifts to Ford's efforts to prevent the industrial organization of its Dallas workers. The Ford Terror provides a fascinating example of the Dallas elite's willingness to condone violence and protect its perpetrators when repression served the elite's interests, and foreshadows the business community's response to a revival of Ku Klux Klan–style terrorism directed at blacks in the 1950s.[12]

I

Dallas's rapid expansion to the north and east and the annexation of 21.6 square miles during the 1920s nearly doubled its physical size and increased both the geographic and social distance between most middle-class residents and those who worked in the dress factories that rimmed the southern edge of the business district. By 1935 many downtown workers commuted by automobile from the new neighborhoods to the north and did not linger long after the workday ended. A significant number of urban and suburban residents no longer made the trip downtown every day—and an increasing number of those who did never ventured far on foot from their workplaces. Physical changes in the business district made to accommodate cars and buses further lessened the number of pedestrians on city streets. The functional segregation of downtown into financial, shopping, entertainment, warehouse, and manufacturing districts combined with the distance between home and the workplace to limit interaction between middle-class residents and the city's workers.[13]

In addition to the growing homogenization of daily life for much of Dallas's middle class, the disintegration of the early alternative press left many residents more dependent than ever on four major daily newspapers for information. (In 1906, Dallas had sixty periodicals, most of them newspapers. By the Depression's end, only thirteen newspapers survived.[14]) The ability of local business leaders to manipulate public opinion through their control of the daily newspapers proved to be a major factor in the defeat of the International Ladies Garment Workers Union's (ILGWU) attempt to bring the principles of collective bargaining to Dallas dress factories.

Approximately one hundred Dallas dressmakers joined a grassroots "sewing club" in 1934, after the Supreme Court declared unconstitutional the National Industrial Recovery Act (NRA) codes stipulating minimum wages and maximum hours. Dallas manufacturers of overalls and other work clothes reduced wages to pre-code levels, and the dressmakers feared their employers would soon follow suit. The dressmakers patterned their grassroots organization on the familiar model of a social club—an organizational structure with a long history of acceptance by Dallas residents of all social classes. Charlotte Graham, one of the "club's" twelve original members, explained that because of virulent anti-union propaganda disseminated by the Open Shop Association, local organizers determined that a few married women whose husbands were employed would "stick our necks out" first. After several clandestine meetings, members of the group asked Larry Taylor, president of the Dallas Central Labor Council, for advice. Taylor subsequently contacted the ILGWU and requested that an organizer be sent to Dallas.[15]

The actions of Dallas dressmakers likely came as no surprise to ILGWU officials. Under the leadership of David Dubinsky, the union's membership jumped from 40,422 in 1933 to 216,801 in 1935—due largely to fears that even the smallest gains would be lost after the revocation of NRA codes.[16] Dressmakers around the country formed grassroots organizations such as the one in Dallas and affiliated with the ILGWU in the mid-1930s. Dubinsky sent New York organizer Meyer Perlstein, who had served as one of the union's vice presidents from 1910 to 1925, to Dallas in November 1934. Within four months, more than 400 of the almost 1,000 dressmakers in Dallas joined the union. In early 1935 Perlstein told Dallas dress manufacturers that unless wages were increased and hours reduced the ILGWU's two Dallas locals were prepared to strike. Local dress manufacturers refused to recognize either Perlstein or the ILGWU and immediately dismissed workers suspected of union activity. Picketing began in early February. The walkout spread quickly to all fifteen Dallas factories owned by members of the Texas Dress Manufacturers' Association.[17]

The *Dallas Morning News* and its sensational first afternoon affiliate, the *Journal,* carried strike stories almost daily. Coverage in the *Dallas Times Herald* and the *Dallas Dispatch* was less extensive but similar in tone to that of the *Morning News.* The *News* initially refused to take female strikers seriously. On the first day of the walkout, dressmakers were described "chatting good-naturedly as if they were on an outing." Noting less tension than was usually present among crowds that gather after an auto wreck, the *News* concluded that Dallas dressmakers exhibited no tendencies toward violence and instead provided an example of "how even tempered Texans can stage a strike without getting excessively 'riled up' about it." The article did not mention the conditions under which garment workers labored but attributed the strike to "purported discrimination against union members."[18]

Interviews with conservative "experts" and editorials condemning all strikes followed the *Morning News*'s initial attempts to downplay the garment workers' actions.[19] In a prominently placed article, Dr. J. U. Yarborough, head of the psychology department at Southern Methodist University, declared that increased labor unrest meant "the depression is definitely breaking up." Yarborough argued that the public had not responded to the strikers' grievances because of a conservative reaction to New Deal reform measures. Yarborough reinforced the Open Shop Association's contention that "outside elements" were responsible for local disputes with his assertion that more "isms" were "being peddled from door to door than ever before in the history of the Nation."[20]

Keeping with the popular belief that white women, most of whom were from rural Texas or other southern states, would never join together and "man" picket lines on their own accord, the *Morning News* frequently repeated charges by the Texas Dress Manufacturers' Association that Perlstein and Leah Oleve, another New York organizer, and Frank Rather from St. Louis came to Dallas "to agitate the garment workers and instigate a strike."[21] The paper's anticommunist rhetoric and emphasis on the union organizers' backgrounds obscured the conditions responsible for local dressmakers' dissatisfaction and the garment workers' formation of a grassroots organization *before* their affiliation with the ILGWU. The *News* applauded a strikebreaker who responded to an insult with, "I might be yellow, but I'm not red."[22] Ironically (given the paper's preoccupation with Perlstein's background, but not in the context of the Dealeys' anti-union agenda), the *News* ignored the central role Perlstein had played in the ILGWU's expulsion of communists during the mid-1920s.[23]

In what would become a familiar pattern over the next ten months, pickets attempting to keep strikebreakers from entering a dress factory on February 12 clashed with Dallas police. Women blocking the doors to Donovan Manufacturing Company bit, kicked, and beat law officers and private guards who escorted scabs into the facility.[24] Reports of women fighting to enforce picket lines shocked Dallas editors. Both the *Morning News* and the *Journal* supported the often brutal tactics of local police. When a law officer tore a union song sheet from a striker's hands and threw her to the pavement with such force that she was hospitalized with a hip injury, the *News* excused his actions, explaining that the police mistook the song sheet for a court-ordered injunction.[25] The *Journal* admitted that some officers "have erred on the side of vigor rather than on that of mercy" but claimed that the police had performed a "tremendously difficult and distasteful task" admirably.[26] Its editor attempted to lessen the credibility of numerous eyewitness accounts of police brutality by claiming that "the evidence of spectators is confused and unreliable." Another *Journal* editorial belittled union appeals in Austin for an investigation into the conduct of the local police.[27]

In March the *News* printed a sensational photograph of J. D. Goss, a twenty-two-year-old policeman whose hair had been almost completely ripped out during a strike riot. Alongside it ran a picture of union member May Swoffard, "exhibiting a bare spot where her scalp lock once was."[28] Police Chief Claude Trammell admitted that his officers had hit some of the pickets but insisted that in each case, "there was a positive necessity." Trammell was even less tolerant of strikers' husbands, relatives, and friends who provided support on the picket lines. According to the police chief, "Men agitators have been struck with fists, and it is no more than they deserve."[29]

The newspapers' coverage of the strike did not place the dressmakers' militancy into a context that included economic exploitation and the intransigence of local employers, who refused to negotiate a solution to the dispute or abide by collective-bargaining agreements. According to an industry representative, Dallas garment workers who sewed cotton dresses averaged $9.50 per week before NRA codes went into effect in October 1933 (those sewing silk dresses made slightly more). Highly skilled silk-dress cutters, who earned weekly wages of $35 to $50 in other parts of the country, made as little as $10 to $15 in Dallas. The NRA committee raised the Dallas minimum for cutters to $27 and set a $14 weekly standard for dressmakers working in silk. Operators making cotton dresses were to receive a weekly minimum of $12.[30]

Local clothing manufacturers routinely ignored the new codes. "Chiseling" had been common enough in the days before the NRA, but the establishment of regional standards increased Dallas garment workers' awareness of each new violation. Many local employers used the federally mandated minimum-wage scale as a maximum and fired those workers whose piecework earnings did not reach the NRA minimum. Some employers listed almost all garment workers, regardless of skill level, as operators to avoid higher codes for pressers, cutters, and drapers. Others diluted the impact of legislation that reduced the work week by opening factories "off the clock" on Saturdays. Dallas garment workers alleged that in order to circumvent NRA codes, managers routinely fired women who completed "apprenticeships," only to rehire them as "beginners." In a hearing before the Industrial Commission of Texas, local dressmakers described how manufacturers billed matched suits to retailers as two separate items in order to make the garments under cheaper codes. Jackets were called blouses for the same reason, and expensive silk dresses were sewn under the cotton code.[31]

By the time the strike was a month old, Dallas papers printed detailed descriptions of altercations between strikers, scabs, and police officers several times a week. In addition to the heckling, shoving, and occasional beating that occurred as strikers attempted to block access to the dress factories, several strikebreakers had red pepper thrown in their eyes, and one male scab was beaten with a blackjack by three men allegedly aiding the union.[32] Most of the violence, however, stemmed from police efforts to enforce injunctions that restricted the number of pickets allowed outside the factories. Union members rejected Dallas judge Towne Young's order that only one picket be stationed in front of each plant and continued to confront scabs directly.

Unlike the major strikes in 1898 and 1919, the garment workers' walkout generated few rallies in which union speakers explained their positions to the general public. Although riots involving strikers, scabs, and police still attracted large numbers of onlookers, the downtown area was no longer conducive to spontaneous gatherings. The dress-makers' hopes for a greater share of the benefits of urban growth were lost amid sensationalist newspaper coverage of the melees. Union demands went unreported after the first few weeks of the strike.[33] The major dailies never printed accounts of the working conditions that motivated the strikers even though the downtown newspaper build-ings were within blocks of (and in the case of the *Morning News* across the street from) the dress factories. The press's attention remained nar-rowly focused on the pronouncements of union organizers and the militancy of the strikers.

Perhaps the most damaging aspect of the Dallas newspapers' pre-sentation of the "dressmakers' war" was that the strikers themselves remained in the background. The women were portrayed in the news-paper accounts of the strike as pawns of the union's "imported" lead-ership.[34] Although 90 percent of the ILGWU's local members had dependents (many of those without children cared for elderly parents or had injured or unemployed spouses), the union could not erase the popular perception that working women only supplemented the incomes of fathers and husbands.[35]

The belief that long-term factory work made women coarse and unladylike persisted despite the presence in the dress factories of mar-ried women such as Bessie Havens, a veteran dressmaker who impressed members of the Industrial Commission of Texas with both her testimony and her demeanor. After almost six years as a dress-maker, Havens no longer considered herself a temporary worker. She worked because her husband, a regularly employed barber, did not make enough money for her to remain at home. The couple had no children or other dependents but needed two incomes to live com-fortably in the depressed economy of the 1930s. Although Havens never made more than $12 per week in five years at Morten-Davis Manufacturing, her employer promised $18 weekly if she remained on the job during the strike. Havens told commissioners at a hearing on the garment industry in Dallas that she joined the ILGWU because her work was undervalued and she thought that a union could improve conditions. In one of the first strike riots, Havens was beaten by police and taken to the hospital emergency room. A subsequent trip to jail, where she was "put in with the street walkers and everybody else," did not lessen her commitment to the union.[36]

A few Dallas residents did question the accounts they read in local papers. In a letter to the *Morning News*, Edward Mather, a University Park resident with no union connections, declared that "all the publicity on the current struggle so far . . . fails to inform us of a number of things." Mather asked why the *News* had not questioned the dress manufacturers' refusal to arbitrate the dispute. He found the coverage of the strike lacked analysis and raised three substantive questions: (1) Why did the governor's committee, with the sole exception of the manufacturers' representative, find in favor of the strikers? (2) Why was the State Department of Labor not allowed to make public local wage scales? and (3) Why was the national standard considered too high in Dallas? Mather doubted the sincerity of "companies who 'couldn't afford' wage hikes" yet bought newspaper space during the strike and hired "fleets of taxicabs" to transport strikebreakers to and from the factories.[37]

Despite the arrests of at least 86 women (whose names appeared in the *Morning News*), all of the daily papers continued to print manufacturers' estimates that the strikers numbered no more than 50. The ILGWU claimed it paid 150, an estimate more in line with the experience of one policeman who commented, "Who said there were only 50 on strike? Who are those people on picket duty?"[38] In contrast to newspaper depictions of the strikers as easily led and relatively naive girls, those arrested during the walkout ranged in age from their late teens to early fifties. Almost half were married, or had been at some time.[39]

Examples of southern folk humor in the "Strikers Streak," a grassroots newsletter distributed by local dressmakers, further contradict the newspapers' insistence that the strike was simply the work of Meyer Perlstein and his fellow organizers. One issue jokingly describes a mock funeral conducted by strikers arrested during a confrontation with police. Protesting inadequate jail facilities for women and a lack of prompt medical attention for injured pickets, one of the so-called jail birds "died" of her wounds and was "buried" in jail. The amateur editors of the newsletter skillfully used the strikers' singing of the funeral dirge and the laughing "corpse" as symbols of solidarity and defiance.[40]

In addition to presenting a distorted picture of the strikers and ignoring their grievances, Dallas newspapers did not report local business leaders' attempts to thwart the new union, intimidate potential members, and discourage further attempts to organize Dallas workers.

Lester Lorch, the dress manufacturers' representative at a hearing before the Industrial Commission of Texas, admitted that Dallas dress manufacturers blacklisted women. The dress manufacturers routinely evaded questions concerning the tenets of their organization and its contributions to the Open Shop Association. Factory owners feigned ignorance of frequent luncheons and meetings. The Dress Manufacturers' Association set up a fund to pay for full-page advertisements in local newspapers and hired "investigators to find out one thing or another relative to the strike that we thought we should know about."[41]

Soon after the manufacturers established their strike fund, incidents of police brutality increased and special guards augmented the local force. As many as a hundred private guards wore uniforms like those of the Dallas police and carried pistols during the strike. The Dress Manufacturers' Association paid $2,256.11 to "detectives" and spent over $100 taking pictures of the strikers. Ironically, factory owners who claimed they could not afford to pay skilled dressmakers more than $12 per week paid private guards a weekly wage of $25 to stand at the factory doors.[42]

The relationship between the dress manufacturers and the Open Shop Association similarly was not reported by local papers or discussed publicly, although the two organizations were closely related. In a letter written during the second month of the strike, C. A. Jay, the Open Shop Association's vice president and general manager, urged members to call or write city councilors to express support for the police. Jay warned that other industries would soon face the same trouble if "imported labor union agitators" gained a foothold in the garment industry. He concluded, "That right prevails is of tremendous importance to this city."[43] The Industrial Commission was amazed when a ten-year veteran of the Dallas police department testified that he had never heard of the Open Shop Association (described by one of the commissioners as the most powerful organization in Dallas, "the Ku Klux excepted"). A more forthright policeman admitted that there were officers on duty at the dress factories who were not paid by the city.[44]

Throughout the strike's first six months, ILGWU attempts to combat inaccurate depictions of its Dallas members and national organizers proved ineffective. In the absence of an alternative press, the union was also unable to expose the behind-the-scenes maneuvering of the

Open Shop Association. Support from other Dallas unions was limited by the Dallas Central Labor Council's commitment to arbitration; a general strike was never seriously considered.[45] Members of the Dress Manufacturers' Association ignored the recommendation of the state Industrial Commission and refused to recognize the ILGWU or submit to an arbitrated settlement of the strike.

As the fall buying season approached, the Dallas pickets became restless. When regional buyers appeared downtown to purchase goods made by scab labor, union members' frustration peaked. On the morning of August 7, striking dressmakers unleashed their anger on strikebreakers entering the Morten-Davis and Lorch Manufacturing companies. In an hour-long riot, ten female employees were stripped of their clothing. Hundreds of spectators crowded the streets and

FIGURE 4: An artist's depiction of the August 7, 1935 "strike stripping" incident in Dallas. Courtesy of Texas Labor Archives, University of Texas at Arlington Libraries.

FIGURE 5: "Strike strippers" Mrs. Charlotte Duncan, Mrs. Jessie Burgett, and Mrs. Mae Senley in the Dallas County jail. Union members interpreted Mrs. Burgett's incarceration with her fourteen-month-old son Roy as symbolic of their resolve. Photograph from the Charlotte Graham Scrapbook, courtesy of Patricia Cumberland.

hung out of nearby office windows to witness the spectacle. The strikers surprised company guards and the few police officers stationed near the plants and, until reinforcements arrived, attacked at will. In addition to the ten women who were partially or completely denuded, a male strikebreaker and a police officer had their shirts ripped off.

"Strike stripping," as the newspapers dubbed the incidents at the two downtown plants, seemed to confirm the public's unflattering perception of female factory operatives. Both the *Morning News* and the *Journal* professed sympathy for the victims but compounded their humiliation by printing their names (and some of their ages). The *Journal* added details of exactly which women were completely disrobed and ran a series of riot pictures, including one of smiling police officers holding up "lost" undergarments.[46] A cartoon published the day after the riot—showing angry strikers in high heels and hats chasing a frantic scab stripped down to her underwear—proved to be an exception to the seriousness with which the Dallas elite took the incident (see Figure 4).[47] Condemnation of the strikers and legal retribution were swift. In less than a week, three of the union women received $25 fines and jail sentences (the strikers spent only one night in jail after writing the judge a letter of apology explaining that they could not pay the fines since they had not worked in over six months). A newspaper photograph of the three convicted "strike strippers" in which Jessie Burgett held her 14-month-old son aloft in the jail cell was intended to demonstrate union members' resolve (see Figure 5). For some middle-class residents, however, the photograph of the child behind jail bars reinforced arguments that linked working women with family suffering.[48]

Despite the judge's leniency and widespread speculation that a local jury would not convict the strike strippers if they were charged with felonious assault, the incidents were roundly condemned by local newspapers. The *Journal* opined that the strikers "disgraced their cause" and added, "three days in jail is a small price to pay for such an outrage."[49] Other editorials accused the strikers of "unwomanly violence" and accurately predicted that public opinion—ambivalent at best before the stripping incidents—would turn away from the union.[50] Both the local newspapers and the courts blamed Meyer Perlstein for inciting the riot. The union organizer received a three-day sentence, which he served, and a fine of $100.[51]

More troublesome for the ILGWU was Perlstein's indictment by Dallas newspapers. Local editors frequently described Perlstein, a U.S. citizen for almost twenty years, as a foreigner—a "Russian-Born Jew"—and an inappropriate choice for negotiations with Dallas employers. No mention was made of the fact that at least one-third of the Dallas members of the Dress Manufacturers' Association also were Jewish.[52] The *Morning News* continued to ignore ample evidence that Perlstein was not a political radical and made no attempt to refute manufacturers' charges to the contrary. The paper buried near the end of a long article reports that William Burrow, who represented factory owners during Perlstein's week-long trial, had received several warnings from the district judge for defaming Perlstein.[53] The Dealeys' afternoon paper followed the *News*'s lead in its condemnation of Perlstein. According to the *Journal*, "The leadership displayed in this strike has been such as to defeat its ends again and again. Methods that terrorize manufacturers in the North and East simply will not stand up in the light of public opinion hereabouts."[54]

Little credence was given to Perlstein's contention that the stripping incidents were spontaneous demonstrations of the dressmakers' anger and frustration. There is certainly no evidence that strike stripping was part of the ILGWU's repertoire of collective actions. More likely, the activity had its roots in shaming behaviors common in the rural South.[55] Forms of ritualized humiliation involving the removal of clothing, which include tarring and feathering, would have been meaningful to southern women and quite alien to Meyer Perlstein. Charles Tilly has noted:

> People learn how to strike, . . . just as they fail to learn a great many other forms of action which they might, in theory, employ to advance their interests. . . . We can thus speak reasonably of any coherent population as having a limited repertoire of collective action within which its members ordinarily make choices when they have collective claims to advance.[56]

In Dallas during the Depression, an extreme form of shaming behavior directed primarily at other women was a viable, if surprising, option for female strikers. More traditional forms of collective violence involving weapons were not.

The literal undressing of strikebreaking dressmakers struck a resonant chord with the ILGWU's Dallas members. There were other outbreaks of violence in September as strikers unsuccessfully attempted to repeat the "wholesale stripping incident."[57] In addition, three union women accosted factory owner Joe Donovan on a downtown street. One split his pants to the waist while the others covered his face so he could not identify them.[58] Strike stripping in Dallas attracted international attention. An Italian artist's sketch of the August melee appeared in Rome's *La Tribuna Illustrata* and subsequently in the *Dallas Morning News*. Accounts of the garment workers' actions appeared in the *New York Times* and in papers as far away as Australia. There was even a copy-cat incident in Memphis, Tennessee, involving cosmetic-industry workers.[59]

The publicity that followed the dressmakers' actions embarrassed Dallas business leaders and made many church-goers fearful that the city would acquire a reputation as an immoral place. The end result of the stripping incidents was the further alienation of striking dressmakers from middle-class residents, and even from nonunion workers. Many women refused to venture downtown alone. Lula Maude French, a dressmaker in a small Dallas shop north of the business district, recalls feeling completely isolated from the garment workers downtown and happy to make $10 a week during the Depression. French made buttons and operated a serging machine in a factory that employed about twenty-five people. Like most Dallas residents who depended on the daily newspapers for information, she knew little of the issues prompting the strike. Ironically, her background was remarkably similar to those of the strikers; French moved to Dallas from a small town in North Texas and found a job through a network of extended family members. Nonunion workers in the city's small factories worked long hours and most, like French, were paid poorly. Although a relative worked in a downtown sweatshop sewing cuffs on men's shirts during the strike, French remained ambivalent toward unions in general and largely uninformed about the "trouble" in the business district. Like many of the recent migrants who composed the bulk of the city's working class, she continued to consider herself fortunate to have any job during hard times.[60]

Unable to force the dress manufacturers into arbitration, in October the union made final appeals to President Roosevelt and to the Dallas Pastors' Association. The federal government refused to intervene, but local pastors joined the state Industrial Commission's call for an arbitrated settlement.[61] It was apparent that the union could not support the strikers much longer, however, and factory owners remained intransigent. A month later, the strikers voted to end the walkout.[62] The city's longest and most colorful strike ended almost without notice and completely without explanation in the daily newspapers.

The ILGWU's inability to force Dallas dress manufacturers to recognize the union and implement collective bargaining measures in 1935 demonstrated that the problems faced by previous Left-liberal coalitions—the intense opposition of the elite, a lack of financial resources, and racism that precluded the full cooperation of potential allies—remained powerful obstacles for those who challenged business leaders' vision of largely unrestrained growth. There were new problems as well. Dallas businessmen's adroit use of local newspapers to distort the motivations, proposals, and even the personal characteristics of their adversaries did not bode well for opponents of laissez-faire capitalism or those who sought its reform. Popular attitudes toward working women proved to be especially persistent and discouraged widespread support for policies that would bring more women into the workplace. Finally, the elite's influence with local judges and use of the police force to protect its interests increased the level of personal danger faced by activists and effectively discouraged widespread participation in movements for social change over the next forty years.

Despite the dressmakers' initial defeat, the ILGWU maintained its two Dallas locals after the strike. Significantly, most of the strikers found work in the area and remained in the union. Meyer Perlstein made frequent trips to Dallas for negotiations, and by 1936 five local dress plants operated as union shops. A 1937 ILGWU strike against Sheba Ann Manufacturing Co., which coincided with rumors of organizing attempts at the local Ford plant and the renewed activity of Dallas socialists, alarmed Open Shop interests.[63] The dressmakers' ability to hold out for almost a year in 1935 taught the local business community to take the organization of industrial workers seriously and increased concern among the elite about its own lack of unity. Certainly the expansion of union activity beyond the traditional crafts threatened the system of low wages that fueled much of the city's growth. Dallas businessmen determined that 1937 was the time and Ford the place to strike back.

II

A series of challenges, both political and ideological, to the Citizens Charter Association convinced the new generation of business leaders that traditional measures of social control—manipulation of the media, inciting race hatred, and co-opting rival leaders—could not by themselves quiet opposing groups during the 1930s. Municipal employees, dissident business interests, and workers organized the Catfish Club and seized control of city government. In addition, black and white unemployed leagues that demanded unprecedented spending on social services, as well as industrial workers who fought for union representation and collective bargaining agreements, threatened to raise the costs of doing business in Dallas. The ability of the garment workers to maintain local unions after losing their 1935 strike and the ILGWU's subsequent break with the increasingly conservative AFL convinced Dallas business interests that the organization of other industrial workers must be prevented.

The revival of the city's Socialist party local and its members' support of industrial unions strengthened the resolve of business leaders. Throughout the mid-1930s, the Socialist party sought to improve Works Progress Administration (WPA) wages by organizing the unemployed as a pressure group. When the City of Dallas cut relief rations in half for the approximately 11,000 area unemployed, Carl Brannin, a socialist from West Texas who returned to Dallas in 1933 after organizing, teaching, and writing in Seattle, established the Workmen's Co-operative League. Brannin coordinated black and white unemployed leagues whose members served on integrated committees. When relief grants were cut again in 1934 (along with the number of local WPA jobs), the unemployed staged a "sit-in" at city hall. Although the city cut off lights, fans, and toilet facilities, between six and seven hundred unemployed workers of both sexes held the city hall auditorium for eleven days and nights. The "strike" ended when police cut off the protesters' food supply. The group continued its pressure on city government, however, and by the end of the year had won an increased grocery allowance for those on relief.[64]

Local newspapers published editorial invectives and cartoons critical of the unemployed leagues. When the Workmen's Co-operative League issued demands for unemployment insurance, disability compensation, and relief funds of $10 weekly for singles, $15 for couples, and an extra $4 per week for each additional family member, both the *Morning News* and the *Times Herald* responded with claims that the unemployed should be grateful for any relief and had no right to demand more from a city making plans for the Texas Centennial Exposition.[65] Although the league was not directly associated with the Socialist party, many of its organizers and supporters were party members. Frequent allegations that the leaders of the league were radicals who advocated the intermarriage of blacks and whites stirred local prejudices and motivated a riot south of Dallas in Lancaster. Angry farmers threw eggs and garbage at Workmen's Co-operative League speakers. According to Brannin, Dallas County sheriff's officers assigned to the rally struck members of the league and prevented them from determining their attackers' identities.[66]

The Socialist party revival of the 1930s, in Dallas and throughout the Southwest, began with "old timers"—veterans of the tenant farmers' movement of the 1910s. Socialist candidates for the Dallas City Council included E. M. Lane and attorneys George Clifton Edwards and Earl Miller—all leaders of the earlier party in Dallas. Carl Brannin, associated with the Dallas local before leaving the city in 1914, ran for governor in 1936 on the Socialist ticket with Lane. Edwards wrote the state party's platform. Since the socialists could not afford radio time and rental fees, Brannin and Lane spoke in city parks throughout the state and on the beach in Galveston. Their rallies in Dallas attracted mostly wage earners and county farmers, although a few professionals and small business owners attended as well. Despite its best efforts, the party of Norman Thomas never proved to be as attractive to Texans as was that of Eugene Debs. By 1938 Brannin and Edwards were reconciled to many New Deal reform measures and were working to "liberalize" the Democratic party and abolish poll taxes.[67] In the middle of the decade, however, Dallas's veteran socialists supported local attempts to organize industrial workers and acted as mentors to the last generation of Dallas radicals until the civil rights struggles of the 1960s.

To George Lambert, a West Virginian in his early twenties sent to Dallas by the Socialist party in 1937, the city's socialists, most of whom were twenty years his senior, seemed like "lost souls." While Lambert found a few Jewish merchants of the Arbeiter Ring still interested in maintaining ties to the party, he concluded that theirs was a "nostalgic interest" and that local labor organizers and younger attorneys were the only potential activists of his generation.[68] The Socialist party never managed to seriously challenge the political hegemony of Dallas business leaders. No socialist candidate of the 1930s received even one-tenth of the total number of votes in a council race. Nevertheless, the professional respectability and social status of Dallas's most visible socialists, the party's history as a factor in Dallas political and cultural life, and its support of the garment workers in 1935 and striking taxi drivers (represented by the Teamsters) in 1936 led business interests to perceive any association of socialists and industrial workers as a threat to growth.[69]

In 1937 the new elite was poised to capitalize on the success of the Texas Centennial Exposition. The volatility of the political and social atmosphere, however, kept the men who formed the Citizens Council on the defensive. When Ford "workers" began their attacks on union organizers and local socialists, the new generation of business leaders and their peers in the Catfish Club turned their heads.

The Ford Motor Company had operated an assembly plant in Dallas without a union since 1915.[70] By 1937 Dallas workers were assembling approximately 290 automobiles per day for distribution throughout the Southwest and abroad. Early in the year, according to testimony deemed credible by the National Labor Relations Board, Ford's plant superintendent summoned to his office Stanley C. Perry, a ten-year employee weighing well over two hundred pounds. The superintendent and general body foreman introduced "Fats" Perry to Warren Worley, who had been sent to Dallas by company officials in Dearborn, Michigan, to "scout around" for information concerning CIO organizing efforts in Dallas. Perry was given access to a company car and, along with Worley, began to cruise through Dallas and surrounding towns lingering near strike sites in search of intelligence. Although Perry and Worley received pay increases, Ford records continued to list them as regular production workers and showed that they punched the factory time clock.[71]

Perry received a second raise in June after he relayed a tip that two representatives of the United Automobile Workers of America (UAW), both Ford employees in Kansas City, were on their way to Dallas to discuss strategies for organizing the Dallas plant. A group of Ford employees led by Perry, Worley, and Rudolph Rutland, the general body foreman, ambushed the two organizers in a drugstore across the street from the plant. They broke up a meeting, in which the union men had compared conditions in Kansas City to those in Dallas, and began beating the organizers just outside the store. One managed to run away. The other was taken to a nearby school yard where Perry's gang beat him again and told him to leave town. Despite cuts, bruises, and broken ribs, the UAW representatives remained in Dallas for several more days. They met secretly with Ford workers and designated W. J. Houston, a young Dallas attorney, as the union's local spokesman.[72]

After Houston announced the UAW's organizing plans to Dallas newspapers, Rutland, Perry, and Worley recruited a permanent strong-arm squad of over twenty Ford production workers. Recruits were warned that if the union succeeded in organizing the Dallas branch, the plant could be closed and "all of the boys would lose their jobs."[73] E. C. Elsik, a veteran of Ford's Houston plant that was closed in 1932, was among those invited to join the strong-arm squad and one of the few to refuse the "offer." Elsik "managed to find some excuse" but subsequently became a target for verbal and physical abuse.[74] Most members of what became known as the "outside" squad were large and muscular. Many were members of the plant's champion tug-of-war team. Rutland dispatched the men in pairs—to the Greyhound bus terminal to watch for the arrival of union organizers and to a downtown garment factory where ILGWU workers were again on strike. Another pair followed Houston, whose high-profile office in the Republic Bank building provided some measure of protection. Inside the plant, two squad members manned a special phone line through which communications were maintained, and another pair worked in the employment office screening prospective employees for evidence of prior union activity. Somewhat later, members of the outside squad received blackjacks manufactured in the maintenance department of the plant. By August squad members had acquired whips and lengths of rubber hose, many of which they kept at the plant in a supervisor's desk.[75]

Ford management also organized "inside" squads to prevent "union talk" during working hours and to distribute anti-union pamphlets. Attempts by the inside squads to influence Ford workers even extended beyond the end of the workday. In early July the maintenance department's night-shift supervisor instructed one of his subordinates to organize six meetings on successive Saturday nights at a hall across the street from the plant. At each meeting, workers were told that joining the union or expressing opinions favoring the organization of industrial workers would cost them their jobs. Although night maintenance personnel did not usually work on Saturdays, the meetings were compulsory and workers were required to sign a register. Ford managers used mandatory meetings in which specific workers were instructed to "talk down" the UAW in front of their peers to create an apparent consensus against the union.

Beneath the surface, however, many workers secretly hoped for change. In a plant where employees were often denied lunch periods and even short breaks were rare, much of the anti-union rhetoric was insincere. During hearings before the National Labor Relations Board, the organizer of the Saturday night meetings testified that despite a lack of real anti-union sentiment, he participated in the repression because "they would have made me wished [*sic*] I had done it, if I hadn't."[76]

During the summer and fall of 1937, Ford strong-arm squads attacked more than fifty people, crippling over a dozen and killing one man.[77] The victims included union organizers, Ford workers, out-of-town visitors associated with the CIO, and Dallas residents who expressed prolabor sentiments. According to the NLRB, which tried Ford in 1940 for violating federal labor laws, these incidents were characterized by "extreme violence, merciless brutality, and banishment from Dallas by threats of immediate bodily harm."[78] One member of the outside squad testified that he could personally recall twenty-five or thirty individual cases. They followed distinctive patterns. Organizers were usually ambushed during meetings arranged by workers cooperating with Ford managers. In early July, one Ford employee invited two UAW organizers to his home where they were severely beaten by twelve to fourteen members of the outside squad.

After a few incidents of this type, squad members grew bolder and less concerned about possible witnesses. W. J. Houston, the Dallas attorney who acted as a spokesman for the UAW, required hospital treatment after he was beaten and kicked by members of the outside squad upon leaving a downtown drugstore. One of Houston's assailants continued to strike the attorney in the presence of the police. A Ford manager arranged bonds for three squad members arrested in the case and persuaded newspaper photographers not to take their pictures. Shortly afterward, members of the outside squad tapped Houston's telephone. As the beatings continued throughout the summer, Houston concluded that the Ford thugs were too well protected to be brought to justice in Dallas. He left the city in October and the charges against his assailants were dropped.[79]

Whenever rumors linked Ford's Dallas employees with the CIO, they were "taken for a ride" by members of the outside squad. The rides usually led to one of three isolated spots where the victims were whipped and beaten. Some were also forced to quit their jobs. Others were "exonerated" after denouncing all unions or passing "tests" in which an "impostor organizer" was sent to their homes to determine their "true" loyalties.

Several Ford employees from Kansas City, where workers maintained an active UAW local, inadvertently walked into violent traps. In

August, L. E. Shepard, an assistant foreman at the Kansas City plant, stopped in Dallas on his way to Galveston to see the factory and visit friends. Members of the strong-arm squad kidnapped Shepard as he left the plant and drove him out of town. Although he was threatened repeatedly, Shepard convinced his captors that as a foreman he was ineligible for union membership and that he opposed the CIO in any case. Other Kansas City employees were not so lucky. Charles Elliott brought his wife to the Dallas plant after spending several days in Fort Worth. As Elliott approached the factory to inquire about a tour, members of the outside squad forced him into a waiting car. Mrs. Elliott watched as her husband's captors drove away. After finding a union card in Elliott's wallet, the kidnappers stopped at White Rock Lake on the eastern edge of the city and beat the Kansas City man with switches cut from a nearby tree.

The outside squad operated with complete impunity and made few attempts to hide its activities. Indeed, for the beatings to deter union activity, they had to be common knowledge. Sometimes squad members welcomed spectators. Two regular employees of the plant (not ordinarily involved in the strong-arm squad's repressive activities) witnessed the attack on Elliott. One of them testified that "mighty near everybody" working at the plant knew that the beatings were taking place but that he was impelled by curiosity to see for himself what was happening. After the thugs were through with Elliott, "Fats" Perry told his wife where to find him and added that if she loved her husband, she should get him out of the state immediately. Three weeks later, Harold Bowen, another Kansas City worker, received similar treatment from ten members of the outside squad. A Ford gang patrolling the fairgrounds during the Pan-American Exposition spotted CIO stickers on Californian Orville Phillips's car. Several members of the outside squad ambushed Phillips, his wife, and relatives when the group returned to the parking lot. The Californians succeeded in reversing the usual order of events, however, and forced the strong-arm squad to flee the area.[80]

According to the NLRB, persons from other cities who applied for jobs at the Dallas plant were *prima facie* considered union organizers and "destined for treatment by the outside squad." Richard Sowers, one of the job applicants beaten by Perry's men, ignored the usual death threats and remained in town long enough to identify four of his attackers. After discussing the matter with police officers in the factory showroom, a Ford supervisor told three of the men Sowers named as his assailants to go downtown with the policemen and "everything would be taken care of." The group stopped for drinks on the way to the police station, where the Ford men were quickly released on bail. Despite Sowers's willingness to press charges and the identification of the same squad members by a second victim, Dallas prosecutors dismissed the case.[81]

By the end of the summer, most Dallas residents were afraid to give public support to any union. Repression once aimed at CIO organizers, receptive local workers (whether their interest was actual or perceived), and out-of-town members of CIO unions spread to include all union organizers and any local resident who advocated an organized work force. Archie Lewis, owner of a small business, died of wounds received during an attack intended for his twin brother, who had expressed pro-union sentiments to a neighbor who worked for Ford.[82] In sharp contrast to the patterns established in the 1880s, where Dallas residents based their attitudes toward labor unions on the circumstances surrounding particular disputes and engaged in lively debates concerned with fairness, few Dallas residents in 1937 dared to discuss labor issues.

The city's increasingly conservative craft unions, which opposed the CIO's efforts to organize industrial workers, also remained silent during Ford's campaign of terror. According to Wallace Reilly, whose family published the *Craftsman*, the city's "labor paper" did not run articles about Ford's anti-union activities because they were directed against the CIO.[83] Despite Reilly's contention that the indiscriminate violence of the outside squads did not concern the city's trade unions, the Dallas Central Labor Council's failure to take a stand against anti-union terrorism lessened its credibility with the rank and file and stymied future organizing efforts. Socialist organizer George Lambert claimed that the conservative AFL hierarchy that barred radical delegates in favor of industrial unions from the Central Labor Council joined with the Chamber of Commerce and the Open Shop Association to keep the CIO out of Dallas. The craft unions' association with Dallas business interests, in Lambert's estimation, won the unions "only a temporary aura of respectability and no more."[84] Dallas's AFL-affiliated unions never regained their status of the 1910s, when building tradesmen employed militant tactics in defense of their right to organize.

The passivity of the city's trade unions proved nearly fatal to George Baer, a young organizer for the AFL's Millinery Workers' Union. Dallas hat manufacturers reduced wages immediately after the abolition of NRA codes, and by 1937 wages had fallen to about $12 per week. Workers complained that much of that went to foremen in the form of kickbacks. Because Max Zaritsky, the Millinery Workers' international president, expressed an interest in industrial unions, Dallas AFL leaders were suspicious of Baer and offered him no support. Baer's uncertain status was enough to make him a target of Ford's strong-arm squad. After receiving a tip from a local police inspector, Ford men abducted Baer from the office of a Dallas hat manufacturer (who cooperated in the organizer's entrapment). Baer was beaten so severely with blackjacks that he sustained more than twenty cuts on his head, lost several teeth, and was blinded in one eye. His assailants left him for dead in a field near the Trinity River. Sometime later, Baer told Carmen Lucia, who replaced him as the hatmakers' Dallas organizer, that he crawled to the highway where a passing motorist agreed to drive him to the hospital. The Samaritan was so terrified upon discovering that he had assisted a union man that he dumped Baer in front of the hospital and sped away. Even after Baer regained consciousness and told his story, the Dallas police refused to provide him with protection. Indeed, members of the outside squad were allowed on an upper floor of the hospital where they attempted unsuccessfully to throw Baer out the window. Shortly afterward, Baer's family and the international union transported the organizer out of Dallas to another hospital.[85]

On the evening of August 9, the same day as the assault on Baer, Rutland and Perry instructed Ford workers to disrupt a rally sponsored by Dallas socialists. Earlier that week, a general organizational film, *Millions of Us*, and Pere Lorentz's *The Plow that Broke the Plains* were shown without incident at the city hall auditorium. Local socialists wanted to show the films again at Fretz Park in the city's cotton mill district. The South Dallas cotton mill, surrounded by Dallas's first slum, was established in the 1870s, and its reputation for low pay, long hours, and a severe lack of ventilation had remained unchanged since the turn of the century. Members of the Socialist party local asked two young organizers sent to the city by the national organization to introduce the city's textile workers to the goals and strategies of industrial unions. They advertised the program with handbills and placed notices in local newspapers. Many textile workers brought their children to the park to eat picnic suppers, see the "movies," and hear the radical speakers.[86]

About seventy-five Ford employees, members of the outside squad and selected members of the teams that reinforced anti-union sentiment inside the plant, appeared at the rally. Perry ensured that the park policeman was not on duty that evening although it was customary for a patrolman to attend all park events. The NLRB later rejected Ford lawyers' claim that segments of *Millions of Us* portraying black and white workers marching arm-in-arm caused the ensuing disturbance, because the crowd of approximately five hundred remained calm during the film and listened attentively as veteran socialist E. M. Lane began to speak. On cue from one of Perry's lieutenants, the Ford men shouted obscenities and rushed the speaker's platform. They smashed the projector, stole the sound recordings, and knocked one of the organizers to the ground. Carl Brannin, who rushed to the younger man's aid, was left alone, probably because his family was well respected in Dallas. Barto Hill, whose duty it was to kidnap the speaker, considered Lane, also a well-known Dallas native, too old for the punishment Ford managers had in mind. Instead, Hill instructed his men to grab Herbert Harris, an organizer from Tennessee who operated the projector.

Hill's gang took Harris to a whipping place on the outskirts of town where he was beaten, partially stripped, and covered with tar and feathers. The Ford men dumped Harris in front of the *Dallas Morning News* building, where a photographer waited. A sympathetic crowd formed immediately and shielded Harris from the photographer, but Dallas police officers restrained onlookers and forced the socialist into the open. In contrast to the almost immediate presence of the police at the site of Harris's public humiliation and despite the fact that Dallas squad cars were equipped with radios, it took police twenty minutes to respond to the riot at Fretz Park.[87] The presence of many witnesses at both locations led to widespread speculation that local law enforcement officers operated on the instructions of city officials and their supporters in the business community.

The melee and its attendant lawlessness moved Gov. James Allred to send a detachment of Texas Rangers to Dallas. Citizens Charter Association business leaders joined Catfish Club–backed mayor George Sprague in denouncing the governor's action and declared the police force capable of maintaining law and order in Dallas.[88] When Allred called Dallas police chief Bob Jones several days after the riot to inform him of the Rangers' eminent arrival, Jones dismissed the complaints of local socialists. In a move that foreshadowed Dallas authorities' increasing lack of tolerance for those who protested the policies or politics of the local elite, Jones made light of the summer's violence and declared, "It's only a couple of Goddamned red sons o' bitches."[89] After unprecedented group hearings before the Dallas County Grand Jury yielded little evidence, Allred assured Brannin that the Rangers would remain in Dallas indefinitely and donated $500 to a reward fund for evidence leading to the conviction of the rioters (donations by Texas socialists and the American Civil Liberties Union pushed the reward total to $1,600). Most witnesses were afraid to testify during the open hearings although one woman, who watched Ford employees destroy the projector, wrote down license numbers of three getaway cars.[90]

Some local socialists considered Allred's dispatch of the Rangers only a political move, since the violence continued and police made no arrests. After the Rangers broke up protests by striking workers in Fort Worth, many in Dallas suspected that the Rangers, too, had received instructions not to interfere with the activities of the outside squad. Before a speech by Norman Thomas at city hall, George Clifton Edwards claimed that the violence would end only when Dallas business leaders took a stand against Ford's anti-union campaign. His sentiments were echoed by Thomas in an interview with the *Dallas Times Herald*. Thomas laid the blame for the summer's attacks "largely upon the interests which . . . dominate Dallas."[91]

III

By the fall of 1937, public outrage at the indiscriminate violence began to rise. The tarring and feathering of Herbert Harris was a public reminder that the vigilante activity of antilabor groups bore a peculiar resemblance to that of the Ku Klux Klan. Like the open welcome accorded Klan members in the early 1920s, the protection of those who controlled Dallas institutions was given to Ford's anti-union vigilantes as long as they were perceived as protecting the existing social order. Similarly, the Klan and Ford's outside squad were disavowed when they became threats to continued growth and civic coherence.[92] A reputation for violence hurts business, and by the end of the summer, Dallas was considered by many to be a dangerous place.

After the August riot at Fretz Park and the beatings that killed

Archie Lewis and blinded George Baer, Rutland told Perry and two of his men, "this town is really on fire. You better lay low." The foreman then gave the group money and sent them to McKinney, a county seat north of Dallas, where they joined a fellow employee whose car had been linked to the park disturbance. On numerous occasions after that, Rutland provided funds to defray travel expenses when business associates or police officials warned him that members of the outside squad were "hot" and should leave the county. The presence of the Rangers and widespread condemnation of the riot forced Ford and the police to change their tactics. Police Chief Jones tried to silence all dissent, but his order barring controversial speakers from holding rallies at city hall or in parks proved so unpopular that it was quickly rescinded.[93] Although the beatings continued until the end of October, future CIO speakers were silenced by hecklers instead of by physical attacks. Workers told that the CIO would "pack the plant with Blacks" chased one such speaker, Roy Sessions of the Houston Oil Workers' local, to his car before he had a chance to begin.[94]

By the end of 1937, CIO efforts in Dallas were at a standstill. Houston, Harris, and Baer had been driven out of town, and Lambert was sent to San Antonio to assist a grassroots organization of pecan shellers. Dallas's socialist local fell into disarray—its financial and emotional resources exhausted. Aware of Dallas business leaders' growing impatience with the excesses of the outside squad, Rutland returned its members to ordinary production work in early 1938 (although the inside squads remained intact for some time afterward). During the meeting in which the group disbanded, Rutland congratulated squad members, saying that "everybody was satisfied the way us boys [*sic*] handled ourselves" and acknowledging that organizing efforts were "just about over with." What contemporaries referred to as the "Ford Terror" would have remained the subject of speculation in Dallas had not Rutland fired several members of the strong-arm squad, including "Fats" Perry, more than a year later. Perry had been promised job security in exchange for his role in the repression of CIO organizing efforts and considered his discharge a "dirty deal." During the fall of 1939, he traveled to Detroit three times to speak to Ford officials. On one of these trips, a companion warned him that Rutland was plotting his murder. Perry and most of his former squad members agreed to testify against Ford after another discharged member of the strong-arm squad told their story to an NLRB field examiner in Fort Worth who promised them immunity.[95]

The NLRB presented its case against Ford in Dallas during the spring of 1940—three years after the violence began. Dallas business leaders first tried to ignore the proceedings. When that failed, they used the press to challenge the credibility of CIO witnesses and the skill of NLRB attorneys. Six months before NLRB hearings attracted national attention to the case, the *Dallas Morning News*, which by 1940 consistently presented the views of the Dallas Citizens Council, rejected a former Ford employee's offer to tell his story because it allegedly had lost its news value.[96]

The *News* ignored the hearings completely until the twelfth day of testimony. In contrast, the *New York Times* sent Louis Stark, a nationally known journalist, to Dallas to cover the case. Newspaper audiences in New York, Washington, Detroit, and Cincinnati read reports of Ford's anti-union activities in Dallas before the *Morning News* printed its first reports. When the *News* finally acknowledged the hearings, it ran a slanted story under headlines that charged, "All Rules of Evidence are Cast Overboard." The city's most influential newspaper reminded Dallas residents that the NLRB was "one of the most bitterly criticized federal agencies created by the new deal" and favorably compared the talents of Ford's prestigious local attorneys to the "youthful" NLRB prosecutors.[97] As the hearings progressed, yielding over one million words of testimony, the *News* allocated a relatively scant 112 column inches (including headlines) to the case. Although the *Journal* and the *Times Herald* covered the hearings in slightly more detail, they too were critical of the NLRB and the trial examiner. In keeping with Dallas trade unions' refusal to denounce the violence three years earlier, the *Craftsman* ignored the Ford case. Oddly, the AFL paper's owner and editor left town just as the case began to make national headlines and pack the local courtroom.[98]

In addition to the daily newspapers' inattention to the evidence obtained during the hearings, Dallas business leaders embraced Ford managers who either participated in or covered up the anti-union campaign (the *Dispatch* had merged with the *Journal* by 1940, so all three of the daily papers were owned by members of the Citizens Council). Rudolph Rutland had been promoted to the position of factory service foreman in late 1937 and, according to a prominent Dallas attorney, enjoyed a great deal of social prestige during the 1940s.[99] The NLRB rejected the testimony of John McKee, Ford's employment officer who falsified records to cover up discrimination against union members, as "incredible," but McKee's subsequent promotions coincided with invitations to join the interlocking directorates through which the Citizens Council maintained its grip on urban institutions (during the 1950s, McKee was an active member of ten boards, leagues, and commissions).[100]

The Ford executive's ability to provide Lincoln limousines for out-of-town dignitaries was especially well received by Citizens Council leaders. McKee took an active interest in the conservative wing of the state Democratic party, became one of the most powerful Masons in Texas, and presided over the locally influential Dallas Crime Commission from 1957 to 1972. His attempts to conceal evidence of Ford's anti-union activities were not isolated incidents but fit into a lifelong pattern of illegal activity and deception. After his retirement in 1971 as Ford's regional director of civic and governmental affairs (covering a nineteen-state area), McKee was convicted of embezzling Scottish Rite funds. A background check revealed that the Ford manager had deserted from the U.S. Navy in 1929 while charged with forgery and the misappropriation of funds. He obtained his position with Ford using a false name and claiming a bogus degree from New York University. Even after his exposure, Citizens Council members stood by McKee. One prominent leader blamed McKee's legal troubles on a mysterious "injury" or "some kind of loss of memory."[101]

The repression of CIO organizing efforts during 1937 had its intended effect—industrial unions made few significant gains in Dallas and young radicals were driven out of town. More significantly perhaps, the city acquired a reputation for hostility toward union activity that deterred the formation of future grassroots organizations like that of the garment workers in the mid-1930s and obscured an earlier legacy of trade union militancy. After CIO and socialist activity in favor of industrial unions ended, wages at the South Dallas cotton mill fell from an average of $16 per six-day week to around $14.[102] Dallas factory workers in other important industries were paid significantly less than the national averages for those industries (see Table 4).[103] Significantly, Dallas's female garment workers and the city's auto workers were among the few local manufacturing operatives whose wages approached or exceeded the national averages for their industries in 1940.

The Open Shop Association's well-funded propaganda continued to link all labor organizations with "trouble"—a vague but common synonym for violence and economic suffering. During the course of two

TABLE 4

A COMPARISON OF ANNUAL WAGES OF MANUFACTURING OPERATIVES IN 1939

AREA, INDUSTRY & SEX	% DISTRIBUTION BY INCOME			
	$0 – $599	$600 – $1,199	$1,200 – $1,999	$2,000 PLUS
Dallas, Food Products, Male	34.7	47.6	16.6	0.6
U.S., Food Products, Male	24.5	35.2	33.8	5.0
Dallas, Machinery, Male	24.0	44.3	27.7	4.2
U.S., Machinery, Male	20.9	34.1	38.3	5.6
Dallas, Automobiles, Male	7.4	33.5	56.6	1.4
U.S., Automobiles, Male	15.2	30.8	50.0	3.3
Dallas, Apparel, Male	32.5	54.6	11.3	1.1
U.S., Apparel, Male	28.7	38.8	23.8	7.2
Dallas, Apparel, Female	60.8	37.2	0.8	0.04
U.S., Apparel, Female	62.8	33.2	2.6	0.1

Source: U.S. Census Bureau

unsuccessful strikes by millinery workers in Dallas and Garland, a suburb to the northeast, strikers were again beaten by gangs of thugs and employees told that unions would give white workers' jobs to blacks. These tactics reinforced the fear instilled by the Ford Terror and further divided Dallas workers. One of the city's daily papers inaccurately labeled front-page pictures of bandaged Garland strikers to indicate that the victims in this round of violence were not union members but scabs (a brief retraction appeared weeks later but neglected to explain the actual situation).[104] Millinery Workers' Union organizer Carmen Lucia and local labor activist Arvil Inge, discouraged by the hostility of their environment, joined the list of young radicals who left Dallas between 1935 and 1940.

George Lambert, who returned to the city at the end of the decade, claimed that as a result of Dallas's five-year war on labor, local liberals, including several prominent ministers, SMU professors, and professionals, were understandably "weak-kneed, scared stiff even to stick their necks out on as flagrant violations of civil liberties as were going on in Dallas a couple of years ago."[105] Lambert's wife Latane, an organizer for the Textile Workers of America, described the Texas Socialist party as "something of an empty shell" and considered joining the Communists in 1939.[106] In the absence of other local radicals of their generation, however, the Lamberts returned to the Democratic party along with George Clifton Edwards, Carl Brannin, and the rest of the city's aging socialists.[107]

During the 1940s, Dallas business leaders solidified relationships with conservative trade-union leaders. Wallace Reilly, a second-generation Dallas printer previously known for his fiery criticism of the Open Shop Association while an official with the State Federation of Labor, became a close friend and ally of R. L. Thornton after World War II. At a dinner in Reilly's honor, attended by former Charter Association–backed mayor Woodall Rodgers and the president of the Chamber of Commerce, Dallas leaders congratulated the *Craftsman*'s editor for his effective opposition to radical elements within the city's labor organizations and for earning the respect of business and civic leaders. Reilly remained one of the most influential voices within the Central Labor Council until the late 1960s (long after the reunification of the AFL and the CIO).[108]

A collective bargaining agreement between Ford's corporate officials and the UAW resulted in the unionization of the Dallas plant in 1941. The victory was a hollow one, however, won by the militancy of northern auto workers and enforced through the federal courts.[109] Among the new members of UAW Local 870 were both employees victimized in 1937 and those who had coerced co-workers into anti-union stances as members of the inside squads. The new union was never able to overcome the climate of suspicion instilled during the campaign of terror. Like the rank and file of local trade unions whose leaders had been co-opted by the Dallas elite, the city's industrial workers distrusted union organizers *and* company officials. In this context, many workers could only hope that the election of Charter Association candidates who promised to work for the good of the entire city and the Citizens Council programs that they touted would in fact benefit all of Dallas. Ford's local employees remained relatively passive until the mid-1960s, when a brief flurry of activism preceded the plant's closure in 1970.

By 1940 the voices of those who had traditionally opposed the policies of Dallas business leaders had been effectively silenced. The new elite

used its control of local newspapers and radio stations and the anticommunist fervor that intensified after World War II to discourage dissent and reinforce the idea that Charter Association council candidates
and Citizens Council–sponsored bond issues benefited the city "as a
whole." During and immediately after the war, business-backed
municipal governments provided incentives to new and expanding
industries and determined the modern city's primary transportation
arteries with little attention to the effects that loosely regulated growth
had on neighborhoods, schools, and traffic patterns. Without a doubt,
those primarily concerned with the exchange value of land surrounding the city benefited from the new elite's domination of Dallas after
1940. The effects of largely unchecked growth on the majority of the
city's residents—those whose primary concerns lay in the use values of
urban land and in the quality of city life—were less beneficent. It
would be thirty-five years, however, before new coalitions mounted
effective challenges to the Dallas Citizens Council. Organized labor's
minimal role in those coalitions was not coincidental.

*Perhaps the worst
tyranny is that which is
created for our own good.*
— Henry Miller in
"The Air Conditioned
Nightmare"

WITH THE ELECTION OF THE ENTIRE
Charter Association city council slate in
1939, the stage was set for the Dallas Citizens Council to solidify the hegemony of
business over municipal government and
urban institutions. The Citizens Council did
not corrupt city government or maintain a political "machine" in the
usual sense of the term but extended its influence by reinforcing the
notion that business leaders worked for the benefit of the city as a
whole and by denying the legitimacy of partisan city politics and professional politicians.[1] During the mid-1940s, several Charter Association city council candidates ran unopposed—an unprecedented
occurrence in the history of local government. In 1955 the association's entire council slate was elected without opposition. Between
1939 and 1985, only two Dallas mayors lacked the support of the
Charter Association (one was an arch-conservative defector from both
that organization and the Citizens Council, the other a local sports-
caster).[2]

Much of the apparent consensus during the 1940s and 1950s
stemmed from the city's phenomenal growth (see Table 5).[3] To many
Dallas residents, it appeared that the policies of the city's leaders did
indeed benefit the entire city. Solid endorsements from the *Dallas
Morning News* and the *Dallas Times Herald* played a crucial role in the
Citizens Council's ability to maintain its beneficent image.[4] Local
newspapers attributed the acquisition of a naval reserve aviation base
and one of the country's largest airplane-assembly plants to the joint
efforts of the Citizens Council and the Chamber of Commerce. Extensive coverage of the elite's aggressive lobbying for new manufacturing
facilities and military installations obscured demographic changes and

TABLE 5
DALLAS POPULATION, 1930–1990

CENSUS	POPULATION
1930	260,475
1940	294,734
1950	434,462
1960	679,684
1970	844,000
1980	905,000
1990	1,006,877

Source: U.S. Census Bureau

geographic advantages that attracted war industries to Dallas. The presence of a large body of unskilled workers lured labor-intensive assembly plants. Even the city's location in the center of the country, which had traditionally deterred manufacturers from establishing operations in the Southwest, served as an advantage throughout the war. Dallas was generally perceived as a site from which aircraft and ordnance factories, as well as those processing primary metal products (especially steel, magnesium, aluminum, and tin), could be easily protected.[5]

The expansion of the local economy built on Dallas's historical foundations as a market center and continued after the war. Improved communication and distribution networks stimulated both the relocation of new industry to Dallas and enlarged markets for established industries. North American Aviation employed a wartime high of approximately 30,000 workers in its B-24 bomber assembly plant just outside the Dallas city limits. After the war, Texas Engineering and Manufacturing Company (Temco) and Chance-Vought leased the giant factory. The two companies employed up to 25,000 at the site well into the 1950s.[6] Dallas's apparel industry, which achieved national prominence during the war and in the decades that followed, took an

F 3 94. D2157
H35 1996

increasing share of regional business away from manufacturers in New York and Los Angeles.[7]

Between 1940 and 1953, the number of Dallas County workers employed in manufacturing jumped 184 percent—three times the national average. During this period, the percentage of local residents employed by industry grew faster than that of any other urban center with the exception of Los Angeles, and the city's population increased by more than 270,000.[8] Wage increases also continued after the war. According to Latane Lambert, a Dallas organizer with the Amalgamated Clothing Workers, the average wage in union apparel plants throughout the state increased by over 100 percent during the 1940s. Nonunion workers shared in the overall gains, but their wages lagged behind those of union workers. By the end of the decade, CIO workers in Dallas's apparel plants had obtained a forty-hour week and averaged a little more than 70 cents hourly, a full 10 cents per hour better than their nonunion peers.[9]

In the decades following World War II, business interests dominated public policy making in other southwestern and western cities. In Houston, Phoenix, and San Diego, for example, growth elites led by businessmen have successfully promulgated an ideology of laissez-faire capitalism.[10] Modern Dallas differs from other "Sunbelt" cities primarily because of the remarkable duration of Citizens Council influence and the relative weakness of the coalitions that challenged elite rule in the 1960s and 1970s. Although the Charter Association died after a federal court put an end to at-large city council elections, the Citizens Council remains the most powerful policy-oriented group in town. In addition, Dallas business leaders have retained successfully the council-manager form of city government long after its popularity waned in other large cities and two decades after the reintroduction of single-member council districts. The pace of political change has been slow in Dallas, prompting questions such as, "Did the civil rights movement bypass the city?" and assertions that Dallas, "a well-run predemocratic city-state," has only recently become an integral part of the United States.[11]

By the 1960s city government by a small coterie of unelected businessmen was referred to locally as "The Dallas Way." With the notable exception of R. L. Thornton, most Dallas leaders remained remote, inaccessible, and at times almost anonymous. They conducted their affairs in private and rarely engaged in public debate. The presence of a professional city manager—accountable to the city council but not directly to the electorate—contributed to the "faceless" nature of municipal government. The Citizens Council perpetuated a nonpartisan, even nonpolitical image despite the fact that the men who chose Charter Association candidates for the city council, the school board, and a host of municipal and county offices were members of the Citizens Council's inner circle. The Charter Association discouraged its city council candidates from campaigning as individuals or raising campaign funds on their own and generally refused to support candidates after their second two-year term (Woodall Rodgers and Thornton both served four terms as mayor, and Erik Jonsson served three and a half). Such short-term support precluded a potential defector's establishing a personal political base and ensured a succession of like-minded businessmen on the city council.

The Charter Association masterfully co-opted labor leaders, blacks, and white liberals while sharing little real power. The association received the support of AFL-affiliated unions and the *Dallas Craftsman* when it backed the council campaign of local AFL president Bill Harris in 1953 and 1955. Despite public proclamations that labor deserved representation on the council, the association's support of Harris was calculated to defuse any potential challenge from the city's trade unions after the popular labor leader ran a strong council campaign in 1949.[12] At the height of its power by the end of Harris's second term, the Charter Association once again filled its slate with businessmen and lawyers committed to R. L. Thornton's brand of single-option city government.

Citizens Council members offered unusual financial opportunities in exchange for loyalty to the slate of candidates presented by the Charter Association and adherence to the Citizens Council agenda. James Rankin, a senior vice president at Thornton's Mercantile Bank, noted leadership qualities and keen political judgment in George Allen, a young African American accountant, and enlisted him as an ally in the early 1950s. On Rankin's recommendation, Thornton loaned Allen $60,000, accepting stock shares in a black insurance company as collateral. Allen turned the quite unexpected windfall into a "small fortune" and wove his way into the interlocking directorate of urban institutions through which Citizens Council leaders expanded their influence (because of his race, Allen was barred from membership in the organization). In 1955 Allen became the first black to serve on the board of directors of the Red Cross and Community Chest (now the United Way). At the same time, Allen maintained his position as a leader in the black community, serving on the board of the local NAACP and participating in early civil rights demonstrations.

In exchange for Allen's political support, Senator George Parkhouse provided government jobs for middle-class African Americans. The relationship with Parkhouse was particularly instructive; according to Allen, it taught him that not all Dallas leaders were ultraconservative ideologues. Some displayed "that conservative front, facade, because it's unpopular to admit they're liberal." Allen noted that, during the 1960s, a faction of the elite was less hostile to social and political change than appearances would indicate. He concluded that this group paid lip service to conservative rhetoric for fear of alienating the powerful banking contingent. After an unsuccessful city council campaign without the Charter Association, Allen was appointed to an expanded council in 1968 and received the association's backing in subsequent elections. As a Charter Association–backed council member, Allen supported desegregation, open housing, and environmental measures but criticized members of the black community who demanded immediate change. "If you don't have the so-called Establishment," declared Allen, "where are the jobs? . . . If you need money, where are you going to borrow it?"[13]

White liberals and moderates who sought civic influence found it almost impossible to avoid co-optation by—or at least cooperation with—the Citizens Council. In 1946 the leaders of that organization recognized in Wallace Savage a dangerous opponent and enlisted one of the young attorney's close friends to persuade him to run as a Charter Association council candidate. Despite early misgivings about the way business leaders ran Dallas city government, Savage served on the council and as mayor during the city's postwar population and construction booms.[14] Similarly, Stanley Marcus served for decades as the liberal conscience of the Citizens Council, and Charles Meyer, the regional head of Sears Roebuck, helped moderate extreme views. Unlike George Allen, who remained an outsider primarily because of his skin color, prominent white liberals who were considered "team players" and did not demand rapid change were offered positions as

TABLE 6
AFRICAN AMERICAN POPULATION IN DALLAS
1900–1990

CENSUS	% BLACK POPULATION OF TOTAL
1900	21.3
1910	19.6
1920	15.2
1930	14.9
1940	17.1
1950	13.2
1960	19.3
1970	24.9
1980	29.4
1990	29.5

Source: U.S. Census Bureau

Charter Association candidates or, if they met the criteria, Citizens Council membership.

In the decades after World War II, white voters outnumbered blacks by such a large margin that nonmilitant black demands could be largely discounted (see Table 6).[15] Citizens Council leaders skillfully accommodated the racism of the white electorate and obscured a shortage of segregated housing for blacks after a series of bombings in the early 1950s threatened plans to "reclaim" for industry a large tract of land along the Trinity floodplain. White residents who could not afford to abandon their South Dallas neighborhoods for deed-restricted suburbs north of downtown destroyed several houses purchased by blacks, issued death threats, and vandalized the property of their new neighbors. Fearful that Ku Klux Klan–style violence in South Dallas would attract attention to a Citizens Council–backed project that exacerbated the housing shortage by removing poor blacks from shantytowns along the Trinity River, city leaders established a blue-ribbon grand jury to investigate the bombings. The grand jurors, all members of the Citizens Council, concluded, "There was evidence that lay and religious and community groups, through misguided leadership, entered an action, perhaps unwittingly, that resulted in violence and destruction."[16] The degree of complicity of "respectable" members of the white community in South Dallas convinced the elite that to pursue those who orchestrated and carried out the violence would be political suicide.

Although thirteen people were indicted in connection with the bombings, the only man brought to trial in the case was acquitted on all charges. The grand jury, after public proclamations that it lacked only bits of corroborating evidence before more indictments could be handed down, asked to be disbanded. Perhaps not coincidentally, the bombings ceased. Jim Schutze, formerly a columnist for the *Dallas Times Herald* and author of a book on race relations in Dallas, notes that after dominating the headlines for two years, "the entire matter disappeared one day like a rock dropped in a lake."[17]

The Citizens Council's decision not to seek a legal resolution to the violence in South Dallas demonstrates the commitment of the Dallas elite to maintaining an urban image favorable to business—better to accommodate the racist excesses of white voters and put a quick end to the violence than to allow the full story to shame the community and give national exposure to the forced relocation of blacks from the Trinity floodplain. It reveals as well the Citizens Council's ability to manipulate both the legal system and the media. The position taken by a mature Citizens Council in the early 1950s mirrored the emerging elite's response to Ford's anti-union campaign in the late 1930s. African Americans, like an earlier generation of industrial workers, could not avoid the conclusion that Dallas leaders were motivated to stop the violence only when it threatened business interests.[18]

Moderate voices within the elite were silenced by the Citizens Council's political dependence on a white population that was virulently segregationist and increasingly drawn to highly visible political reactionaries. As a result, the Citizens Council tolerated the proclamations and innuendoes of the local John Birch Society and did not speak out against extremists and eccentrics, including Congressman Bruce Alger (the first Republican to be elected from Dallas County since Reconstruction), reactionary publisher Dan H. Smoot, retired general Edwin A. Walker, and oil billionaire H. L. Hunt.[19]

In the decade that followed the assassination of John Kennedy, the Citizens Council's fear that racial violence would do irreparable harm to the city's reputation motivated civic leaders to include moderate minority leaders in forums such as Goals for Dallas and resulted in the election of several blacks to the city council. The pace of change quickened after federal courts mandated single-member districts for school board elections in 1974 and for city council elections a year later.[20]

Other factors also played a role in loosening the Citizens Council's grip on city government. An influx of migrants from the Midwest and from northern states invigorated neighborhood groups in East and North Dallas, Oak Lawn, and, later, Oak Cliff. Many of the newcomers liked living in the city and objected to Citizens Council proposals that would bisect established residential areas with thoroughfares serving suburbs to the north and east. The ability of Evelyn Dunsavage and a well-connected group of East Dallas homeowners to win historical designations and backzoning for racially and economically mixed neighborhoods surrounding Swiss Avenue left many city leaders shaking their heads.[21]

The Citizens Council operated on the dated theory that whites would move north as soon as they could afford new homes in homogeneous neighborhoods (financed and built by members of the Citizens Council). For decades commuters had provided a relatively affluent constituency for the construction of new thoroughfares and transit routes. As gentrification movements, such as those supported by the Swiss Avenue homeowners and a group called the Bois d'Arc Patriots, gained momentum, more residents of inner city neighborhoods and the older sections of North Dallas had the resources to fight growth policies that threatened the quality of urban life. Not long after the victory in East Dallas, neighborhood activists in Oak Lawn blocked Citizens Council plans to make the old M.K.T. rail line through Turtle Creek the centerpiece of a new mass transit system.[22]

The focus of neighborhood groups on quality-of-life issues and increased concerns about the environment combined with single-member election districts to force city council members to pay more attention to their constituents. Grassroots campaigns opposing projects endorsed by local business leaders were no doubt encouraged by national movements and by their improved chances for success in the more inclusive political atmosphere of the mid-1970s. There were unmistakable signs, however, that the Citizens Council represented only one vision among many. One such sign was the defeat of a bond issue that would realize the dream of early Dallas business leaders and convert the Trinity River into a navigable canal to the Gulf of Mexico. This defeat proved that the time-honored Citizens Council argument that all growth benefited the entire city had lost much of its effectiveness. Although the Citizens Council deluged the public with arguments in favor of the canal and derided opponents as "environmental extremists," voters responded to concerns that the project would destroy shellfish breeding grounds near the Gulf, pollute drinking water, and disproportionately benefit local business interests.[23]

In addition to electoral changes that allowed popular leaders to develop power bases in specific parts of the city and the intensified demands of minorities and neighborhood activists, changes in the composition and inclinations of the oligarchy itself began to emerge in the 1970s. The founding members of the Citizens Council failed to groom replacements who shared their zeal for local politics. The Dallas Assembly, formed in 1962 to groom future Citizens Council leaders, did not produce a new generation committed to their elders' policy of single-option government. According to Dallas author A. C. Greene, "the heirs never seemed to want the job."[24] Some of the Charter Association's new council candidates even insisted on managing their own campaigns.[25]

The amendment of Texas banking laws to allow the formation of statewide holding companies enlarged the focus of younger leaders in area financial institutions. Executive positions began to be filled by people from within the larger corporation or the national occupational pool, squeezing out managers with ties to the original Citizens Council leadership. The Citizens Council had begun as a banker's club and remained one in its heyday. With the passing of its founding generation, younger bankers and merchants competed with insurance company heads, utility managers, developers, and a few oil men for control of the organization (merchants faced the same predicament as Dallas banking executives after the consolidation of locally owned department stores into national chains).[26] Although the business community has remained the most powerful force in Dallas politics and civic affairs, since the mid-1970s its leaders have found it increasingly difficult to speak with one voice.

At the end of the decade, Elsie Faye Heggins, a veteran of the South Dallas homeowners movement that fought eminent domain near Fair Park, and independent whites, including Pleasant Grove hardware-store owner Max Goldblatt, won council elections in sections of the city where the benefits of growth had failed to trickle down.[27] Heggins unabashedly represented the black voters of her district. She made no attempt to speak for the city as a whole and resented white business-men from North Dallas who presumed to do so. The success of seem-ingly disparate political actors like Heggins and Goldblatt indicates that Dallas's political economy had completed its slow transformation from what Stephen Elkin calls the "pure" entrepreneurial stage and had begun to resemble the "complex" systems of most modern Amer-ican cities.[28] In the 1980s connections between the business commu-nity and civic leaders would not be as direct as before; members of the Dallas Citizens Council and elected officials were no longer a society of peers.

The Citizens Council now has approximately 270 members but remains almost exclusively a white, male bastion of civic influence (in 1985, the organization admitted as members presidents and directors of the city's largest law and accounting firms). As late as 1987, the group had only three female and three minority members.[29] Yet very recently, voters chose attorney Ron Kirk to be Dallas's first black mayor. Kirk had the support of most African American voters *and* the city's business elite. In addition, Dallas's new long-range plan acknowledges the serious needs of areas outside the business district and rhetorically includes all of the city's residents.[30]

The complexity of municipal government in the 1980s and 1990s has caused some to yearn nostalgically for a time when things "just happened." Because power struggles between competing groups were repressed for over forty years and the city remains cut off from its early history, a highly competitive, often acrimonious, politically charged atmosphere is difficult for many in Dallas to accept. Neither the media nor residents of New York City, Boston, or Chicago denounce feuding council members for vigorously defending the interests of their constituents.

The political atmosphere of contemporary Dallas corresponds closely to that of the city prior to the 1920s—when the elite spoke in multiple voices and the politics of competition and cooperation char-acterized urban life. A lack of historical inquiry and the extent of business leaders' dominance since World War II have allowed popular perceptions of the Dallas of the Citizens Council to be transposed onto the more than eighty years before a new elite closed the door on dissent. Most of Dallas's past remains undocumented. Residents of the contemporary city can only benefit from an awareness that they share an urban legacy in which calls for fairness, cooperation, and greater attention to human services accompanied rapid growth.

ABBREVIATIONS USED IN NOTES

DHS   Dallas Historical Society
ETSU   East Texas State University
ILGWU   International Ladies Garment Workers Union
LA, UTA   Labor Archives, University of Texas at Arlington Library
MR, DPL   Municipal Reference, Dallas Public Library
NTSU   North Texas State University (now the University of
                     North Texas)
SMU   Southern Methodist University
T/D, DPL   Texas/Dallas History and Archives Division, Dallas
                     Public Library
UI, DPL   Urban Information, Dallas Public Library
UTD   University of Texas at Dallas

INTRODUCTION

1. Eric H. Monkkonen has found the adjective "improbable" used to describe many American cities. See *America Becomes Urban: The Development of U.S. Cities and Towns, 1780–1980* (Berkeley: University of California Press, 1988), p. 2.

2. See for example Gunther Barth, *Instant Cities: Urbanization and the Rise of San Francisco and Denver* (New York: Oxford University Press, 1975), Lawrence H. Larsen, *The Urban West at the End of the Frontier* (Lawrence: The Regents Press of Kansas, 1978), and Kenneth W. Wheeler, *To Wear a City's Crown: The Beginnings of Urban Growth in Texas, 1836–1865* (Cambridge: Harvard University Press, 1968).

3. David Hamer, *New Towns in the New World: Images and Perceptions of the Nineteenth-Century Urban Frontier* (New York: Columbia University Press, 1990), pp. 5, 10.

4. Joe R. Feagin, *Free Enterprise City: Houston in Political-Economic*

Perspective (New Brunswick: Rutgers University Press, 1988), pp. 107, 117, 151–152, 275.

5. Stephen L. Elkin, *City and Regime in the American Republic* (Chicago: University of Chicago Press, 1987), pp. 61, 84. For more on Sunbelt cities after World War II, see Carl Abbott, *The New Urban America: Growth and Politics in Sunbelt Cities* (Chapel Hill: University of North Carolina Press, 1987); Richard M. Bernard and Bradley R. Rice, eds., *Sunbelt Cities: Politics and Growth Since World War II* (Austin: University of Texas Press, 1983); Robert B. Fairbanks and Kathleen Underwood, eds., *Essays on Sunbelt Cities and Recent Urban America* (College Station: Texas A&M University Press, 1990); and Raymond A. Mohl, ed., *Searching for the Sunbelt: Historical Perspectives on a Region* (Knoxville: University of Tennessee Press, 1990).

6. Monkkonen, *America Becomes Urban*, pp. 5–8.

7. Warren Leslie, *Dallas Public and Private: Aspects of an American City* (New York: Grossman, 1964), p. 23; "The Dydamic Men of Dallas," [*sic*] *Fortune*, February 1949, pp. 98–103, 162–166.

8. *Memorial and Biographical History of Dallas County, Texas* (Chicago: Lewis Publishing, 1892), pp. 275–276; Philip Lindsley, *A History of Greater Dallas and Vicinity*, vol. 1 (Chicago: Lewis Publishing Co., 1909), pp. 33, 88, 122–123, 125.

9. John H. Cochran, *Dallas County* (Dallas: Service Publishing Co., 1928), pp. 15, 88, 249–250; Justin F. Kimball, *Our City—Dallas: A Community Civics* (Dallas: Kessler Plan Association, 1927), see chapter 2 and p. 80.

10. "Dallas: The Centennial City Host to a Nation," *Southwest Business*, June 1936, p. 15. Writing several years after the Texas Centennial Exposition, Sam Acheson, a local historian and reporter for the *Dallas Morning News*, still attributed the city's early growth to its location and rich agricultural hinterland. See *35,000 Days in Texas: A History of the Dallas News and its Forbears* (New York: Macmillan, 1938), pp. 79, 99.

11. "The Dydamic Men of Dallas"; Quoted in "The Dallas Way," *Dallas Times Herald*, 15 November 1987, sec. H, p. 16.

12. See *Dallas City Directory*, 1936; "Dallas: The Centennial City Host to a Nation," p. 15. The city directory for 1934–1935 lists "people" before agriculture and commerce as key determinants of the city's growth. Nevertheless, there is no mention of the city lacking a reason to exist.

13. Unless otherwise noted, material on early Dallas comes from the following sources: Sam Acheson, *Dallas Yesterday*, ed. Lee Milazzo (Dallas: Southern Methodist University Press, 1977); Cochran, *Dallas County*; Lindsley, *A History of Greater Dallas and Vicinity*, vol. 1; Andrew Morrison, *The City of Dallas and the State of Texas* (St. Louis: George W. Englehardt, n.d.); Darwin Payne, *Dallas: An Illustrated History* (Woodland Hills, Calif.: Dallas Historic Preservation League and Windsor Publications, 1982); John William Rogers, *The Lusty Texans of Dallas* (New York: E. P. Dutton, 1951;

reprint ed. [expanded], Dallas: Cokesbury Book Store, 1965); George H. Santerre, *Dallas's First Hundred Years, 1856–1956* (Dallas: Book Craft, 1956); Texas Writers Project (Works Progress Administration), *Dallas Guide and History*, chronology, 1940; and L. A. Wilson, *History and Opportunity* (Dallas, 1911).

14. *Encyclopedia of Texas*, 2d ed. (St. Clair Shores, Mich.: Somerset Publishers, 1985), pp. 174–175; comments of A. C. Greene at "Dallas Past and Present: A Sesquicentennial Symposium," sponsored by the Dallas Public Library, 15 November 1986.

15. Seymour V. Connor, "A Statistical Review of the Settlement of the Peters Colony, 1841–1848," *Southwestern Historical Quarterly* 57 (July 1953):55.

16. Single men over the age of 17 received 320 acres. Peters Colony settlers were required to build a cabin, cultivate at least 15 acres, and live on a claim for three years before receiving a deed. See Kimball, *Our City—Dallas*, p. 6.

17. Ibid., pp. 53–54, 64; Seymour V. Connor, *Texas: A History* (Arlington Heights, Ill.: AHM Publishing, 1971), pp. 137–140.

18. For information on the La Reunion colony, see Rogers, *The Lusty Texans of Dallas*, pp. 77–88 and *Encyclopedia of Texas*, pp. 175–176.

19. *Encyclopedia of Texas*, p. 176.

20. Shirley Achor, *Mexican Americans in a Dallas Barrio* (Tucson, Ariz.: University of Arizona Press, 1978), pp. 55–56.

21. An ironic example was the "Momentum" campaign of Mercantile Bank, which Thornton founded.

22. David Dillon begins a recent work on Dallas architecture by calling the myth Dallas's "oldest cliche." He then reinforces the myth. See *Dallas Architecture, 1936–1986* (Austin: Texas Monthly Press, 1985), p. 1.

23. U.S. Bureau of the Census, *Statistical Abstract of the United States: 1913* (Washington, D.C.: U.S. Government Printing Office, 1914), p. 42; U.S. Bureau of the Census, *Statistical Abstract of the United States: 1960* (Washington, D.C.: U.S. Government Printing Office, 1960), p. 18. Prior to 1880, the census reports only Dallas County population totals (2,743 in 1850 and 8,665 in 1860). See U.S. Bureau of the Census, *Statistical View of the United States: A Compendium of the Seventh Census: 1850* (Washington, D.C.: A. O. P. Nicholson, 1854), p. 308; and U.S. Bureau of the Census, *United States Census of Population: 1870*, vol. 1 (Washington, D.C.: U.S. Government Printing Office, 1872), p. 63.

24. Homer L. Kerr, "Migration into Texas, 1860–1880," *Southwestern Historical Quarterly* 70 (October 1966):190–194, 199.

25. Texas Writers Project, *Dallas Guide and History*, chronology pp. 00700–00701.

26. Vera Lea Dugas, "Texas Industry, 1860–1880," *Southwestern Historical Quarterly* 59 (October 1955):179.

27. Ibid., p. 169.

28. *Bureau of the Census, United States Census of Population: 1800*, vol. 2, *Report of Social Statistics of Cities* (Washington, D.C.: U.S. Government Printing Office, 1887), pp. 186–189, 369–371. Dallas possessed Texas's largest single ice plant in 1880. With factories in Dallas, Houston, San Antonio, and Austin, Texas led the nation in ice production with a third of the national total. Artificial ice cost Dallas consumers about 2 1/2 cents per pound. Local inventor Thomas L. Rankin expanded the county's ice-based industry through his development of production techniques for refrigerated breweries, storage houses, slaughterhouses, and box cars. See Dugas, "Texas Industry, 1860–1880," p. 178.

29. David R. Goldfield, *Cotton Fields and Skyscrapers: Southern City and Region, 1607–1980* (Baton Rouge: Louisiana State University Press, 1982), pp. 93–94.

30. Payne, *Dallas: An Illustrated History*, pp. 76–77.

31. Rogers, *The Lusty Texans of Dallas*, pp. 141–142.

32. Larsen, *The Urban West*, p. 87.

33. Ibid., p. 24; Norma Adams Wade, "E. Dallas School Named for Pioneer Teacher," *Dallas Morning News*, 15 February 1987, sec. A, p. 33.

34. *U.S. Census: 1880*, vol. 2, pp. 311–312.

35. John W. Reps, *Cities of the American West: A History of Frontier Urban Planning* (Princeton, N.J.: Princeton University Press, 1979), p. 670.

36. *Encyclopedia of Texas*, p. 177.

37. Fidel J. Gonzalez, Jr., *P. P. Martinez: Texas Pioneer, Civic Leader, Philanthropist, Real Estate Tycoon and Tobacco Manufacturer, Dallas, Texas 1880–1935* (Dallas, 1980), p. 25; William L. McDonald records the destruction of Dallas landmarks and the frequency with which they were replaced by parking lots in *Dallas Rediscovered: A Photographic Chronicle of Urban Expansion, 1870–1925* (Dallas: Dallas Historical Society, 1978).

38. Texas Writers Project, *Dallas Guide and History*, chronology pp. 00700–00705. As late as the 1960s, local newspapers still compared "the Dallas summer musicals to Broadway, the Dallas Civic Opera [first established in 1957] to the Metropolitan, and the Dallas Symphony Orchestra to the New York Philharmonic." Leslie, *Dallas Public and Private*, pp. 26–27.

39. *Memorial and Biographical History of Dallas County*, pp. 308, 310, 321.

40. Detail from Sam Street's Map of Dallas County, Texas, 1900, T/D, DPL. See also Sanborn Insurance Maps of Dallas, Texas, 1885, T/D, DPL.

41. Department of Urban Planning, City of Dallas, "Comprehensive Land Use Policy Plan for Dallas," 1976 (typewritten), II-26–28, UI, DPL; Acheson, *Dallas Yesterday*, p. 134; Payne, *Dallas: An Illustrated History*, p. 83.

42. Texas Writers Project, *Dallas Guide and History*, chronology pp. 00699–00700. Texas law did not permit Home Rule until 1913. See William Neil Black, "Empire of Consensus: City Planning, Zoning, and Annexation in Dallas, 1900–1960" (Ph.D. dissertation, Columbia University, 1982), pp. 122–124.

43. W. Lee Armstrong, "City of Dallas Mayors and City Councils, 1856–1963," typewritten and unpaginated, 1962, T/D, DPL.

44. Gerda Lerner considers "contribution histories" a necessary first step toward the historical inclusion of previously neglected groups. See "Placing Women in History: Definitions and Challenges," *Feminist Studies* 3 (Fall 1975):5–8.

45. Anne Firor Scott uses the phrase "organized womanhood" as a designation for a wide variety of women's associations. See *Natural Allies: Women's Associations in American History* (Urbana: University of Illinois Press, 1991).

46. See Black, "Empire of Consensus."

CHAPTER 1

1. Don H. Doyle, *New Men, New Cities, New South: Atlanta, Nashville, Charleston, Mobile, 1860–1910* (Chapel Hill: University of North Carolina Press, 1990), p. 137.

2. Hamer, *New Towns in the New World*, pp. 5, 10. Hamer argues that boosters were more aware that they were competing for migrants in a movement that transcended national boundaries than historians have generally acknowledged.

3. Quoted in Alma Cunningham, "Periwinkle Pen Aided Humanity," *Dallas Morning News*, Centennial Edition, 11 April 1942, sec. 3, p. 12.

4. Marsha Wedell, *Elite Women and the Reform Impulse in Memphis, 1875–1915* (Knoxville: University of Tennessee Press, 1991), p. 4.

5. Stuart M. Blumin notes the irony of "a class that binds itself together as a social group in part through the common embrace of an ideology of social atomism." See *The Emergence of the Middle Class: Social Experience in the American City, 1760–1900* (Cambridge: Cambridge University Press, 1989), pp. 9–10. Robert H. Wiebe discusses the difficulties with which middle-class American businessmen "sacrificed a jot of their independence" in *Businessmen and Reform: A Study of the Progressive Movement* (reprint ed., Chicago: Elephant Paperbacks/Ivan R. Dee, Inc., 1989), p. 16.

6. "Lynn Lawther: An Oral History Interview Conducted by Alan Mason on March 6, 1981" (ETSU and DPL, typewritten transcript, 1983), p. 11.

7. Payne, *Dallas: An Illustrated History*, p. 65; Ralph W. Widener, Jr., *William Henry Gaston: A Builder of Dallas* (Dallas: Historical Publishing, 1977), pp. 20–21.

8. Texas Writers Project, *Dallas Guide and History*, chronology p. 00700; *Encyclopedia of Texas*, p. 176.

9. Widener, *William Henry Gaston*, pp. 21–23. In contrast, at about the same time voters in Sherman declined to extend a subsidy to the Missouri-Kansas-Texas railroad since the town already possessed one line. See Payne, *Dallas: An Illustrated History*, pp. 66–67.

10. *Encyclopedia of Texas*, p. 176.

11. Texas Writers Project, *Dallas Guide and History*, chronology pp. 00700, 00703; Payne, *Dallas: An Illustrated History*, p. 70.

12. See Doyle, *New Men, New Cities, New South*, pp. 89–90.

13. Acheson, *Dallas Yesterday*, pp. 131–133; Cochran, *Dallas County*, pp. 124, 134; Ben Cabell's oldest son was Dallas mayor pro-tem. His youngest, Earle, became mayor in 1961 and was re-elected in 1963. Earle Cabell also served four successive terms in the U.S. House of Representatives between 1965 and 1972. See Sarah Boulton Evans, "A Guide to the Collection of Earle Cabell," MSS 16, 1983, Fikes Hall of Special Collections and DeGolyer Library, SMU; Rogers, *The Lusty Texans of Dallas*, pp. 155–161; Widener, *William Henry Gaston*, pp. 33, 46.

14. Rogers, *The Lusty Texans of Dallas*, pp. 103–104.

15. Ibid., pp. 120–122, 155–161; Acheson, *Dallas Yesterday*, pp. 131–133, 310.

16. Marilynn Wood Hill, "A History of the Jewish Involvement in the Dallas Community" (Master's thesis, SMU, 1967), pp. 96, 135.

17. Samuel Paul Maranto, "A History of Dallas Newspapers" (Master's thesis, NTSU, 1952), pp. 83–84; Acheson, *35,000 Days in Texas*, pp. 96, 100; Ernest Sharpe, *G. B. Dealey of The Dallas News* (New York: Henry Holt, 1955), pp. 43, 109.

18. In his socialist labor weekly, George Clifton Edwards questions the sincerity of the *News* after that paper suggests New Yorkers evicted from tenement districts move to Texas and "camp out." Edwards complains that the *News* ignores the often prohibitive cost of such a move and comments that workers in Texas, where the "earth is the landlord's and the fullness thereof," receive no respite from rent collectors. *Dallas Laborer*, 15 April 1904, p. 4. The following quotation from editor J. C. McNealus, whose *Dallas Democrat* provided state and national political news on a weekly basis beginning in 1883, is another example of the kind of criticism the *Morning News* regularly received before most of the city's small periodicals failed during the Depression of the 1930s. McNealus comments on the *News*'s harsh criticism of former Dallas mayor Henry D. Lindsley while Lindsley served in Woodrow Wilson's cabinet. "When Henry D. Lindsley was in the hey-day of power and influence, The Dallas Morning News out-slobbered all other slobberers in its publicity laudations of him. He was 'the greatest Mayor in the United States.' Now that Lindsley seems to be 'down and out,' The Dallas Morning News out-kicks all other kickers in helping along the downing. . . . This is characteristically News-like: it knows no fealty except to the powerful." "Kicking the Man That's Down," *Dallas Democrat*, 24 May 1919, p. 1.

19. Prior to 1917, the state legislature did not distinguish between annexation and consolidation. See Black, "Empire of Consensus," pp. 245–247.

20. Apparently, legislators extrapolated the citizenry's support for annexation from its election of pro-annexation officials. See Acheson, *Dallas*

Yesterday, pp. 40–43; *Memorial and Biographical History of Dallas County*, pp. 755–756; Steve Mabry, "History of the City of East Dallas," Texas Historical Marker Application, typescript, T/D, DPL; East Dallas Clippings Files, T/D, DPL; A. C. Greene, "Rail Lines' Location Made East Dallas a City Apart," *Dallas Morning News*, 16 June 1991, sec. A, p. 42.

21. Acheson, *Dallas Yesterday*, pp. 29–31.

22. Black, "Empire of Consensus," pp. 247–248. The state's annexation law is ambiguous during this period. A local election on the issue of disincorporation was usually considered a prerequisite to the annexation of incorporated areas. In the East Dallas case, however, the town both lost its charter and was annexed by Dallas through an act of the state legislature.

23. Acheson, *Dallas Yesterday*, pp. 52–56.

24. Black, "Empire of Consensus," pp. 122–124, 246, 252–254.

25. "Highland Park," *Dallas Democrat*, 9 August 1919, p. 4.

26. Kimball, *Our City—Dallas*, p. 272.

27. Kenneth T. Jackson, *Crabgrass Frontier: The Suburbanization of the United States* (New York: Oxford University Press, 1985), p. 151.

28. See "Citizens Association Holds First Political Rally," *Dallas Morning News*, 8 May 1907, p. 3, and "Citizens Association Ticket Makes Clean Sweep," *Dallas Morning News*, 22 May 1907, p. 4, for details regarding supporters of the charter changes in 1907.

29. Bradley Robert Rice, *Progressive Cities: The Commission Government Movement in America, 1901–1920* (Austin: University of Texas Press, 1977), pp. xiv, 25–26, 28, 110. For a recent case study or for comparison, see David E. Alsobrook, "Mobile's Commission Government of 1910–1911," *Alabama Review* 44 (January 1991):36–60.

30. "Dallas Trades Council," *Dallas Morning News*, 16 January 1899, p. 8.

31. Rice, *Progressive Cities*, pp. 28, 30, 32–33; Acheson, *35,000 Days in Texas*, p. 245.

32. Kimball, *Our City—Dallas*, pp. 244–247, 333–334.

33. *Encyclopedia of Texas*, p. 177; William H. Wilson, "Adapting to Growth: Dallas, Texas, and the Kessler Plan, 1908–1933," *Arizona and the West* 25 (1983):248–250.

34. Texas Writers Project, *Dallas Guide and History*, chronology p. 00707.

35. See William H. Wilson, *The City Beautiful Movement* (Baltimore: Johns Hopkins University Press, 1989).

36. W. H. Wilson, "Adapting to Growth," p. 253.

37. George E. Kessler, *A City Plan for Dallas*, 1911, p. 22, MR, DPL.

38. Goldfield, *Cotton Fields and Skyscrapers*, pp. 101–102. Goldfield claims that much of the impetus for "city beautiful" campaigns throughout the South came from women's clubs. As in Dallas, business communities in many southern cities supported small-scale measures to beautify the urban environment— "occasional shrubs, 'comely' waste receptacles, and flower beds"—but ignored major aesthetic aspects of city plans.

39. Kessler, *A City Plan for Dallas*, pp. 19–20.

40. W. H. Wilson, "Adapting to Growth," pp. 252, 255, 258.

41. Ibid., p. 260.

42. Louis P. Head, *The Kessler City Plan for Dallas*, reprinted articles from the *Dallas Morning News*, 1924–1925, p. 25, T/D, DPL.

43. W. H. Wilson, "Adapting to Growth," p. 257.

44. See Larsen, *The Urban West*, p. 55.

45. Kimball, *Our City—Dallas*, pp. 72, 100–101.

46. *Dallas City Directory*, 1906, p. 6.

47. Cochran, *Dallas County*, pp. 134, 296.

48. Mason interview with Lynn Lawther, pp. 15–16.

49. Ibid., p. 11; "Mrs. Frank W. Wozencraft and Frank M. Wozencraft, Sr.: An Oral History Interview Conducted by Alan Mason on November 22, 1980" (ETSU and DPL, typewritten transcript, 1983), pp. 7–9; Acheson, *Dallas Yesterday*, pp. 174–177. Although Lawther's administration was routinely characterized as a utility-dominated "machine" by local newspapers and in the political rhetoric of his opponents, one must question the accuracy of the term considering Lawther's tenure as mayor spanned only two years.

50. Mason interview with Mrs. Frank W. Wozencraft and Frank M. Wozencraft, Sr., p. 6.

51. Acheson, *Dallas Yesterday*, p. 173.

52. Mason interview with Mrs. Frank W. Wozencraft and Frank M. Wozencraft, Sr., pp. 6–7.

53. Ibid., p. 8; *Dallas Democrat*, 29 March 1919, p. 1.

54. Mason interview with Mrs. Frank W. Wozencraft and Frank M. Wozencraft, Sr., pp. 8–9.

55. Dallas was the smallest city in the nation to acquire a regional bank. The addition of a financial institution with $6.5 million in capital (Dallas banks combined possessed $5 million in 1913) and the Robertson Law, a 1907 statute which required insurance companies operating in Texas to reinvest at least 75 percent of their Texas profits in Texas businesses, reinforced the city's position as a regional financial center and extended its scope. See Payne, *Dallas: An Illustrated History*, pp. 162–164, and Black, "Empire of Consensus," p. 64.

56. Blaine A. Brownell, "The Urban South Comes of Age, 1900–1940," in *The City in Southern History: The Growth of Urban Civilization in the South*, edited by Blaine A. Brownell and David R. Goldfield (Port Washington, N.Y.: Kennikat Press, 1977), p. 142.

57. Quoted in Eric F. Goldman, *Rendezvous with Destiny: A History of Modern American Reform* (New York: Alfred A. Knopf, 1952; reprint ed., New York: Vintage Books, 1977), p. 144.

58. Rogers, *The Lusty Texans of Dallas*, pp. 342, 359. As late as the mid-1920s, members of the Dallas Woman's Club reported on garden club activities in Philadelphia and commissioned a study of national trends before orga-

nizing the Dallas Garden Club in 1926. For details regarding early Dallas literary clubs, see Michael V. Hazel, "Dallas Women's Clubs: Vehicles for Change," (Dallas County Heritage Society) *Heritage News* (Spring 1986):18–21, and Elizabeth York Enstam, "The Forgotten Frontier: Dallas Women and Social Caring, 1895–1920," *Legacies* (Spring 1989):20–28.

59. See Karen J. Blair, *The Club Woman as Feminist: True Womanhood Redefined, 1868–1914* (New York: Holmes & Meier, 1980) for an analysis of the activities of club women in northern and eastern cities.

60. Rogers, *The Lusty Texans of Dallas*, p. 341.

61. Ibid., pp. 341–343.

62. Kathleen D. McCarthy, *Noblesse Oblige: Charity and Cultural Philanthropy in Chicago, 1849–1929* (Chicago: University of Chicago Press, 1982), p. 47.

63. "A Flattering Attendance," *Dallas Morning News*, 11 May 1899, p. 10; Acheson, *Dallas Yesterday*, p. 205; Rogers, *The Lusty Texans of Dallas*, pp. 265, 342.

64. Quoted in "The First Fifty Years of *The Dallas Morning News*: Second Ten Years Are Eventful—1896–1905," *Dallas Morning News*, Fiftieth Anniversary Jubilee Edition, 1 October 1935, sec. 3, p. 6.

65. Mrs. E. B. Reppert, "First Woman's Editor of *News* Led Fight for Each Big Improvement," *Dallas Morning News*, Fiftieth Anniversary Jubilee Edition, 1 October 1935, sec. 5, p. 10.

66. Ibid.; Mary Carter Toomey, "Dallas' First Woman's Club Born Two Months After *The Dallas News*," *Dallas Morning News*, Fiftieth Anniversary Jubilee Edition, 1 October 1935, sec. 5, p. 8; Cunningham, "Periwinkle Pen Aided Humanity."

67. Quoted in Cunningham, "Periwinkle Pen Aided Humanity."

68. James Leiby, *A History of Social Welfare and Social Work in the United States, 1815–1972* (New York: Columbia University Press, 1978), p. 146.

69. Goldman, *Rendezvous with Destiny*, pp. 93–95.

70. Reppert, "First Woman's Editor of *News*."

71. Blair, *The Clubwoman as Feminist*, p. 119. Chicago women shared these concerns. Leiby credits the Chicago Women's Club with efforts to improve conditions for women and children in police stations and jails as early as 1883. See *A History of Social Welfare*, pp. 146–147.

72. Reppert, "First Woman's Editor of *News*." Although the idea of making rent payments and paying the salary of the city's first probation officer probably came from Chicago, it is important to note that in Dallas women's clubs assumed this role because the city initially refused to do so. In Chicago, club women deliberately paid salaries and even chose the probation officers themselves in order to keep the program out of the hands of "political spoilsmen." See Leiby, *A History of Social Welfare*, p. 147.

73. Texas Writers Project, *Dallas Guide and History*, chronology p. 00705; Department of Urban Planning, City of Dallas, "Comprehensive Land Use

Policy Plan for Dallas," II-11.

74. Reppert, "First Woman's Editor of *News*."

75. Goldfield, *Cotton Fields and Skyscrapers*, p. 96.

76. Acheson, *Dallas Yesterday*, pp. 205–206.

77. "Barry Miller to the Men," *Dallas Democrat*, 3 May 1919, p. 3.

78. *Dallas Craftsman*, 8 August 1919, p. 4.

79. Texas Writers Project, *Dallas Guide and History*, chronology p. 00707; Cochran, *Dallas County*, pp. 213, 237, 240–241; Kirk Dooley, *Hidden Dallas* (Dallas: Taylor Publishing, 1988), p. 188. Dooley incorrectly lists the 1908 female Board of Education members as Mrs. E. P. Turner and Mrs. T. T. (instead of P. P.) Tucker. The size of the Board of Education and length of members' terms varied throughout the 1920s, resulting in irregularly spaced elections. See also Diana Church, "Mrs. E. P. Turner: Clubwoman, Reformer, Community Builder," (Dallas County Heritage Society) *Heritage News* (Summer 1985):9–14.

80. Manuel Castells, *The City and the Grassroots: A Cross-Cultural Theory of Urban Social Movements* (Berkeley: University of California Press, 1983), p. 68.

CHAPTER 2

1. For this and similar announcements see *Dallas Laborer*, 8 April 1904, p. 5; 15 April 1904, p. 4.

2. Throughout, I capitalize "Populist" when the term refers specifically to the radical farmers' movement of the late nineteenth century (associated with the People's party). In lower case, "populist" refers to individuals or groups advocating some of the principles of the original movement or attempting to revive its legacy of grassroots activism. "Socialist" is capitalized only when it refers to the Socialist Party of America or its members. Dallas "socialism" included many (workers, reformers, women, adherents of the social gospel) who were not formally affiliated with the Socialist party.

3. In 1900, 1,975 Dallas County farmhouses were occupied by white owners, while renters occupied 2,295 county farmhouses. See Sam Street's Map of Dallas County, Texas, 1900, T/D, DPL.

4. Acheson, *Dallas Yesterday*, p. 320.

5. James R. Green, *Grass-roots Socialism: Radical Movements in the Southwest, 1895–1943* (Baton Rouge: Louisiana State University Press, 1978), p. 64; see also "From Our Correspondents," *Dallas Laborer*, 29 August 1908, p. 4.

6. "Victory for the People of Dallas," *Dallas Laborer*, 1 July 1911, p. 1; Sam Acheson, *35,000 Days in Texas*, p. 245. Although Acheson acknowledges the presence of socialist George Clifton Edwards on the charter committee, he oddly describes Edwards and union printer (also contractor and attorney)

Gilbert H. Irish as nonpolitical figures. The careers of both men, their election by workers to the 1907 City Charter Commission, and Irish's service as an alderman between 1902 and 1906 indicate otherwise. See Armstrong, "City of Dallas Mayors and City Councils," unpaginated. Acheson's de-politicization of the workings of municipal government is an example of a rhetorical technique frequently used by the new elite (and its chroniclers) that emerged in the 1920s and gained power throughout the 1930s.

7. Sam Bass Warner, Jr., *The Urban Wilderness: A History of the American City* (New York: Harper & Row, 1972), pp. 15–19.

8. J. R. Green, *Grass-roots Socialism*, p. 1.

9. Connor, *Texas*, pp. 273–274.

10. Lawrence Goodwyn, *Democratic Promise: The Populist Moment in America* (New York: Oxford University Press, 1976), p. xiii. Goodwyn's is the finest study of southwestern Populism. On the origins of southern Populism, see Robert C. McMath, Jr., *Populist Vanguard: A History of the Southern Farmers' Alliance* (Chapel Hill: University of North Carolina Press, 1975). For details of Populism in Texas, see Roscoe C. Martin, *The People's Party in Texas: A Study in Third Party Politics* (1933; reprint ed., Austin: University of Texas Press, Texas History Paperback, 1970); Worth Robert Miller, "Building a Progressive Coalition in Texas: The Populist–Reform Democrat Rapprochement, 1900–1907," *Journal of Southern History* 52 (May 1986): 163–182; and Ralph Smith, "The Farmers' Alliance in Texas, 1875–1900," *Southwestern Historical Quarterly* 48 (January 1945):346–369. Daniel J. Elazar's *Cities of the Prairie: The Metropolitan Frontier and American Politics* (New York: Basic Books, 1970) discusses Populism in midwestern cities, although the farmers' movement is not the focus of the book.

11. Acheson, *Dallas Yesterday*, p. 320.

12. See Leon Fink's history of the Knights, *Workingmen's Democracy: The Knights of Labor and American Politics* (Urbana: University of Illinois Press, 1983) and Melton Alonza McLaurin's *The Knights of Labor in the South* (Westport, Conn.: Greenwood Press, 1978).

13. Robert W. Larson's research indicates that empathy for organized labor was not unique to Texas Alliance members. The farmers' movement frequently raised labor issues in the Rocky Mountain states. See Larson's *Populism in the Mountain West* (Albuquerque: University of New Mexico Press, 1986).

14. Goodwyn, *Democratic Promise*, pp. 56–57.

15. Quoted ibid., pp. 61–63.

16. Ibid., p. 65.

17. See Fink, *Workingmen's Democracy*, p. 112, for similar effects of the strike in other cities.

18. Quoted in Acheson, *Dallas Yesterday*, pp. 238–239.

19. "Mr. Lang on the Alliance," *Dallas Morning News*, 15 May 1886, p. 2.

20. Quoted in Goodwyn, *Democratic Promise*, p. 66.

21. Quoted ibid., pp. 75–76.

22. Maranto, "A History of Dallas Newspapers," p. 54; Acheson, *Dallas Yesterday*, pp. 319–320. Acheson related Rust's reaction to a Chamber of Commerce news release that boasted of Dallas's 119 lawyers and 107 physicians—"There are but few necks broken for legal cause and but few deaths from natural causes."

23. *Southern Mercury*, 7 June 1888.

24. Goodwyn, *Democratic Promise*, pp. 84, 125–126.

25. Ibid., p. 128.

26. Ibid., pp. 126–134.

27. Charles W. Macune, Jr., "The Wellsprings of a Populist: Dr. C. W. Macune before 1886," *Southwestern Historical Quarterly* 90 (October 1986):150–151.

28. Goodwyn, *Democratic Promise*, pp. 135–137; "State Alliance Meets," *Dallas Morning News*, 24 August 1888, p. 5.

29. "State Alliance Meets," *Dallas Morning News*, 25 August 1888, p. 8.

30. *Southern Mercury*, 23 October 1888.

31. J. R. Green, *Grass-roots Socialism*, p. 8; "People's Party," *Fort Worth Gazette*, 18 August 1891, p. 1.

32. "Alliance in Session," *Dallas Morning News*, 19 August 1891, p. 1; "People's Party," *Fort Worth Gazette*, 18 and 19 August 1891, p. 1; "The People's Party," *Dallas Morning News*, 18 August 1891, p. 1. For details of the earlier work of Golden and Loe with the Texas State Federation of Labor, see "The Labor Convention," *Dallas Morning News*, 5 July 1889, p. 8.

33. J. R. Green, *Grass-roots Socialism*, p. 8.

34. Goodwyn, *Democratic Promise*, p. 286; "Registration in Dallas," *Dallas Herald*, 1 February 1868, p. 2; Rogers, *The Lusty Texans of Dallas*, pp. 100–101.

35. Armstrong, "City of Dallas Mayors and City Councils," unpaginated.

36. "Registration in Dallas," *Dallas Herald*, 1 February 1868, p. 2; *Dallas Herald*, 8 August 1868, p. 2.

37. "The Labor Convention," *Dallas Morning News*, 5 July 1889, p. 8.

38. Quoted in "People's Party," *Fort Worth Gazette*, 18 August 1891, p. 1.

39. Ibid.

40. Goodwyn, *Democratic Promise*, pp. 290–291.

41. "The People's Party," *Fort Worth Gazette*, 18 August 1891, p. 1.

42. Dallas possesses neither a study of area Populists nor a history of nineteenth-century trade unions. I believe an inquiry into either topic would reveal others who, like Golden and Kearby, combined political activity at the state level with local activism. I emphasize their careers because they were the city's most visible Populists.

43. *Members of the Texas Legislature 1846–1962* (Austin, Tex., 1962), pp. 152–153.

44. In 1892, moderate Democrats (and the *Dallas Times Herald*) support-

ed James S. Hogg in his bid for reelection as governor. Conservative Democrats (including most Dallas business leaders, the railroad companies, and the *Dallas Morning News*) supported George Clark. Hogg won the election. See Maranto, "A History of Dallas Newspapers," pp. 98–102, 133.

45. *Memorial and Biographical History of Dallas County*, pp. 310, 938–939.

46. For information regarding the Henderson Substitute for Golden's mechanics' lien law, see "A Call," *Fort Worth Gazette*, 20 August 1891, p. 1, and "Minutes of AF of L, Dallas Branch, Regular and Special Meetings, September 20, 1891–March 4, 1894," Collection 5, Box 11, Folder 2a, LA, UTA.

47. AFL Minutes, LA, UTA; Charles MacGibson, "Organized Labor in Texas from 1890 to 1900," Collection 134, Box 1 (chronology of events taken from the *Dallas Morning News*), LA, UTA.

48. "Mayor's Message and Annual Reports of City Officers of the City of Dallas, Texas," 1889, T/D, DPL.

49. "Ordinances and Resolutions of the Council of the City of Dallas from October 1, 1886 to June 25, 1888," T/D, DPL.

50. Ibid.; Sanborn Insurance Maps of Dallas, Texas, 1899, T/D, DPL. The office of street superintendent was created for Golden in 1894. He served sporadically until 1897; the office remained vacant during the periods between Golden's several resignations and reappointments. After resigning in September of 1897, Golden was replaced, but the street superintendent remained a feature of city government until the city commission, which included an elected commissioner in charge of streets, replaced the council of aldermen in 1907. See Armstrong, "City of Dallas Mayors and City Councils," unpaginated.

51. Armstrong, "City of Dallas Mayors and City Councils," unpaginated; *Members of the Texas Legislature 1846–1962*, pp. 81, 89, 96, 112, 144, 152, 177, 186.

52. *Memorial and Biographical History of Dallas County*, pp. 690–691; Goodwyn, *Democratic Promise*, pp. 331, 478–479; Lindsley, *A History of Greater Dallas and Vicinity*, vol. 1, p. 404.

53. Philip Lindsley, *A History of Greater Dallas and Vicinity*, vol. 2, ed. L. B. Hill (Chicago: Lewis Publishing, 1909), p. 88.

54. Goodwyn, *Democratic Promise*, p. 509.

55. Quoted ibid., pp. 478–479, 492.

56. J. R. Green, *Grass-roots Socialism*, pp. 9–11.

57. Lindsley, *A History of Greater Dallas and Vicinity*, vol. 2, p. 88. The careers of other radical Dallas attorneys will be discussed in the context of their activities as local socialists and work on behalf of organized labor.

58. J. R. Green, *Grass-roots Socialism*, pp. 3, 26–27.

59. Ibid., pp. 12–13, 39. By 1913, when socialism reached its peak in Dallas, the *Appeal to Reason* claimed 761,747 subscribers. See James Weinstein, *The Decline of Socialism in America, 1912–1925* (New York:

Vintage Books, 1969), p. 96.

60. Louis H. Hicks Collection, Collection 228, Boxes 1 and 2, LA, UTA.

61. J. R. Green, *Grass-roots Socialism*, pp. 3, 12–13, 24.

62. Ibid., pp. 65, 124, 232; Oral History 39, Interview with Carl Brannin, conducted by Harriet Hamilton, 28 November 1973, p. 15, LA, UTA.

63. J. R. Green, *Grass-roots Socialism*, pp. 19, 22–23, 66.

64. "Roster," *Dallas Laborer*, 2 April 1904, p. 8; see also editions 15 April, 7 May, and 11 June 1904 for additional unions supporting the *Laborer*.

65. "Organization," *Dallas Laborer*, 2 April 1904, p. 4. See also Oral History 1, Interview with Carl Brannin, conducted by Dr. George Green, 12 April 1967, p. 23, LA, UTA. Like Edwards, long-time Dallas Socialist Carl Brannin envisioned the local party as the focal point of an educational movement rather than as a practical, political alternative. Brannin continued to hold this view into the 1930s when New Deal Democrats implemented many of the policies endorsed decades earlier by Dallas socialists.

66. The *Dallas Morning News*, which touted itself as the "largest and cheapest Newspaper in the South," also cost five cents per copy ($7.50 per year). See 1 April 1904, p. 6.

67. Lindsley, *A History of Greater Dallas and Vicinity*, vol. 2, pp. 195–196; Armstrong, "City of Dallas Mayors and City Councils," unpaginated.

68. Oral History 19, Interview with George Lambert conducted by Dr. George Green, pt. 1, 9 September 1971, p. 24, LA, UTA.

69. Weinstein, *The Decline of Socialism in America*, p. 101.

70. "The Laborer," *Dallas Laborer*, 2 April 1904, p. 4.

71. "Commercial Club Courtesy," *Dallas Laborer*, 15 April 1904, p. 4.

72. *Dallas Laborer*, 2 April 1904, p. 5; "Free Lectures on Economics," *Dallas Laborer*, 30 April 1904, p. 4; "Socialist Local Entertains," *Dallas Laborer*, 9 July 1904, p. 1.

73. "By a Dallas Author," *Dallas Laborer*, 1 July 1911, p. 2.

74. In "The Capitalist Dailies and the Workers," Edwards examines the gulf that separates the interests of workers and those of publishers and major advertisers supporting local papers. He claims that the *Dallas Morning News* was the strongest Texas opponent of turn-of-the-century legislation to regulate child labor (considered essential by local socialists in order to raise wages and increase levels of education among workers). See *Dallas Laborer*, 22 April 1904, p. 4.

75. J. L. Hicks, "From the Worker's Viewpoint," *Dallas Laborer*, 28 March 1914, Louis H. Hicks Collection, Collection 228, Box 1, Scrapbook II, LA, UTA.

76. J. R. Green, *Grass-roots Socialism*, pp. 186–187; *Dallas Laborer*, 11 November 1911, p. 3, and 25 November 1911, p. 1; Acheson, *Dallas Yesterday*, pp. 170–172.

77. For information concerning Edwards's activities described below and for biographical information, see his son's (George Edwards) *Pioneer-at-Law*

(New York: W. W. Norton, 1974), especially pp. 20–28. Unless otherwise noted, quotations are from a typewritten memoir of the elder Edwards found in the George and Latane Lambert Papers, Collection 127, Box 4, Folder 5, LA, UTA. See also "Book Learnin' Got Strong Toehold Before City Officially Organized," *Dallas Times Herald*, 28 August 1949, sec. G, p. 6; Sam Acheson, "Edwards Backed Freedom of Speech," *Dallas Morning News*, 23 February 1970, sec. D, p. 2; and James Dunlap, "Author's Creed Served Integrity," *Dallas Morning News*, 7 November 1974, sec. A, p. 14. Acheson claims that, while serving as a missionary archdeacon in Alaska several years after his work with Edwards and Hinsdale in Dallas, Stuck became the first white man to climb Mount McKinley (Denali).

78. See "No Man Liveth to Himself," *Dallas Morning News*, 21 November 1898, p. 8, the text of a Sunday sermon on feeding the hungry and developing social consciousness, as an example of Stuck's urban vision.

79. Kenneth Foree, "Dangerous Man," *Dallas Morning News*, 7 September 1947, sec. 4, p. 2.

80. Ibid.

81. Edwards began practicing law after being discharged from his teaching position because of his political views. Rev. George W. Owens, a wealthy Oak Cliff minister, led the campaign to oust him. The Board of Education refused to fire the socialist, claiming that since Edwards taught Latin and algebra, his political views were irrelevant (although Dallas artist Olin Travis recalled a Latin lesson during which Edwards compared government corruption in Rome to the Dallas City Council; see Edwards, *Pioneer-at-Law*, p. 26). In the next election, Owens and his followers defeated the old Board of Education, and the newly elected members promptly fired Edwards. The Socialist read law with his father and quickly passed the bar examination. By 1910, there was a firm of Edwards and Edwards in the Dallas bar. Edwards's firing is the only incident of repression against a Dallas socialist I have found prior to World War I. See sources cited in notes 77 and 79 above for biographical information.

82. Oral History 19, Interview with George Lambert conducted by Dr. George Green, pt. 2, 6 February 1972, p. 4, and Oral History 1, Interview with Carl Brannin, conducted by Dr. George Green, 12 April 1967, pp. 29–30.

83. Interview with James P. Simpson, Jr., Dallas, Texas, 14 June 1987.

84. Miriam Allen DeFord, *On Being Concerned: The Vanguard Years of Carl and Laura Brannin* (Dallas, 1969), pp. 1–3; Oral History 34, Interview with Carl Brannin, conducted by Jan H. Cohen, 6 March 1973, p. 8, LA, UTA.

85. In a letter to the Dallas Public Library's Lillian M. Bradshaw, 25 July 1975, Clippings Files, Biography—Carl Brannin, T/D, DPL.

86. DeFord, *On Being Concerned*, p. 5.

87. Ibid., pp. 5–7.

88. Eulogy read by Brannin at the funeral of George Clifton Edwards, C. P. Brannin Papers, A6268, DHS.

89. DeFord, *On Being Concerned*, pp. 5–7, 12, 33, 37.

90. Ibid.

91. Oral History 19, Interview with George Lambert, pt. 2, p. 5.

92. *Dallas Morning News*, 27 June 1915, Louis H. Hicks Collection, Collection 228, Box 2, LA, UTA.

93. See *Dallas Democrat*, 18 January 1919, p. 8, for a typical ad promoting radical, labor, or liberal periodicals.

94. Willis Andrews, "Bolshevism," *Dallas Democrat*, 8 March 1919, p. 1.

95. DeFord, *On Being Concerned*, p. 15.

96. *Dallas Democrat*, 8 November 1919, p. 4; Willis Andrews, "Political Amnesty," *Dallas Democrat*, 28 June 1919, p. 1.

97. Weinstein, *The Decline of Socialism in America*, p. 138.

98. Wallace C. Reilly Papers and Memorabilia, Collection 115, Folder 5, LA, UTA.

99. I have found no indication in any biographical or autobiographical materials that George Clifton Edwards especially regretted the loss of the *Laborer*. With the national movement in disarray, he may have felt the paper had run its course. Edwards remained a member of the socialist local and continued to work closely with the Dallas union leaders who created a nonpartisan labor movement.

100. Quoted in Edwards, *Pioneer-at-Law*, p. 26.

101. "The Federal Labor Union," *Dallas Laborer*, 18 June 1904, p. 8.

102. J. R. Green, *Grass-roots Socialism*, pp. 96, 117–119, 138; Weinstein, *The Decline of Socialism in America*, see table pp. 94–102. On Nat Hardy, see *Dallas Laborer*, 17 June 1911, and J. R. Green, *Grass-roots Socialism*, p. 148.

103. J. R. Green, *Grass-roots Socialism*, p. 382.

104. Quoted in Weinstein, *The Decline of Socialism in America*, p. 235.

CHAPTER 3

1. "Another Mass Meeting," *Dallas Morning News*, 15 November 1898, p. 8.

2. For an analysis of early unions in Texas, see Frank H. Smyrl, "Unionism in Texas 1856–1861," *Southwestern Historical Quarterly* 68 (October 1964):172–195.

3. James V. Reese, "The Early History of Labor Organizations in Texas, 1838–1876," *Southwestern Historical Quarterly* 72 (July 1968):7, 18.

4. Maranto, "A History of Dallas Newspapers," p. 119.

5. See notes on Golden and Irish in chapter 2. Max Hahn's activities as a Dallas alderman (1898–1900) will be discussed later in this chapter.

6. "Dallas Central Labor Council History," n.d., Dallas AFL-CIO Records, Collection 5, Box 15, Folder 8, LA, UTA. See also *Members of the Texas Legislature 1846–1962*, pp. 247, 257, 266.

7. Between 1911 and 1921, Dallas unionists provided solid political support for *Dallas Democrat* editor J. C. McNealus. McNealus died while serving his sixth term in the state Senate. After his participation in the 1898 streetcar workers' strike, during which he made speeches and negotiated on behalf of the union, McNealus continued to advocate public control of utilities, land reform, and worker organization. Despite liberal stances on these issues, McNealus's commitment to the Democratic party and support for progrowth policies like land reclamation and annexation made his candidacy acceptable to most Dallas business leaders.

8. "Organized Labor Dates Back 60 Years in Dallas," *Dallas Times Herald*, 28 August 1949, sec. G, p. 4. For general labor and working-class history, see Stanley Aronowitz, *False Promises: The Shaping of American Working-Class Consciousness* (New York: McGraw-Hill, 1973); Milton Cantor, ed., *American Workingclass Culture: Explorations in American Labor and Social History* (Westport, Conn.: Greenwood Press, 1979); Herbert G. Gutman, *Work, Culture, and Society in Industrializing America: Essays in American Working-Class and Social History* (New York: Vintage Books, 1977); David Montgomery, *The Fall of the House of Labor: The Workplace, the State, and American Labor Activism, 1865–1925* (Cambridge: Cambridge University Press, 1987); Joseph G. Rayback, *A History of American Labor* (New York: Macmillan, 1959); and Irwin Yellowitz, *The Position of the Worker in American Society, 1865–1896* (Englewood Cliffs, N.J.: Prentice-Hall, 1969). For more specific studies and for comparison, see Bruce Laurie, *Working People of Philadelphia, 1800–1850* (Philadelphia: Temple University Press, 1980); John C. Leggett, *Class, Race, and Labor: Working-Class Consciousness in Detroit* (New York: Oxford University Press, 1968); and Harold C. Livesay, *Samuel Gompers and Organized Labor in America* (Boston: Little, Brown, 1978).

9. "The Dallas Typographical Union Was Chartered Oct. 5, 1885 with 442 Members," *Dallas Craftsman*, 1958, Louis H. Hicks Collection, Collection 228, Box 1, Folder 10, LA, UTA.

10. Paul Crume, "Big D," *Dallas Morning News*, 4 September 1962, p. 1.

11. *Memorial and Biographical History of Dallas County*, p. 310; AFL Minutes, Collection 5, Box 11, Folder 2a, LA, UTA; *Dallas City Directory*, 1891–1892, pp. 63–64.

12. "Dallas Stenographers," *Dallas Morning News*, 21 September 1890, p. 8.

13. *Memorial and Biographical History of Dallas County*, p. 310; AFL Minutes, LA, UTA; *Dallas City Directory*, 1891–1892, pp. 63–64.

14. *Memorial and Biographical History of Dallas County*, p. 310.

15. "The Waiters Will Organize," *Dallas Morning News*, 15 October 1890, p. 3.

16. AFL Minutes, LA, UTA.

17. Ibid.

18. Ibid.

19. Ibid.

20. Ibid.

21. "The Labor Convention," *Dallas Morning News*, 5 July 1889, p. 8.

22. Ibid.

23. "Dallas City Council," *Dallas Morning News*, 16 February 1890, p. 11.

24. "Dallas City Council," *Dallas Morning News*, 6 March 1890, p. 8.

25. "Dallas City Council," *Dallas Morning News*, 10 April 1890, p. 4.

26. AFL Minutes, LA, UTA; "Central Labor Demands," *Dallas Morning News*, 30 August 1892, p. 8.

27. AFL Minutes, LA, UTA.

28. Ibid. In April of 1893, Golden reported to the Dallas Trades Assembly that the Texas House had passed a bill making it a misdemeanor for a corporation to discharge an employee because of union membership. The bill was pending before the Senate, and he urged Dallas workers to make some effort to ensure its passage.

29. Ibid.

30. "Street Car Men on Strike," *Dallas Morning News*, 11 November 1898, p. 8. A closed-shop contract requires that all employees be members of the union.

31. Ibid.

32. Ibid.

33. "Status of the Strike," *Dallas Morning News*, 14 November 1898, p. 8.

34. Ibid.

35. "Another Mass Meeting," *Dallas Morning News*, 15 November 1898, p. 8.

36. The Freethinkers maintained a lively discussion group that met regularly on Sunday nights. A typical program included a sermon by a local minister, a review by one of the freethinkers, and then a rejoinder by the pastor. Dr. David MacKay, the city's best-known white Republican, was a prominent member of the Dallas Freethinkers. Although almost exclusively middle-class professionals, Dallas's freethinkers often supported the Populist-Labor coalition and later that of socialists and workers. Populist attorney Jerome Kearby was extremely popular among Dallas's middle and professional classes, who did not react negatively to reports of his immoderate drinking and lack of religious fervor as did Populists in rural counties. See "Dallas Freethinkers," *Dallas Morning News*, 14 February 1898, p. 8, and Roscoe Martin's *The People's Party in Texas*, pp. 59, 118–119. For details regarding meetings at which Paget spoke, see "Strikers' Mass Meeting," *Dallas Morning News*, 18 November 1898, p. 8 and "The Labor Unions of Dallas," *Dallas Morning News*, 21 November 1898, p. 8.

37. See "Status of the Strike," *Dallas Morning News*, 14 November 1898, p. 8, and "Another Mass Meeting," *Dallas Morning News*, 15 November 1898, p. 8.

38. "Another Mass Meeting," *Dallas Morning News*, 20 November 1898, p. 4.

39. "The Labor Unions of Dallas," *Dallas Morning News*, 21 November 1898, p. 8.

40. "Striking Street Car Men," *Dallas Morning News*, 1 December 1898, p. 8.

41. "Street Cars Dynamited," *Dallas Morning News*, 3 December 1898, p. 8.

42. "It's Ancient History Now," *Dallas Morning News*, 7 December 1898, p. 10.

43. Ibid.

44. See for example "Dallas Trades Council," *Dallas Morning News*, 16 January 1899, p. 8.

45. "A Noted Labor Leader," *Dallas Morning News*, 15 May 1899, p. 8.

46. In August of 1892, managers of the State Fair Association still owed members of the musicians union for performances at the 1891 fair. Two months later, the Lone Star Collar Company moved to Rusk, in East Texas, to employ convicts. See AFL Minutes, LA, UTA. In 1893 a contractor imported nonunion stonecutters to end a work stoppage at the Episcopal cathedral. Organized labor's influence in Dallas benefited the strikebreakers, who were offered eight-hour days and received union wages. See "Stonecutters' Strike," *Dallas Morning News*, 21 December 1893, p. 12.

47. "Roster," *Dallas Laborer*, 2 April 1904, p. 8; see editions 15 April, 7 May, and 11 June 1904 for additional unions supporting the *Laborer*; "Labor Temple Rentals," *Dallas Craftsman*, 5 December 1919, p. 3.

48. "Commercial Club Courtesy," *Dallas Laborer*, 15 April 1904, p. 4.

49. "Typographical," *Dallas Laborer*, 11 June 1904, p. 1. See also "The Trades Assembly," *Dallas Laborer*, 14 May 1904, p. 1. and "Victory for the Barbers," *Dallas Laborer*, 18 June 1904, p. 5, for typical socialist reporting of union activities.

50. "The Dallas Typographical Union Was Chartered Oct. 5, 1885 with 442 Members," *Dallas Craftsman*, 1958, Louis H. Hicks Collection. The article is in Hicks's scrapbook. The headline is misleading; the 1885 union consisted of just over 100 members. The 442 figure refers to the membership level in the late 1950s, at the time of the article.

51. Maranto, "A History of Dallas Newspapers," pp. 142–146.

52. "Directory," *Dallas Laborer*, 11 November 1911, p. 3; Dallas AFL-CIO Records, Collection 5, Box 15, Folder 8, LA, UTA.

53. Dallas AFL-CIO Records, LA, UTA.

54. Michael Kazin's analysis of San Francisco unions reveals a similar chronology in which the city's unions, led by the building trades, gained power steadily after 1890. By World War I, the local AFL advocated a reformed version of American capitalism. In San Francisco, as in Dallas, union leaders used Populist-inspired rhetoric to articulate their reform vision. San Francisco's building-trades unions, like those in Dallas, lost power in the early 1920s due to their own racist exclusivity, employer organization, and a rightward shift in national politics. See *Barons of Labor: The San Francisco Building*

Trades and Union Power in the Progressive Era (Urbana: University of Illinois Press, 1987), pp. 4, 170–171.

55. "The Dallas Typographical Union Was Chartered Oct. 5, 1885 with 442 Members," *Dallas Craftsman*, 1958, Louis H. Hicks Collection. The article lists nine father-son combinations among early Dallas union printers. A saying among the typographers emphasized "when a member comes into the union, . . . if his father was a union man, that he had it half made."

56. Dallas Central Labor Council, "Trade Unions: Past, Present, Future," n.d., Fred Webster Miscellaneous Vertical File, T/D, DPL.

57. "300 Carpenters Fail to Report For Work," *Dallas Morning News*, 2 July 1918, p. 3.

58. Ibid.; "All Carpenters Return to Work At More Pay," *Dallas Morning News*, 9 July 1918, p. 4.

59. "Nine Unions Have Voted to Strike," *Dallas Morning News*, 1 June 1919, p. 6.

60. Ibid.; "Arbitration Board Reports on Strike," *Dallas Morning News*, 8 June 1919, p. 2.

61. "Nine Unions Have Voted to Strike," *Dallas Morning News*, 1 June 1919, p. 6.

62. Ibid.

63. "Eleven Unions Are Now Out on Strike," *Dallas Morning News*, 4 June 1919, p. 11.

64. Louise Tilly has noted that in periods of "extraordinary ferment" collective actions are "often a continuation of past politics and an acceleration or increase in scale of old disputes." See Louise A. Tilly and Charles Tilly, eds., *Class Conflict and Collective Action* (Beverly Hills: Sage Publications, 1981), p. 235.

65. Dallas coopers, for example, were working a regular eight-hour day as early as 1904. See "The Trades Assembly," *Dallas Laborer*, 14 May 1904, p. 1. The Dallas Central Labor Council used the typographers' evidence that the eight-hour workday increased workers' life spans in its pamphlet, "Trade Unions: Past, Present, Future."

66. "Police to Stop All Unlawful Assemblies," *Dallas Morning News*, 4 June 1919, p. 8; "Strike Causes Mayor to Depart for Home," *Dallas Morning News*, 3 June 1919, p. 8.

67. "Arbitration Board Reports on Strike," *Dallas Morning News*, 8 June 1919, p. 2.

68. "One Man Killed in Strike Riot," *Dallas Morning News*, 12 June 1919, p. 5; "Eighth Arrest Made as Result of Riot," *Dallas Morning News*, 13 June 1919, p. 4.

69. "One Man Killed in Strike Riot," *Dallas Morning News*, 12 June 1919, p. 5; "Arguments Begin in Shrum's Trial," *Dallas Morning News*, 25 October 1919, p. 8.

70. "Four Strike Cases Set for Trial July 21," *Dallas Morning News*, 26 June

1919, p. 9; "Trial of Union Men Continued Sept. 29," *Dallas Craftsman*, 29 August 1919, p. 1. Despite the fact that the *Dallas Morning News* gave the "strike riot" cases almost constant attention throughout the summer of 1919, I could find no mention of the doctor's crucial testimony except in the labor paper, the *Craftsman*.

71. "Arguments Begin in Shrum's Trial," *Dallas Morning News*, 25 October 1919, p. 8; "Shrum is Convicted of Manslaughter," *Dallas Morning News*, 27 October 1919, p. 16; "Al Shrum Found Guilty of Manslaughter," *Dallas Craftsman*, 31 October 1919, p. 1.

72. "The Strike Lesson," *Dallas Craftsman*, 4 July 1919, p. 1.

73. "Strike Situation Remains Unchanged," *Dallas Craftsman*, 2 June 1919, p. 3.

74. "The Strike Lesson," *Dallas Craftsman*, 4 July 1919, p. 1.

75. "Dallas Typo. Union," *Dallas Craftsman*, 8 August 1919, p. 1; "Dallas Typo. Union Met Last Sunday," *Dallas Craftsman*, 10 October 1919, p. 1.

76. "Royce Is Surprised," and "Rapid Growth of Union," *Dallas Craftsman*, 7 November 1919, p. 3.

77. "Will Aid Galveston," *Dallas Craftsman*, 31 October 1919, p. 3; "A Liberal Contribution," *Dallas Craftsman*, 12 December 1919, p. 3.

78. Co-Operative Store," *Dallas Craftsman*, 14 November 1919, p. 3; "Labor Temple Ball Is Well Patronized," *Dallas Craftsman*, 5 September 1919, p. 1; "Many at Temple Dance," *Dallas Craftsman*, 24 October 1919, p. 2; "Labor Temple Rentals," *Dallas Craftsman*, 5 December 1919, p. 3.

79. "Local Waiters' Union Signs New Wage Scale," *Dallas Craftsman*, 29 August 1919, p. 1; "Waiters Union Prosperous, Says Glauberg," *Dallas Craftsman*, 12 September 1919, p. 1.

80. Many Join Waiters," *Dallas Craftsman*, 24 October 1919, p. 3.

81. "Local Butcher Workers in Splendid Condition," *Dallas Craftsman*, 12 September 1919, p. 1; "Butchers Consider Wages," *Dallas Craftsman*, 31 October 1919, p. 3.

82. "Iron Workers Want New $8 Wage Scale," *Dallas Morning News*, 14 October 1919, p. 15; "Iron Workers Quit," *Dallas Craftsman*, 17 October 1919, p. 1.

83. "Dallas Contractors Peeved at Union Men?" *Dallas Craftsman*, 31 October 1919, p. 1; "Carpenters' New Scale," *Dallas Craftsman*, 14 November 1919, p. 3.

84. "Businessmen Favor 'Open Shop' Policy," *Dallas Morning News*, 19 November 1919, p. 15. Although literacy levels are difficult to determine, charges that Dallas's building-trades unions were led by or under the influence of foreign agitators, bolshevists, or members of the Industrial Workers of the World (IWW) were completely unfounded. The leadership of all Dallas unions (except the segregated black locals) was white and American by birth. Dallas unions resisted all IWW organizing efforts and did not support the city's democratic socialists after 1917.

85. Ibid.; The *Craftsman* blamed daily newspapers subscribing to the Associated Press for printing misleading stories in "a state-wide effort . . . to discredit, if not to totally disrupt labor unions in Texas." The *Craftsman* specifically cited the *Dallas Times Herald*. See "Dallas Contractors Peeved at Union Men?" *Dallas Craftsman*, 31 October 1919, p. 1.

86. Jay Littman Todes, "Organized Employer Opposition to Unionism in Texas, 1900–1930" (Master's thesis, The University of Texas, 1949), pp. 70–71. The Central Labor Council and the Building Trades Council boycotted the State Fair of Texas in 1911 because its directors contracted with Mosher for a cattle-exhibition building. See "Unfair Dallas Fair," *Dallas Laborer*, 15 July 1911, p. 3.

87. "Businessmen Favor 'Open Shop' Policy," *Dallas Morning News*, 19 November 1919, p. 15.

88. "Open Shop Declaration of Chamber of Commerce," *Dallas Craftsman*, 21 November 1919, p. 1.

89. "Central Labor Council," *Dallas Craftsman*, 5 December 1919, p. 3.

90. "Labor Mass Meeting," *Dallas Craftsman*, 21 November 1919. p. 3; letter from Oscar Calvert, *Dallas Craftsman*, 5 December 1919, p. 3.

91. "Painters Demand Increase," *Dallas Craftsman*, 21 November 1919, p. 3.

92. "Printers Quit Work In Seven Dallas Shops," *Dallas Morning News*, 3 May 1921, p. 13.

93. "The Dallas Typographical Union Was Chartered Oct. 5, 1885 with 442 Members," *Dallas Craftsman*, 1958, Louis H. Hicks Collection.

94. Telegram from W. G. Lee to H. H. Jones, 1 August 1922, and letter from Lee to Jones, 15 August 1922, Brotherhood of Railroad Trainmen Cherry Blossom Lodge No. 671, Dallas, Texas, Collection 240, Box 3, Folder 11, LA, UTA.

95. William Z. Foster, "RR Workers Amalgamate!" *Chicago Labor Herald*, November 1922, Brotherhood of Railroad Trainmen Cherry Blossom Lodge No. 671, Dallas, Texas, Collection 240, Box 3, LA, UTA.

96. Elmer Scott, *88 Eventful Years* (Dallas: Civic Federation of Dallas, 1954), pp. 135–136. Dana Frank argues that the decline of Seattle's labor movement in the 1920s was due in large part to low-risk tactics such as cooperatives, boycotts, and union label campaigns that allied union members with middle-class consumers and reformers. See *Purchasing Power: Consumer Organizing, Gender, and the Seattle Labor Movement, 1919–1929* (Cambridge, England: Cambridge University Press, 1994).

CHAPTER 4

1. Quoted in Rogers, *The Lusty Texans of Dallas*, p. 167. As Harold Platt has noted, "Progressivism's blend of uniformity and diversity makes comparative

analysis of individual case studies vital to an understanding of the period." With Dallas businessmen's early interest in structural reform, the late institutionalization of social reforms, and the simultaneous revival of the Ku Klux Klan, Progressivism in Dallas differed substantially from the national model that has the period ending with the United States's entry into World War I. Ironically, the politics of race (and of racists) enhanced the status of the Dallas elite at the expense of the white middle and working classes. See Harold L. Platt, "City-Building and Progressive Reform: The Modernization of an Urban Polity, Houston, 1892–1905," in *The Age of Urban Reform: New Perspectives on the Progressive Era*, edited by Michael H. Ebner and Eugene M. Tobin (Port Washington, N.Y.: Kennikat Press, 1977), p. 28.

2. Acheson, *Dallas Yesterday*, pp. 172–174; E. Scott, *88 Eventful Years*, p. 37. For an interesting biographical profile of another reform mayor, see Michael H. Ebner, "Redefining the Success Ethic for Urban Reform Mayors: Fred R. Low of Passaic, 1908–1909," in *The Age of Urban Reform*.

3. Ruth Hutchinson Crocker's recent study of the settlement movement in two "second-tier" industrial cities indicates that some institutions devoted to social reform blossomed and others remained vital despite a change in emphasis long after the traditional "end" of the Progressive Era. See *Social Work and Social Order: The Settlement Movement in Two Industrial Cities, 1889–1930* (Urbana: University of Illinois Press, 1992). On social welfare and social work during the Progressive Era, see Clark A. Chambers, *Paul U. Kellogg and the Survey: Voices for Social Welfare and Social Justice* (Minneapolis: University of Minnesota Press, 1971); Goldman, *Rendezvous with Destiny*; Richard Hofstadter, *The Age of Reform* (New York: Random House, 1955); Michael B. Katz, *In the Shadow of the Poorhouse: A Social History of Welfare in America* (New York: Basic Books, 1986), *The Irony of Early School Reform* (Cambridge: Harvard University Press, 1968), and *Poverty and Policy in American History* (New York: Academic Press, 1983); Gabriel Kolko, *The Triumph of Conservatism: A Re-Interpretation of American History* (Glencoe, Ill.: The Free Press, 1963); Leiby, *A History of Social Welfare*; Roy Lubove, *The Professional Altruist* (Cambridge: Harvard University Press, 1963); Walter I. Trattner, *From Poor Law to Welfare State: A History of Social Welfare in America* (New York: The Free Press, 1974) and Trattner, ed., *Biographical Dictionary of Social Welfare in America* (Westport, Conn.: Greenwood Press, 1986).

4. See Chapter 1 for an analysis of this important mayoral campaign.

5. See E. Scott, *88 Eventful Years*. Scott's autobiography was written shortly before his death in the 1950s. It is an especially useful account for students of reform in Dallas because it includes membership lists and excerpts from Civic Federation minutes and programs.

6. Carole Sadovnick Cohen, "Elmer Scott and the Civic Federation of Dallas" (Master's thesis, SMU, 1979), pp. 18, 26. Scott's 1908–1909 playgrounds predate those of Elizabeth Williams and Charles Stover in New York

City. See also Larry Cavitt, "History of the Civic Federation of Dallas" (Master's thesis, SMU, 1971).

7. E. Scott, *88 Eventful Years*, p. 30.

8. City of Dallas, "First Annual Report, Department of Welfare, 1915–1916," G. B. Dealey Papers A6667, Box 6, Folder 47, DHS; Brownell, "The Urban South Comes of Age, 1900–1940," pp. 148–149.

9. E. Scott, *88 Eventful Years*, p. 32.

10. Ibid., pp. 35–36. Results of the 1916 study indicate the average annual expenses reported by 50 Dallas families as $1,134.55. The lowest "bare existence" costs for a family of five were determined to be $747.00.

11. Ibid., pp. 32–33.

12. Ibid., pp. 33, 35.

13. Acheson, *Dallas Yesterday*, pp. 174–176.

14. K. D. McCarthy, *Noblesse Oblige*, p. 107.

15. E. Scott, *88 Eventful Years*, pp. 38–39.

16. Chambers, *Paul U. Kellogg and the Survey*, p. 29.

17. E. Scott, *88 Eventful Years*, pp. 38–39.

18. Ibid., p. 39.

19. Quoted Ibid., pp. 42–43, 100. See also Edward Devine, *Misery and Its Causes* (New York: Macmillan, 1909), in which Devine, Scott's mentor and friend, outlines his Progressive vision.

20. E. Scott, *88 Eventful Years*, pp. 55–57.

21. Quoted Ibid., p. 57.

22. Ibid., p. 58.

23. Ibid., pp. 100–101; *American Jewish Year Book*, 1966, vol. 11, p. 608. The following is a partial list of early Civic Federation members and contributors: (1) academics and professionals: Dr. J. H. Black, Dr. Edward H. Cary, Judge Joseph E. Cockrell, Dr. J. W. Embree, Jules Hexter, Dr. (later Bishop) Ivan Lee Holt, Dr. May Agnes Hopkins, Fannie Kahn, Dr. Minnie Maffett, Dr. O. M. Marchman, Alecia Brown Paschall, Harry L. Seay, Carl Weisman, and Frank Wozencraft; (2) prominent women and social workers: Annette Black, Mrs. F. T. Buell, May Dickson Exall, Mrs. Kirk Hall, Mrs. John M. Hanna, Corinne Kelly (later Mrs. Steve Munger), Mrs. M. Liebman, Mrs. S. W. Nichols, Mrs. Florence Rodgers, Nina Scanland, Mrs. George R. Scruggs, Mrs. L. S. Thorne, Mrs. E. P. Turner, and Mrs. Lindsley Waters; (3) merchants and businessmen: G. B. Dealey, Henry Lindsley, Karl Hoblitzelle, E. M. Kahn, Linz Brothers, Frank McNeny, Neiman-Marcus Co., Hugh Prather, Alex and Eli Sanger, G. H. Scholellkopf & Co., Edward Titche, and Titche-Goettinger Co.

24. See Leiby, *A History of Social Welfare*, p. 172.

25. "Negro Actors Exhibit Talent," *Dallas Morning News*, 19 December 1928, sec. I, p. 6; Richard Owen Boyer, "Negro Little Theater Gives Green's 'The No 'Count Boy' With Subtle Appreciation," *Dallas Times Herald*, 20 December 1928, sec. I, p. 8; E. Scott, *88 Eventful Years*, pp. 86–87, 115;

Cohen, "Elmer Scott and the Civic Federation of Dallas," pp. 21–22. The Council of Jewish Women directed one of the few local programs that specifically sought to aid Dallas minorities. The "Penny Lunches" that began in 1913 provided meals for Hispanic school children at the Cumberland Hill School until the early 1920s, when lunchrooms were opened. In 1914, the Council of Jewish Women began supplying fresh milk, food, and clothing to tuberculosis victims, many of whom were black or Hispanic. See Marilynn Wood Hill, "A History of the Jewish Involvement in the Dallas Community," p. 126.

26. E. Scott, *88 Eventful Years*, p. 146.

27. See K. D. McCarthy, *Noblesse Oblige*, p. 169.

28. J. R. Green, *Grass-roots Socialism*, p. 404; see also Kenneth T. Jackson, *The Ku Klux Klan in the City, 1915–1930* (New York: Oxford University Press, 1967).

29. Brownell, "The Urban South Comes of Age," p. 147.

30. Charles Alexander, *The Ku Klux Klan in the Southwest* (Lexington: University of Kentucky Press, 1965), pp. 28, 127.

31. "Reaping the Whirlwind," *Dallas Democrat*, 25 October 1919, p. 1.

32. Rogers, *The Lusty Texans of Dallas*, p. 167.

33. "Dallas KKK [1920s]," A42166, DHS; Alexander, *The Ku Klux Klan in the Southwest*, pp. 79, 96, 193–197; Texas Writers Project, *Dallas Guide and History*, chronology p. 00707.

34. Payne, *Dallas: An Illustrated History*, pp. 166, 169; Alexander, *The Ku Klux Klan in the Southwest*, p. 247.

35. Marilynn Wood Hill, "A History of the Jewish Involvement in the Dallas Community," pp. 52–53.

36. Acheson, *35,000 Days in Texas*, pp. 275–280; Memoir of Alonzo Wasson, 1952, G. B. Dealey Papers, A6667, Box 22, Folder 182, DHS.

37. Correspondence between February and March of 1922, G. B. Dealey Papers, A6667, Box 36, Folder 314, DHS.

38. Letters to Dealey from Jeannette B. Peabody, Nov. and Dec. 1922, G. B. Dealey Papers, A6667, Box 22, Folder 182, DHS; Correspondence 1922–1925, G. B. Dealey Papers, A6667, Box 36, Folders 314-18 and Box 37, Folder 319, DHS.

39. Maranto, "A History of Dallas Newspapers," pp. 165–166; Maranto cites Chester T. Crowell, "Journalism in Texas," *American Mercury* 4 (April 1926):477–478.

40. Information on the MNPPA is taken from "Minutes 3 May 1924–31 Jan. 1925 of Dallas County Farm-Labor Political Conference," Collection 159, LA, UTA.

41. Alexander, *The Ku Klux Klan in the Southwest*, pp. 162, 196–197; Connor, *Texas*, pp. 307, 329–331.

42. Acheson, *35,000 Days in Texas*, pp. 275–280.

43. Allen Safianow, "'Konclave in Kokomo' Revisited," *The Historian* 50

(May 1988):334.

44. Interview with James P. Simpson, Jr., Dallas, Texas, 14 June 1987.

45. Alexander, *The Ku Klux Klan in the Southwest*, pp. 92–94, 222–223.

46. In March, 1931, Klansmen kidnapped socialist attorney George Clifton Edwards and two clients at gunpoint on the steps of city hall. Three members of the district attorney's staff were among the eight kidnappers. Several Dallas police officers also were involved in the incident. See Edwards, *Pioneer-at-Law*, pp. 107–121; "Citizens to Ask Aid of Governor to Catch Kidnappers of Lawyer," *Dallas Morning News*, 7 March 1931, sec. II, p. 1; "Federal and State Probes Asked in Dallas Kidnapping," *Dallas Times Herald*, p. 1. The Edwards kidnapping was typical of Klan terrorism after 1926; the perpetrators were civil servants or clerks. Neither R. L. Thornton, Ben E. Cabell, Sr., the Skillerns, nor the Cullums were themselves associated with the Klan by the end of the decade. However, many major Dallas employers, including Dealey, later admitted that they knew of employees' Klan activities.

47. Black, "Empire of Consensus," pp. 75, 82–83.

48. Ibid., p. 85; Payne, *Dallas: An Illustrated History*, p. 152.

49. City Planning Department, Map of Dallas Texas Showing Street Improvements Recommended by the Ulrickson Committee, 1927, T/D, DPL; Black, "Empire of Consensus," p. 88.

50. Black, "Empire of Consensus," p. 87.

51. Minutes, Opposition Meeting, Corner Hampton Road and Kingston, 5 December 1927, G. B. Dealey Papers, A6667, Box 3, Folder 21, DHS.

52. Ibid.

53. In addition to Ulrickson, committee members included Alex Weisberg, attorney and head of the City Plan Commission; Leslie A. Stemmons, a businessman with interests in steel, oil, and Trinity River land development; realtor Frank McNeny; and H. A. Olmsted, general manager of Southwest Paper Company. See Ulrickson Committee, "Forward Dallas!: Report of the Ulrickson Committee, 1925–1927," UI, DPL (also at DHS); Black, "Empire of Consensus," p. 85.

54. Memorandum from John E. Surratt to Simon Linz, 15 January 1929, G. B. Dealey Papers, A6667, Box 3, Folder 21, DHS.

55. Black, "Empire of Consensus," p. 87.

56. Memorandum from John E. Surratt to G. B. Dealey, 25 January 1929, G. B. Dealey Papers, A6667, Box 3, Folder 21, DHS.

CHAPTER 5

1. Quoted in "The Dallas Way," *Dallas Times Herald*, 15 November 1987, sec. H, p. 16.

2. Key issues that established these patterns before 1930 were the expansion of Fair Park and the fight over the city charter's recall provision in the first

decade of the twentieth century, the debates surrounding increased spending on social services and plans to annex Highland Park in the late 1910s, and the implementation of aspects of Kessler's city plan in the 1920s (especially the decision to remove grade-level railroad crossings from the business district and the passage of a zoning ordinance).

3. In 1906 Dallas had sixty periodicals, most of them newspapers. By 1940, the city had only thirteen newspapers. Edwin J. Kiest (publisher of the *Dallas Times Herald*) established WRR, the state's first radio station, in the early 1920s and purchased KRLD in 1924. The Dealey family, of the rival *Morning News*, began radio station WFAA in 1923. See Maranto, "A History of Dallas Newspapers," p. 159; *Dallas Times Herald*, 28 August 1949, sec. H, p. 7; *Dallas Morning News*, 1 October 1935, sec. 3, p. 12.

4. See Elkin, *City and Regime*, p. 84.

5. Roger Biles, "The New Deal in Dallas," *Southwestern Historical Quarterly* 95 (1991):3.

6. Dealey published articles favoring the council-manager form as early as 1911. See Acheson, *Dallas Yesterday*, pp. 188–189.

7. Brownell, "The Urban South Comes of Age," p. 150.

8. Biles, "The New Deal in Dallas," pp. 3–4. See *Dallas Morning News*, 8 April 1931, sec. I, p. 5, for a history of the charter changes; also see Acheson, *Dallas Yesterday*, p. 189.

9. Acheson, *Dallas Yesterday*, pp. 190–193.

10. Rogers, *The Lusty Texans of Dallas*, pp. 221–223, 382–383.

11. Elkin, *City and Regime*, pp. 63, 69.

12. Figures from *1931–1934 Annual Report of the City of Dallas*, T/D, DPL.

13. Biles, "The New Deal in Dallas," p. 8.

14. Unless otherwise noted, information on the Citizens Charter Association and the Catfish Club is from Acheson, *Dallas Yesterday*, pp. 194–196; Harold Stone et al., *City Manager Government in Dallas* (Chicago: Public Administration Service, 1939), pp. 28–76; articles in the *Dallas Morning News*, 8 and 28 February 1939; and the *Dallas Express*, 1 April 1939.

15. "City Court Licenses Vice, Civics Inform Amen Crowd," *Dallas Morning News*, 30 March 1935, sec. II, p. 1.

16. "City Election Tuesday Next," *Dallas Morning News*, 30 March 1935, sec. II, p. 6; "Civic Ticket Runs Away with Election," *Dallas Morning News*, 3 April 1935, p. 1.

17. Black, "Empire of Consensus," p. 94.

18. Sam Acheson, "City Hall's Hectic Era," *Dallas Morning News*, 24 March 1964, in Mrs. Herbert Gambrell Papers, A6439, DHS.

19. Quoted in Acheson, *Dallas Yesterday*, p. 196.

20. For a discussion of East Texas oil's impact on Dallas, see Biles, "The New Deal in Dallas," pp. 6–7.

21. U.S. Bureau of the Census, *Statistical Abstract of the United States: 1960*

(Washington, D.C.: U.S. Government Printing Office, 1960), p. 18.

22. Acheson, *Dallas Yesterday*, pp. 193–194; Other accounts give $9 million as the total Dallas bid; $2.5 million in bond money, and over $1 million to be raised from local businessmen. See Dillon, *Dallas Architecture*, p. 12.

23. "The Dallas Way," *Dallas Times Herald*, 15 November 1987, sec. H, p. 16.

24. Dillon, *Dallas Architecture*, p. 12.

25. Gonzalez, *P. P. Martinez*, p. 80; Acheson, *35,000 Days in Texas*, pp. 300–303; Joel H. Bernstein, "The Artist and the Government: The P.W.A.P.," in *Challenges in American Culture*, edited by Ray B. Browne, Larry N. Landrum, and William K. Bottorff (Bowling Green, Ohio: Bowling Green University Popular Press, 1970), p. 73. See also Kenneth B. Ragsdale, *The Year America Discovered Texas: Centennial '36* (College Station: Texas A&M University Press, 1988). Nancy Wiley's *The Great State Fair of Texas* (Dallas: Taylor Publishing Co., 1985) is a largely uncritical look at the Dallas institution but includes a chapter on the Centennial Exposition and many color reproductions of fair memorabilia.

26. Dillon, *Dallas Architecture*, p. 11; "Visitors and Citizens Surge Along Streets in Gigantic Welcome," *Dallas Dispatch*, 12 June 1936, p. 1.

27. Dillon, *Dallas Architecture*, p. 24

28. "Dallas" and "Facts and Figures" in introductory section of *Dallas City Directory*, 1936.

29. John R. Logan and Harvey L. Molotch discuss the roles growth-oriented elites play in the acquisition and management of fairs and expositions, as well as the tendency of these events to lose money, in *Urban Fortunes: The Political Economy of Place* (Berkeley: University of California Press, 1987), pp. 78–79.

30. "Buildings at Centennial to be Nice Turkish Baths," *Dallas Dispatch*, 24 July 1935, p. 1.

31. "Henry Kucera: An Oral History Interview Conducted by Gerald Saxon on June 11, 1981," (ETSU and DPL, typewritten transcript, 1983), p. 14.

32. "No Excuse to Kill Centennial," *Dallas Dispatch*, 2 November 1934, p. 1.

33. "Centennial Labor Dispute Before Board of Control," no citation on clipping, Wallace C. Reilly Papers and Memorabilia, Collection 115, LA, UTA; I also thank Sarah Hunter of the DHS, who has prepared a chronology of the Centennial Exposition, for details concerning labor disputes.

34. Dillon, *Dallas Architecture*, p. 16.

35. "Fort Worth Celebration," *Dallas Dispatch*, 24 July 1935, p. 1.

36. J. Frank Dobie, "Minority Report of the Advisory Board of Texas Historians to the Commission of Control for Texas Centennial Celebrations," 1 October 1935, Herbert Gambrell Papers, A42207, DHS; letter of 7 October 1935 from L. W. Kemp, Chairman of the Advisory Board of Texas Historians and co-author of the majority report to the Commission of

Control, Virginia Leddy Papers, A42122, DHS.

37. "To President Roosevelt," *Dallas Dispatch*, 12 June 1936, p. 1.

38. Quoted in "The Dallas Way," *Dallas Times Herald*, 15 November 1987, sec. H, p. 16.

39. "Dallas Is Last to See the Fair," *Southwest Business*, October 1936, p. 13.

40. "Visitors and Citizens Surge Along Streets in Gigantic Welcome," *Dallas Dispatch*, 12 June 1936, p. 1.

41. For a brief biography of Thornton, see Carol Estes Thometz, *The Decision-Makers: The Power Structure of Dallas* (Dallas: Southern Methodist University Press, 1963), pp. 87–88.

42. "The Dallas Way," *Dallas Times Herald*, 15 November 1987, sec. H, p. 16.

43. Ibid.

44. As of 1987, the Dallas Citizens Council was still limited to company presidents and CEOs and membership rolls were not available to the public. See "Quietly Influential Citizens Council Marks 50th Year," *Dallas Times Herald*, 8 February 1987, sec. B, p. 1.

45. Mason interview with Robert Cullum, p. 16.

46. The Citizens Council does not make its membership rolls public. In 1981, Comer Cottrell, a businessman from Los Angeles, became the first black to join the group. See Jim Schutze, *The Accommodation: The Politics of Race in an American City* (Secaucus, N.J.: The Citadel Press, 1986), p. 175.

47. A. C. Greene, "Power and Politics," in *The Book of Dallas*, edited by Evelyn Oppenheimer and Bill Porterfield (Garden City, N.Y.: Doubleday, 1976), pp. 241, 246.

48. The same was true in Houston. See Logan and Molotch, *Urban Fortunes*, p. 84.

49. Acheson, *Dallas Yesterday*, pp. 194–195.

50. "Wallace Savage: An Oral History Interview Conducted by Alan Mason on September 18, 1980," (ETSU and DPL, typewritten transcript, 1983), pp. 23–24.

51. "R. L. Thornton, Jr.: An Oral History Interview Conducted by Alan Mason on November 8, 1980" (ETSU and DPL, typewritten transcript, 1983), pp. 17–18.

52. Elkin, *City and Regime*, p. 85.

53. See for example, *Dallas Morning News*, 8 February 1939.

54. See Logan and Molotch, *Urban Fortunes*, p. 36.

55. See Thometz, *The Decision-Makers*, p. 93.

56. Mason interview with Lynn Lawther, p. 11; Mason interview with Robert Cullum, pp. 8–10, 22–23. See also "Robert S. Folsom: An Oral History Interview Conducted by Alan Mason on February 20, 1981" (ETSU and DPL, typewritten transcript, 1983), pp. 16–17.

57. A contemporary Dallas business leader made a similar remark about the city's ballet company. See "Alive and Kicking," *Dallas Observer*, 9 April 1987,

and "Letters," *Dallas Observer*, 23 April 1987. See Lee Cullum, "Radiant Music at the Meyerson—Apotheosis on Flora St.," *Dallas Times Herald*, 17 September 1989, sec. A, p. 22, for a recent retelling of the Thornton–symphony anecdote.

58. E. Scott, *88 Eventful Years*, p. 98; see also p. 68 for another example of Dallas business leaders' parochialism.

CHAPTER 6

1. Quoted in "Ford's Thugs Beat Up Workers," *Southern News Almanac*, 7 March 1940.

2. *Dallas City Directory*, 1934–1935, preface.

3. "Final Day of Labor Meeting Almost Quiet," *Dallas Dispatch*, p. 2; Oral History 3, Interview with Carmen Lucia, conducted by Dr. Howard Lackman and Dr. George Green, 22 November 1967, p. 33, LA, UTA.

4. Heloise M. Foreman, "Negro Life in Dallas," for Texas Writers Project City Guide, 1937 (typewritten), p. 2, T/D, DPL.

5. "Police Prevent Fight as C.I.O. Workers Talk," Clipping from a Dallas newspaper dated 6 March 1935, ILGWU Records, 1935–1970, Collection 167, LA, UTA.

6. "Hearing No. 1 Before the Industrial Commission of Texas, Garment Industry in Dallas Co., July–Aug. 1935," p. 28, George and Latane Lambert Papers, Collection 127, Box 11, LA, UTA.

7. Oral History 3, Interview with Carmen Lucia, pp. 32–33.

8. "Hearing No. 1," p. 104, George and Latane Lambert Papers.

9. See Barbara Welter, "The Cult of True Womanhood: 1820–1860," in *The American Family in Social-Historical Perspective*, edited by Michael Gordon, 3d ed. (New York: St. Martin's Press, 1983), pp. 372–392.

10. See *Dallas City Directory*, 1934–1935, p. 2075; *Dallas City Directory*, 1936, p. 1886.

11. "Hearing No. 1," pp. 88–89, George and Latane Lambert Papers; *Decisions and Orders of the National Labor Relations Board*, vol. 26, 1940 (Washington, D.C.: U.S. Government Printing Office, 1942), p. 382; hereafter cited as *NLRB Decisions*.

12. For an account of the racially motivated bombings of the 1950s, see Schutze, *The Accommodation*.

13. Black, "Empire of Consensus," p. 286. See also Ira Katznelson's *City Trenches: Urban Politics and the Patterning of Class in the United States* (Chicago: University of Chicago Press, 1981).

14. Maranto, "A History of Dallas Newspapers," p. 159. Edwin J. Kiest of the *Times Herald* and the Dealey family of the *Morning News* also owned the local radio stations. Both Kiest and the Dealeys were members of the Citizens Charter Association and the Dallas Citizens Council.

15. "Hearing No. 1," pp. 86–87, 359, George and Latane Lambert Papers; Oral History 43, Interview with Charlotte Graham, conducted by Patsy Putnam, 1973, p. 4, LA, UTA.

16. ILGWU *Report and Record* for 1968, p. 39, ILGWU Records, Collection 167, LA, UTA.

17. "Hearing No. 1," pp. 7, 90–91, 107, 319, George and Latane Lambert Papers; ILGWU *Report and Record* for 1937, p. 92, ILGWU Records, Collection 167, LA, UTA.

18. "Portion of Dress Company Workers Go Out On Strike," *Dallas Morning News*, 8 February 1935, p. 11.

19. See, for example, "More Strikes," *Dallas Evening Journal*, 15 February 1935, p. 6.

20. Quoted in Maureen Osburn, "Strikes Mean Depression's End, Educator Says," *Dallas Morning News*, 31 March 1935, sec. II, p. 1.

21. "Injunction, Fights Mark Beginning of Dress Plant Strike," *Dallas Morning News*, 8 March 1935, sec. II, p. 1.

22. Quoted ibid.

23. "Hearing No. 1," p. 319, George and Latane Lambert Papers. Although the *News* frequently described Perlstein as a Russian-born Jew, the paper did not report his long history of anticommunism until September of 1935, a full seven months after the strike began. See "Strike Leader Takes Stand in Contempt Case," *Dallas Morning News*, 19 September 1935, sec. II, p. 1.

24. "Garment Workers' Pickets and Cops Clash at Factory," *Dallas Morning News*, 13 February 1935, sec. II, p. 1.

25. "Injunctions, Fights Mark Beginning of Dress Plant Strike," *Dallas Morning News*, 8 March 1935, sec. II, p. 1.

26. "Do You Want Their Jobs?" *Dallas Evening Journal*, 11 March 1935, p. 4.

27. Ibid.; "Won't Let Them Fight," *Dallas Evening Journal*, 30 March 1935, p. 10.

28. "Not Dandruff Cases but Strike," *Dallas Morning News*, 10 March 1935, sec. II, p. 1.

29. Quoted in "Police Are Remaining Neutral in Strikers' Difficulty, Chief Says," *Dallas Evening Journal*, 9 March 1935, p. 3.

30. "Hearing No. 1," pp. 20, 28, 92–93, George and Latane Lambert Papers.

31. Ibid., pp. 27–28, 94, 237–238, 361; Oral History 43, Interview with Charlotte Graham, pp. 3–4.

32. "28 Women Jailed After Strike Fight . . . ," *Dallas Morning News*, 3 April 1935, sec. II, p. 1; "Workers of Dress Concern Attacked at Hotel by Trio," *Dallas Morning News*, 2 April 1935, sec. II, p. 1.

33. Before the strike actually began, an occasional article discussed the garment workers' grievances. Usually these were quite brief. See "Issues

Confused in Dress Factory Spat, Claim Union Leaders," *Dallas Times Herald*, 1 January 1935, ILGWU Records, Collection 167, LA, UTA. Issue-oriented reporting disappeared altogether after the initial strike riots in February 1935.

34. For a typical reference to union organizers, see "The Peaceableness of It," *Dallas Evening Journal*, 9 March 1935, p. 8.

35. "Hearing No. 1," p. 99, George and Latane Lambert Papers.

36. Ibid., pp. 231–238.

37. "Strikers' Side," *Dallas Morning News*, 16 October 1935, sec. II, p. 6.

38. "Hearing No. 1," pp. 108, 333; Quoted in "Strikers Streak," 27 March 1935, ILGWU Records, Collection 167, LA, UTA.

39. Of the 86 women arrested during the strike (whose names appeared in the *Dallas Morning News*), 46.5 percent either used Mrs. before their names in the 1934–1935 *Dallas City Directory* or were listed as living with their husbands.

40. See "Strikers Streak," 27 March 1935, ILGWU Records.

41. "Hearing No. 1," pp. 62, 74–75, George and Latane Lambert Papers.

42. Ibid., pp. 203, 257, 287–289.

43. Quoted ibid., pp. 302–303.

44. Ibid., pp. 199, 221–222.

45. See "City's Unions Unite to Support Walkout of Garment Workers," *Dallas Morning News*, 23 September 1935, sec. II, p. 1.

46. "Strikers Strip Ten Women on Dallas Streets," *Dallas Morning News*, 8 August 1935, sec. I, p. 1; "Women Stripped on Street in Strike Riot," *Dallas Evening Journal*, 7 August 1935, p. 1.

47. See "Dress Makers' War," *Dallas Evening Journal*, 8 August 1935, ILGWU Records, Collection 167, LA, UTA.

48. "Strippers of Women Fined $25 and Sent to Jail for Three Days," *Dallas Morning News*, 14 August 1935, p. 1; "Strippers Freed After Apologizing to Court," *Dallas Morning News*, 15 August 1935, sec. II, p. 1.

49. "More Contempt Sentences," *Dallas Evening Journal*, 17 August 1935, p. 8.

50. "Argument by Assault," *Dallas Evening Journal*, 8 August 1935, p. 8; "Investigation," *Dallas Evening Journal*, 14 August 1935, p. 6.

51. "Labor Unions Call Session to Plan Course on Strike," *Dallas Morning News*, 22 September 1935, sec. II, p. 1.

52. "Hearing No. 1," pp. 25, 261–263, George and Latane Lambert Papers.

53. "Strike Leader Takes Stand In Contempt Case," *Dallas Morning News*, 19 September 1935, sec. II, p. 1.

54. "Investigation," *Dallas Evening Journal*, 14 August 1935, p. 6.

55. According to Robert P. Ingalls, the shaming rituals of the American South date back to pre-Christian Europe; see *Urban Vigilantes in the New South: Tampa, 1882–1936* (Knoxville: University of Tennessee Press, 1988), p. 184.

56. Tilly and Tilly, eds., *Class Conflict and Collective Action*, p. 19.

57. "Two Strikers Fined in City Court Trials," *Dallas Morning News*, 28 September 1935, sec. II, p. 1.

58. Oral History 43, Interview with Charlotte Graham, pp. 20–21.

59. Ibid., p. 15; "Italian Publication's Sketch of Stripping in Dallas Dress Strike," *Dallas Morning News*, 10 September 1935, sec. II, p. 1; "Dallas Stripping Topic of Interest to Australians," *Dallas Morning News*, 13 September 1935, sec. II, p. 1; "Memphis Girls Are Stripped to Waist in Strike," *Dallas Morning News*, 15 October 1935, p. 11.

60. Interview with Lula Maude French, Garland, Texas, 21 October 1987; Interviews with Mrs. Franklyn Runyon, Dallas, Texas, 30 September and 4 November 1987.

61. "President's Aid Asked in Local Strike Case," *Dallas Morning News*, 2 October 1935, p. 3; "Will Stop Strike If Pastors Find No Reason for It," *Dallas Morning News*, 9 October 1935, sec. II, p. 1.

62. ILGWU *Report and Record* for 1937, p. 93.

63. Ibid., pp. 93–94.

64. Oral History 1, Interview with Carl Brannin, pp. 8–10, 13–14; Darwin Payne, ed., *Dissenting Opinion: Carl Brannin's Letters to the Editor, 1933–1976* (Austin: American Civil Liberties Foundation of Texas, 1977), pp. 6–7. For additional biographical information on Brannin, see Darwin Payne, "Carl Brannin: Forever the Activist," *Dallas Times Herald Sunday Magazine*, 22 August 1976.

65. DeFord, *On Being Concerned*, p. 30; Oral History 1, Interview with Carl Brannin, pp. 7, 10–11.

66. Oral History 1, Interview with Carl Brannin, pp. 5–7; DeFord, *On Being Concerned*, pp. 29–30.

67. J. R. Green, *Grass-roots Socialism*, p. 414; Armstrong, "City of Dallas Mayors and City Councils," unpaginated; Oral History 1, Interview with Carl Brannin, pp. 11–12, 18, 20–23; Oral History 39, Interview with Carl Brannin, pp. 4, 16.

68. Oral History 19, Interview with George Lambert, pp. 22–24.

69. Armstrong, "City of Dallas Mayors and City Councils," unpaginated; Oral History 1, Interview with Carl Brannin, pp. 14–17; Larry Grove, "Ex-Socialist: No New Panaceas since New Deal," *Dallas Times Herald*, 17 March 1976, sec. F, p. 2.

70. For information on Ford's policies and relationships with labor in Detroit, see Ely Chinoy, *Automobile Workers and the American Dream* (Garden City, N.Y.: Doubleday, 1955); Richard Feldman and Michael Betzold, eds., *End of the Line: Autoworkers and the American Dream* (New York: Weidenfeld & Nicolson, 1988); Leggett, *Class, Race, and Labor;* and Paul Weaver, *The Suicidal Corporation* (New York: Simon & Schuster, 1988). Joyce Shaw Peterson examines conditions in the industry before unionization in *American Automobile Workers, 1900–1933* (Albany: State University of New

York Press, 1987).

71. *NLRB Decisions*, pp. 330–332. The NLRB presented its case against Ford in 1940 after several key participants in the effort to keep the CIO out of the Dallas plant were fired and agreed to cooperate with NLRB investigators. The sequence of events is explained in the text below.

72. Ibid., pp. 332, 335–339.

73. Ibid., pp. 339–340.

74. UAW Local 870 Twentieth Anniversary Banquet Program, in Ford Motor Co. Dallas Plant Memorabilia, Collection 89, Box 1, Folder 4, LA, UTA.

75. *NLRB Decisions*, pp. 340–341.

76. Ibid., pp. 343–344.

77. "The Case Against Ford's" [*sic*], *Friday*, 3 May 1940, pp. 11–13.

78. *NLRB Decisions*, p. 348.

79. Ibid., pp. 349–353.

80. Ibid., pp. 353–362.

81. Ibid., pp. 360–361, 370.

82. Ibid., pp. 362–363.

83. Oral History 10, Interview with Wallace Reilly, conducted by Dr. George Green, 1971, pp. 41–42, LA, UTA.

84. Oral History 19, Interview with George Lambert, pt. 2, pp. 8–9; Oral History 34, Interview with Carl Brannin, p. 54.

85. Oral History 3, Interview with Carmen Lucia, pp. 27–30, 40–41, 44; *NLRB Decisions*, pp. 363–365.

86. *NLRB Decisions*, pp. 364–367; Oral History 19, Interview with George Lambert, pt. 2, pp. 1–4; Cochran, *Dallas County*, p. 130; Herbert Harris, "Terror in Texas," pp. 1–4, pamphlet in Ford Motor Co. Dallas Plant Memorabilia, Collection 89, Box 1, Folder 8, LA, UTA.

87. The photograph of Harris appeared in the *Dallas Morning News*, 10 August 1937. See also *NLRB Decisions*, pp. 364–367; Harris, "Terror in Texas," pp. 8, 17; "Transcript of Testimony," NLRB *v.* Ford Motor Co., 1940, pp. 1008, 1015–1016, Ford Motor Co. Dallas Plant Memorabilia, Collection 89, LA, UTA.

88. Harris, "Terror in Texas," pp. 10–11.

89. Brannin quotes Allred in a letter to George Lambert, 26 September 1937, George and Latane Lambert Papers, Collection 127, Box 6, Folder 2, LA, UTA.

90. Harris, "Terror in Texas," pp. 9, 12–13; Reward Poster, Ford Motor Co. Dallas Plant Memorabilia, Collection 89, Box 1, Folder 4, LA, UTA.

91. "City Warned Against New Violence Here," *Dallas Times Herald*, 10 September 1937, sec. I, p. 12; "Socialist Leader Raps Dallas' Labor Policy," *Dallas Times Herald*, 9 September 1937, sec. II, p. 8.

92. See Ingalls, *Urban Vigilantes*, especially p. 214, for a comparison. See also Logan and Molotch, *Urban Fortunes*, p. 35, for a discussion of the use of police powers by elites.

93. Harris, "Terror in Texas," pp. 13–14, 22.

94. *NLRB Decisions*, pp. 367–370; Oral History 19, Interview with George Lambert, pt. 2, pp. 11, 15.

95. *NLRB Decisions*, pp. 373–377.

96. Ibid., p. 377.

97. Walter C. Hornaday, "All Rules of Evidence Are Cast Overboard . . ." *Dallas Morning News*, 10 March 1940, p. 1; Oral History 1, Interview with Carl Brannin, p. 31; Clippings, Ford Motor Co. Dallas Plant Memorabilia, Collection 89, Box 1, LA, UTA.

98. Oral History 52, Interview with Dr. Edwin Elliot, conducted by Dr. George Green, 7 April 1975, p. 59, LA, UTA; Oral History 1, Interview with Carl Brannin, pp. 31–32.

99. *NLRB Decisions*, p. 384; Interview with James P. Simpson, Jr., Dallas, Texas, 14 June 1987.

100. *NLRB Decisions*, pp. 392–393; Christi Harlan, "Dallas Civic Leader Led Puzzling Double Life," *Dallas Morning News*, 20 March 1983, sec. A, p. 29.

101. See clippings in John McKee's biographical file, T/D, DPL. See also Richard Pruitt, "John McKee: Man in a Glass Booth," *Dallas Morning News Scene Magazine*, 20 March 1977.

102. Dallas Cotton Mill Timebook, 1938, Collection 201, LA, UTA.

103. U.S. Bureau of the Census, *United States Census of Population: 1940*, vol. 3, *The Labor Force*, pt. 1, United States Summary (Washington, D.C.: U.S. Government Printing Office, 1943), pp. 150–155; *U.S. Census: 1940*, vol. 3, pt. 5, Pennsylvania–Wyoming, pp. 528–533.

104. Oral History 3, Interview with Carmen Lucia, pp. 30–31, 47–48.

105. George Lambert to Zilla (an associate with the Textile Workers of America), 30 May 1939, George and Latane Lambert Papers, Collection 127, LA, UTA.

106. An 8 September 1939 letter to Latane Lambert from a friend in North Carolina indicates that Lambert has confided her interest in the Communist Party to another friend. See George and Latane Lambert Papers, Collection 127, LA, UTA.

107. See "Longtime Labor Leader George Lambert Dies," *Dallas Craftsman*, 23 August 1974, p. 1.

108. See clippings and letters of congratulations to be read at testimonial dinner, Wallace C. Reilly Papers and Memorabilia, Collection 115, LA, UTA.

109. John Forsythe, "The Effect of Federal Labor Legislation on Organizing Southern Labor During the New Deal Period," (Master's thesis, NTSU, n.d.), pp. 147–148, Ford Motor Co. Dallas Plant Memorabilia, Collection 89, Box 1, Folder 1, LA, UTA.

EPILOGUE

1. See Elkin, *City and Regime*, p. 70.

2. Ibid., 66; see also *Dallas Morning News*, 6 April 1943.

3. U.S. Bureau of the Census, *Statistical Abstract of the United States: 1960* (Washington, D.C.: U.S. Government Printing Office, 1960), p. 18; *Statistical Abstract of the United States: 1970* (Washington, D.C.: U.S. Government Printing Office, 1970), p. 20; *Statistical Abstract of the United States: 1988* (Washington, D.C.: U.S. Government Printing Office, 1987), p. 32; *1990 Census Snapshot for all U.S. Places* (Milpitas, Calif.: Toucan Valley Publications, 1992).

4. Maranto, "A History of Dallas Newspapers," pp. 172–177; see also editorials in the *Dallas Morning News*, 3 April 1947, and *Dallas Times Herald*, 11 April 1947.

5. Edwin L. Caldwell, "Highlights of the Development of Manufacturing in Texas, 1900–1960," *Southwestern Historical Quarterly* 68 (April 1965):418–419.

6. Ibid., pp. 419–420; "North America Comes to Dallas," *Southwest Business*, October 1940, p. 9.

7. Caldwell, "Manufacturing in Texas," p. 419.

8. Martin V. Melosi, "Dallas–Fort Worth: Marketing the Metroplex," in *Sunbelt Cities: Politics and Growth Since World War II*, edited by Richard M. Bernard and Bradley R. Rice (Austin: University of Texas Press, 1983), p. 164.

9. Typescript biography in George and Latane Lambert Papers, Collection 127, Box 21, Folder 1, LA, UTA.

10. See for example Feagin, *Free Enterprise City*; Robert Fisher, "'Where Seldom Is Heard a Discouraging Word': The Political Economy of Houston, Texas," *Amerikastudien* 33 (1988):73–92; Roger W. Lotchin, *Fortress California 1910–1961: From Warfare to Welfare* (New York: Oxford University Press, 1992); and Bradford Luckingham, *The Urban Southwest: A Profile History of Albuquerque, El Paso, Phoenix, Tucson* (El Paso: Texas Western Press, 1982).

11. Schutze, *The Accommodation*, p. 184.

12. See *Dallas Craftsman*, 3 April 1953; Armstrong, "City of Dallas Mayors and City Councils," unpaginated.

13. "George Allen: An Oral History Interview Conducted by Gerald Saxon on March 13, 1981," (ETSU and DPL, typewritten transcript, 1983), pp. 5, 8, 11, 15–16, 31, 38.

14. Mason interview with Wallace Savage, p. 6.

15. U.S. Bureau of the Census, *Statistical Abstract of the United States: 1913* (Washington, D.C.: U.S. Government Printing Office, 1914), p. 54; *Statistical Abstract of the United States: 1930* (Washington, D.C.: U.S. Government Printing Office, 1930), p. 23; *Statistical Abstract of the United States: 1950* (Washington, D.C.: U.S. Government Printing Office, 1950), p. 55; *Statistical Abstract of the United States: 1970* (Washington, D.C.: U.S. Government Printing Office, 1970), p. 20; *Statistical Abstract of the United States: 1988* (Washington, D.C.: U.S. Government Printing Office, 1987), p.

32; *United States Census of Population: 1950*, vol. 2, *Characteristics of the Population*, pt. 43, Texas (Washington, D.C.: U.S. Government Printing Office, 1952), p. 55; *1990 Census Snapshot for all U.S. Places.* Much work remains to be done on Dallas's African American and Latino populations. One interesting approach would be a study of when and how each group became political "players"—when either through force of numbers, mobilized voters, leadership, or grassroots activity, the city's historically minority populations could no longer be repressed, accommodated, or ignored. For a beginning, see Roy H. Williams and Kevin J. Shay, *Time Change: An Alternative View of the History of Dallas* (Dallas: To Be Pub. Co., 1991).

16. Jim Schutze, "The Accommodation," *D Magazine*, March 1987, p. 129.

17. Ibid., p. 95; see also Schutze's book by the same title (cited above).

18. For more information on the firebombing of black-owned homes in the early 1950s, see Tom Boone and Richard R. Aguirre, "Integrated Dallas Still a Dream," *Dallas Times Herald*, 3 April 1988, sec. A, p. 1.

19. Melosi, "Marketing the Metroplex," p. 179; see also A. C. Greene, "Power and Politics," pp. 246–248.

20. On Goals for Dallas, see "Erik Jonsson: An Oral History Interview Conducted by Alan Mason on June 26, 1980," (ETSU and DPL, typewritten transcript, 1983), p. 5; *Summaries of the Proposals for Achieving the Goals for Dallas* (Dallas, 1969), pp. v, A-1, A-5; Lester T. Potter, *Glitter, Glitter* (Dallas: Lester T. Potter, 1975), and Mason interview with Robert Cullum, pp. 31–33.

21. See "Evelyn Dunsavage: An Oral History Interview Conducted by Alan Mason on May 25, 1981," (ETSU and DPL, typewritten transcript, 1983).

22. Jim Henderson, "Democracy in Dallas," *Dallas Times Herald*, 23 August 1987, sec. K, p. 1.

23. Melosi, "Marketing the Metroplex," pp. 186–187; Logan and Molotch, *Urban Fortunes*, p. 224.

24. Greene, "Power and Politics," p. 249.

25. Mason interview with Robert Folsom, p. 25.

26. See Logan and Molotch, *Urban Fortunes*, p. 203.

27. See "Max Goldblatt: An Oral History Conducted by Gerald Saxon on July 30, 1981," (ETSU and DPL, typewritten transcript, 1983); Schutze, *The Accommodation*, pp. 173–174.

28. Elkin, *City and Regime*, p. 62.

29. "The Dallas Way," *Dallas Times Herald*, 15 November 1987, sec. H, p. 17.

30. Sam Howe Verhovek, "Dallas in Historic Vote, Elects a Black to Be Mayor; Coalition of Blacks and Wealthy Whites," *New York Times*, 8 May 1995; City of Dallas, *The Dallas Plan* (Dallas: Dallas City Plan, Inc., 1994).

SELECTED BIBLIOGRAPHY

ARCHIVAL SOURCES AND MANUSCRIPT COLLECTIONS

Dallas Historical Society

Carl P. Brannin Papers, A6268.
"Dallas KKK" Roster (ca. 1922), A42166.
G. B. Dealey Papers, A6667.
Herbert Gambrell Papers, A42207.
Mrs. Herbert Gambrell Papers, A6439.
Virginia Leddy Papers, A42122.

Dallas Public Library—Texas/Dallas History and Archives Division

1931–1934 Annual Report of the City of Dallas.
Armstrong, W. Lee. "City of Dallas Mayors and City Councils, 1856–1963." Unpaginated and typewritten, 1962.
Clippings Files, Biography—Carl Brannin.
Clippings Files, Subject—East Dallas.
Clippings Files, Biography—John McKee.
Clippings Files, Subject—Riots.
Dallas City Directories, 1891–1892, 1906, 1925, 1934–1935, 1936.
Dallas Mayors Oral History Project. Sponsored Jointly by East Texas State University and the Dallas Public Library. Typewritten transcripts of interviews with: George Allen, 1981; Robert Cullum, 1981; Evelyn Dunsavage, 1981; Robert S. Folsom, 1981; Max Goldblatt, 1981; Erik Jonsson, 1980; Henry Kucera, 1981; Lynn Lawther, 1981; Wallace Savage, 1980; R. L. Thornton, Jr., 1980; Mrs. Frank W. Wozencraft and Frank M. Wozencraft, Sr., 1980.
Foreman, Heloise M. "Negro Life in Dallas." Typescript, written in conjunction with Texas Writers Project City Guide, 1937.
Head, Louis P. *The Kessler City Plan for Dallas.* Reprinted articles from the *Dallas Morning News,* 1924–1925.
Mabry, Steve. "History of the City of East Dallas." Typescript of Texas Historical Marker Application.

Map of Dallas Showing Street Improvements Recommended by the Ulrickson Committee, 1927.

"Mayor's Message and Annual Reports of City Officers of the City of Dallas, Texas," 1889.

Murphy and Bolanz' Index Map of Greater Dallas, 1911.

"Ordinances and Resolutions of the Council of the City of Dallas from October 1, 1886 to June 25, 1888."

Sanborn Insurance Maps of Dallas, Texas.

Sam Street's Map of Dallas County, Texas, 1900.

Fred Webster Miscellaneous Vertical File.

Urban Information

Dallas Master Plan Committee. *A Look at Past Planning for the City of Dallas*, 1956.

Department of Urban Planning, City of Dallas. *Comprehensive Land Use Policy Plan for Dallas*, 1976.

Kessler, George E. *A City Plan for Dallas*, 1911.

Fikes Hall of Special Collections and DeGolyer Library, Southern Methodist University

MSS 16, "A Guide to the Collection of Earle Cabell," 1983.

Labor Archives, University of Texas at Arlington Library

Collection 5, Dallas AFL-CIO Records.

Collection 82, Texas Civil Liberties Union, Dallas.

Collection 89, Ford Motor Co. Dallas Plant Memorabilia.

Collection 115, Wallace C. Reilly Papers and Memorabilia.

Collection 127, George and Latane Lambert Papers.

Collection 134, Charles MacGibson's Chronology, "Organized Labor in Texas From 1890 to 1900."

Collection 159, Minutes of the Dallas County Farm-Labor Political Conference.

Collection 167, ILGWU Records, 1935–1970.

Collection 201, Dallas Cotton Mill Timebook, 1938.

Collection 228, Louis H. Hicks Collection.

Collection 240, Brotherhood of Railroad Trainmen, Cherry Blossom Lodge No. 671, Dallas, Texas.

Oral Histories 1, 34, and 39, Interviews with Carl Brannin, 1967, 1973.

Oral History 3, Interview with Carmen Lucia, 1967.

Oral History 10, Interview with Wallace Reilly, 1971.

Oral History 19, Interview with George Lambert, 2 pts., 1971, 1972.

Oral History 43, Interview with Charlotte Graham, 1973.

Oral History 52, Interview with Dr. Edwin Elliott, 1975.

OTHER PRIMARY SOURCES

Films

Dallas at the Crossroads. Commissioned by the Dallas Citizens Council, 1961.

Government Documents

Decisions and Orders of the National Labor Relations Board, vol. 26. Washington, D.C.: U.S. Government Printing Office, 1942.
U.S. Bureau of the Census. *United States Census of Population: 1870.* Vol. 1. Washington, D.C.: U.S. Government Printing Office, 1872.
———. *United States Census of Population: 1880.* Vol. 2, *Statistics of Cities.* Washington, D.C.: U.S. Government Printing Office, 1887.
———. *United States Census of Population: 1940.* Vol. 3, *The Labor Force*, pt. 1, United States Summary and pt. 5, Pennsylvania-Wyoming. Washington, D.C.: U.S. Government Printing Office, 1943.
———. *United States Census of Population: 1950.* Vol. 2, *Characteristics of the Population*, pt. 43, Texas. Washington, D.C.: U.S. Government Printing Office, 1952.
———. *Statistical Abstracts of the United States.* Vols. for 1913, 1930, 1950, 1960, 1970, 1988. Washington, D.C.: U.S. Government Printing Office.
———. *Statistical View of the United States: A Compendium of the Seventh Census* (1850). Washington, D.C.: A. O. P. Nicholson, 1854.

Interviews by the Author

French, Lula Maude. Garland, Texas, 21 October 1987.
Runyon, Mrs. Franklyn. Dallas, 30 September and 4 November 1987.
Simpson, James P., Jr. Dallas, 14 June 1987.

Newspapers

Chicago Labor Herald.
Dallas Craftsman.
Dallas Democrat.
Dallas Dispatch.
Dallas Evening Journal.
Dallas Express.
Dallas Herald.
Dallas Laborer.
Dallas (later *Southern*) *Mercury.*
Dallas Morning News.
Dallas Observer.
Dallas Times Herald.
Dallas Weekly.

Fort Worth Gazette.
Fort Worth Star Telegram.
New York Times.
Southern News Almanac.

Papers and Addresses

Fairbanks, Robert B. "The Good Government Machine: The Citizens' Charter Association and Dallas Politics, 1930–1960." Presented during the Twenty-third Annual Walter Prescott Webb Memorial Lectures, The University of Texas at Arlington, 17 March 1988.

Greene, A. C. Comments on the "Lack of Scholarly Tradition-Historical Consciousness in Dallas." Presented at Dallas Past and Present: A Sesquicentennial Symposium, Dallas Public Library, 15 November 1986.

Lotchin, Roger W. "The City and the Sword Through the Ages and the Era of the Cold War: The Transformation of Warfare into Welfare." Presented during the Twenty-third Annual Walter Prescott Webb Memorial Lectures, University of Texas at Arlington, 17 March 1988.

Yearbooks and Miscellaneous Reference Works

American Jewish Year Book, 1966, vol. 11.

City of Dallas. *The Dallas Plan.* Dallas City Plan Inc., 1994.

"Dallas From the Ground Up." Chronology prepared in conjunction with an exhibition at the Dallas Museum of Fine Arts, May 19–July 11, 1976.

ILGWU *Report and Record*, 1937, 1968.

1990 Census Snapshot for all U.S. Places. Milpitas, Calif.: Toucan Publications, 1992.

SECONDARY SOURCES

Abbott, Carl. *The New Urban America: Growth and Politics in Sunbelt Cities.* Chapel Hill: University of North Carolina Press, 1987.

Acheson, Sam. *Dallas Yesterday.* Edited by Lee Milazzo. Dallas: Southern Methodist University Press, 1977.

———. *35,000 Days in Texas: A History of the Dallas News and its Forbears.* New York: Macmillan, 1938.

Achor, Shirley. *Mexican Americans in a Dallas Barrio.* Tucson: University of Arizona Press, 1978.

Alexander, Charles. *The Ku Klux Klan in the Southwest.* Lexington: University of Kentucky Press, 1965.

Allen, Frederick Lewis. *Since Yesterday: The 1930s in America, September 3, 1929–September 3, 1939.* New York: Harper & Row, 1939; reprint ed., New York: Perennial Library, 1972.

Alsobrook, David E. "Mobile's Commission Government of 1910–1911." *Alabama Review* 44 (January 1991):36–60.

Angel, William Daniel, Jr. "To Make a City: Entrepreneurship and Urban Rivalry on the Sunbelt Frontier." Ph.D. dissertation, University of Texas, 1978.

Aronowitz, Stanley. *False Promises: The Shaping of American Working-Class Consciousness.* New York: McGraw-Hill, 1973.

Bainbridge, John. *The Super-Americans.* New York: Holt, Rinehart & Winston, 1961.

Barta, Carolyn Jencks. "The *Dallas News* and Council-Manager Government." Master's thesis, University of Texas at Austin, 1970.

Barth, Gunther. *City People.* New York: Oxford University Press, 1980.

———. *Instant Cities: Urbanization and the Rise of San Francisco and Denver.* New York: Oxford University Press, 1975.

Bender, Thomas. *Community and Social Change in America.* Baltimore: Johns Hopkins University Press, 1982.

———. *Toward an Urban Vision: Ideas and Institutions in Nineteenth-Century America.* Lexington: University of Kentucky Press, 1975.

Bernard, Richard M., and Bradley R. Rice. *Sunbelt Cities: Politics and Growth Since World War II.* Austin: University of Texas Press, 1983.

Bernstein, Joel H. "The Artist and the Government: The P.W.A.P." In *Challenges in American Culture*, pp. 69–84. Edited by Ray B. Browne, Larry N. Landrum, and William K. Bottorff. Bowling Green, Ohio: Bowling Green University Popular Press, 1970.

Biles, Roger. "The New Deal in Dallas." *Southwestern Historical Quarterly* 95 (1991):1–19.

Black, William Neil. "Empire of Consensus: City Planning, Zoning, and Annexation in Dallas, 1900–1960." Ph.D. dissertation, Columbia University, 1982.

Blair, Karen J. *The Clubwoman as Feminist: True Womanhood Redefined, 1868–1914.* New York: Holmes & Meier, 1980.

Blumin, Stuart M. *The Emergence of the Middle Class: Social Experience in the American City, 1760–1900.* Cambridge: Cambridge University Press, 1989.

Brownell, Blaine A. *The Urban Ethos in the South, 1920–1930.* Baton Rouge: Louisiana State University Press, 1975.

Brownell, Blaine A., and David R. Goldfield, eds. *The City in Southern History: The Growth of Urban Civilization in the South.* Port Washington, N.Y.: Kennikat Press, 1977.

Browning, Rufus P., Dale Rogers Marshall, and David H. Tabb. *Protest is Not Enough: The Struggle of Blacks and Hispanics for Equality in Urban Politics.* Berkeley: University of California Press, 1984.

Burnham, Robert A. " 'Pulling Together' for Pluralism: Politics, Planning, and Government in Cincinnati, 1924–1959." Ph.D. dissertation, University of Cincinnati, 1990.

Bywaters, Jerry. *Seventy-Five Years of Art in Dallas—The History of the Dallas Art Association and the Dallas Museum of Fine Arts.* Dallas: Dallas Museum of Fine Arts, 1978.

Caldwell, Edwin L. "Highlights of the Development of Manufacturing in Texas 1900–1960." *Southwestern Historical Quarterly* 68 (April 1965):405–431.

Cantor, Milton, ed. *American Workingclass Culture: Explorations in American Labor and Social History.* Westport, Conn.: Greenwood Press, 1979.

"The Case Against Ford's." [*sic*] *Friday*, 3 May 1940, pp. 11–13.

Castells, Manuel. *The City and the Grassroots: A Cross-Cultural Theory of Urban Social Movements.* Berkeley: University of California Press, 1983.

————. *City, Class and Power.* Translated by Elizabeth Lebas. New York: St. Martin's Press, 1978.

————. *The Economic Crisis and American Society.* Princeton: Princeton University Press, 1980.

————. *The Urban Question: A Marxist Approach.* Translated by Alan Sheridan. Cambridge: M.I.T. Press, 1977.

Cavitt, Larry. "History of the Civic Federation of Dallas." Master's thesis, Southern Methodist University, 1971.

Chambers, Clarke A. *Paul U. Kellogg and the Survey: Voices for Social Welfare and Social Justice.* Minneapolis: University of Minnesota Press, 1971.

Chinoy, Ely. *Automobile Workers and the American Dream.* Garden City, N.Y.: Doubleday, 1955.

Church, Diana. "Art and Accommodation in Dallas: Edward G. Eisenlohr (1872–1961)." Master's thesis, University of Texas at Dallas, 1987.

————. "Mrs. E. P. Turner: Clubwoman, Reformer, Community Builder."(Dallas County Heritage Society) *Heritage News* (Summer 1985):9–14.

Cochran, John H. *Dallas County.* Dallas: Service Publishing, 1928.

Cohen, Carole Sadovnick. "Elmer Scott and the Civic Federation of Dallas." Master's thesis, Southern Methodist University, 1979.

Collier, James Lincoln. *The Making of Jazz.* New York: Dell Publishing, 1978.

Connor, Seymour V. "A Statistical Review of the Settlement of the Peters Colony, 1841–1848." *Southwestern Historical Quarterly* 57 (July 1953):38–64.

————. *Texas: A History.* Arlington Heights, Ill.: AHM Publishing, 1971.

Cristol, Geraldine Propper. "The History of the Dallas Museum of Fine Arts." Master's thesis, Southern Methodist University, 1970.

Crocker, Ruth Hutchinson. *Social Work and Social Order: The Settlement Movement in Two Industrial Cities, 1889–1930.* Urbana: University of Illinois Press, 1992.

"Dallas: The Centennial City Host to a Nation." *Southwest Business*, June 1936, p. 15.

Dallas Institute for the Humanities and Culture. *Imagining Dallas.* Dallas: Dallas Institute, 1982.

"Dallas Is Last to See the Fair," *Southwest Business*, October 1936, p. 13.

Davidson, Chandler. *Biracial Politics: Conflict and Coalition in the Metropolitan South*. Baton Rouge: Louisiana State University Press, 1972.

DeFord, Miriam Allen. *On Being Concerned: The Vanguard Years of Carl and Laura Brannin*. Dallas, 1969.

Devine, Edward. *Misery and Its Causes*. New York: Macmillan, 1909.

Dillon, David. *Dallas Architecture*. Austin: Texas Monthly Press, 1985.

Dooley, Kirk. *Hidden Dallas*. Dallas: Taylor Publishing, 1988.

Doyle, Don H. *New Men, New Cities, New South: Atlanta, Nashville, Charleston, Mobile, 1860–1910*. Chapel Hill: University of North Carolina Press, 1990.

Dugas, Vera Lea. "Texas Industry, 1860–1880." *Southwestern Historical Quarterly* 59 (October 1955):151–183.

"The Dydamic Men of Dallas." [*sic*] *Fortune*, February 1949, pp. 98–103, 162–166.

Ebner, Michael H., and Eugene M. Tobin, eds. *The Age of Urban Reform: New Perspectives on the Progressive Era*. Port Washington, N.Y.: Kennikat Press, 1977.

Edwards, George. *Pioneer-at-Law*. New York: W. W. Norton, 1974.

Ekirch, Arthur A., Jr., ed. *Voices in Dissent: An Anthology of Individualist Thought in the United States*. New York: The Citadel Press, 1964.

Elazar, Daniel J. *Cities of the Prairie: The Metropolitan Frontier and American Politics*. New York: Basic Books, 1970.

Elkin, Stephen L. *City and Regime in the American Republic*. Chicago: University of Chicago Press, 1987.

Encyclopedia of Texas. St. Clair Shores, Mich.: Somerset Publishers, 1985.

Enstam, Elizabeth York. "The Forgotten Frontier: Dallas Women and Social Caring, 1895–1920." *Legacies: A History Journal for Dallas and North Central Texas* (Spring 1989):20–28.

Fairbanks, Robert B. "Dallas in the 1940s: The Challenges and Opportunities of Defense Mobilization." In *Urban Texas: Politics and Development*, pp. 141–153. Edited by Char Miller and Heywood T. Sanders. College Station: Texas A&M University Press, 1990.

Fairbanks, Robert B., and Kathleen Underwood, eds. *Essays on Sunbelt Cities and Recent Urban America*. College Station: Texas A&M University Press, 1990.

Feagin, Joe R. *Free Enterprise City: Houston in Political-Economic Perspective*. New Brunswick: Rutgers University Press, 1988.

Feldman, Richard, and Michael Betzold, eds. *End of the Line: Autoworkers and the American Dream*. New York: Weidenfeld & Nicolson, 1988.

Fink, Leon. *Workingmen's Democracy: The Knights of Labor and American Politics*. Urbana: University of Illinois Press, 1983.

Fisher, Robert. "'Where Seldom Is Heard a Discouraging Word': The Political Economy of Houston, Texas." *Amerikastudien* 33 (1988):73–92.

Forsythe, John. "The Effect of Federal Labor Legislation on Organizing

Southern Labor During the New Deal Period." Master's thesis, North Texas State University, n.d.

Frank, Dana. *Purchasing Power: Consumer Organizing, Gender, and the Seattle Labor Movement, 1919–1929.* Cambridge, England: Cambridge University Press, 1994.

Frisch, Michael. "American Urban History." *History and Theory* 18 (1979):350–377.

———. *Town into City: Springfield, Massachusetts, and the Meaning of Community, 1840–1880.* Cambridge: Harvard University Press, 1973.

Fullinwider, John. "Dallas: The City With No Limits?" *In These Times*, December 1980, pp. 17–23.

Goals for Dallas. *The Possible Dream.* Dallas: Goals for Dallas, 1982.

Goldfield, David R. *Cotton Fields and Skyscrapers: Southern City and Region, 1607–1980.* Baton Rouge: Louisiana State University Press, 1982.

Goldfield, David R., and Blaine A. Brownell. *Urban America: From Downtown to No Town.* Boston: Houghton Mifflin, 1979.

Goldman, Eric F. *Rendezvous with Destiny: A History of Modern American Reform.* New York: Alfred A. Knopf, 1952; reprint ed., New York: Vintage Books, 1977.

Gonzalez, Fidel J., Jr. *P. P. Martinez: Texas Pioneer, Civic Leader, Philanthropist, Real Estate Tycoon and Tobacco Manufacturer, Dallas, Texas 1880–1935.* Dallas: Fidel J. Gonzalez, Jr., 1980.

Goodwyn, Lawrence. *Democratic Promise: The Populist Moment in America.* New York: Oxford University Press, 1976.

Graff, Harvey J. "The City, Crisis, and Change in American Culture: Perceptions and Perspectives." In *Transition to the 21st Century: Prospects and Policies for Economic and Urban-Regional Transformation*, pp. 113–152. Edited by Donald A. Hicks and Norman J. Glickman. Greenwich, Conn.: JAI Press, 1981.

———. "How Can You Celebrate a Sesquicentennial If You Have No History: Reflections on Historical Consciousness in Dallas." Sesquicentennial Essay Commissioned by the *Dallas Morning News*, 1986.

———. "The New Social History and the Southwest." *East Texas Historical Journal* 16 (1978):52–62.

Graff, Harvey J., et al. *Dallas, Texas: A Guide to the Sources of Its Social History, to 1930.* Austin: University of Texas Press Services, 1979.

Grantham, Dewey W. *Southern Progressivism: The Reconciliation of Progress and Tradition.* Knoxville: University of Tennessee Press, 1983.

Green, George Norris. *The Establishment in Texas Politics.* Westport, Conn.: Greenwood Press, 1979.

Green, James R. *Grass-roots Socialism: Radical Movements in the Southwest, 1895–1943.* Baton Rouge: Louisiana State University Press, 1978.

Greenberg, Brian. *Worker and Community: Response to Industrialization in a Nineteenth-Century American City, Albany, New York, 1850–1884.* Albany: State University of New York Press, 1985.

Greene, A. C. *Dallas—The Deciding Years—A Historical Portrait.* Austin: Encino Press, 1973.

———. *Dallas USA.* Austin: Texas Monthly Press, 1984.

———. "Power and Politics." In *The Book of Dallas*, pp. 232–251. Edited by Evelyn Oppenheimer and Bill Porterfield. Garden City, N.Y.: Doubleday, 1976.

Gutman, Herbert G. *Work, Culture, and Society in Industrializing America: Essays in American Working-Class and Social History.* New York: Vintage Books, 1977.

Haley, J. Evetts. *Frank Reaugh—Man and Artist.* El Paso: Carl Hertzog, 1960.

Hamer, David. *New Towns in the New World: Images and Perceptions of the Nineteenth-Century Urban Frontier.* New York: Columbia University Press, 1990.

Harris, Neil. "The Drama of Consumer Desire." In *Yankee Enterprise: The Rise of the American System of Manufactures*, pp. 189–216. Edited by Otto Mayr and Robert C. Post. Washington, D.C. Smithsonian, 1981.

———. "The Lamp of Learning: Popular Lights and Shadows." In *The Organization of Knowledge in Modern America, 1860–1920*, pp. 430–439. Edited by Alexandra Oleson and John Voss. Baltimore: Johns Hopkins University Press, 1979.

Harvey, David. *Consciousness and the Urban Experience: Studies in the History and Theory of Capitalist Urbanization.* Baltimore: Johns Hopkins University Press, 1985.

———. *The Limits to Capital.* Chicago: University of Chicago Press, 1982.

Haynes, Robert V. *A Night of Violence: The Houston Riot of 1917.* Baton Rouge: Louisiana State University Press, 1976.

Hazel, Michael V. "Dallas Women's Clubs: Vehicles for Change." (Dallas County Heritage Society) *Heritage News* (Spring 1986):18–21.

Hershberg, Theodore. "The New Urban History." *Journal of Urban History* 5 (1978): 3–40.

———, ed. *Philadelphia: Work, Space, Family and Group Experience in the Nineteenth Century: Essays Toward an Interdisciplinary History of the City.* New York: Oxford University Press, 1981.

Hill, Marilynn Wood. "A History of the Jewish Involvement in the Dallas Community." Master's thesis, Southern Methodist University, 1967.

Hill, Patricia Evridge. "Real Women and True Womanhood: Grassroots Organizing among Dallas Dressmakers in 1935." *Labor's Heritage* 5 (Spring 1994): 4–17.

———. "Women's Groups and the Extension of City Services in Early Twentieth-Century Dallas." *East Texas Historical Journal* 39 (1992): 3–10.

Hobsbawm, Eric J. *Primitive Rebels: Studies in Archaic Forms of Social Movement in the Nineteenth and Twentieth Centuries.* New York: W. W. Norton, 1959.

Hofstadter, Richard. *The Age of Reform.* New York: Random House, 1955.

Hooks, Michael Q. "The Role of Promoters in Urban Rivalry: The Dallas–Fort Worth Experience, 1870–1910." *Red River Historical Review* 7 (1982):4–16.

Ingalls, Robert P. *Urban Vigilantes in the New South: Tampa, 1882–1936.* Knoxville: University of Tennessee Press, 1988.

Jackson, Kenneth T. *Crabgrass Frontier: The Suburbanization of the United States.* New York: Oxford University Press, 1985.

———. *The Ku Klux Klan in the City, 1915–1930.* New York: Oxford University Press, 1967.

Johnson, Yvonne. "Desegregating Dallas, 1936–1961." Master's thesis, University of Texas at Dallas, 1985.

Katz, Michael B. *In the Shadow of the Poorhouse: A Social History of Welfare in America.* New York: Basic Books, 1986.

———. *The Irony of Early School Reform.* Cambridge: Harvard University Press, 1968.

———. *Poverty and Policy in American History.* New York: Academic Press, 1983.

———. *The Social Organization of Early Industrial Capitalism.* Cambridge: Harvard University Press, 1982.

Katznelson, Ira. *City Trenches: Urban Politics and the Patterning of Class in the United States.* Chicago: University of Chicago Press, 1981.

Kazin, Michael. *Barons of Labor: The San Francisco Building Trades and Union Power in the Progressive Era.* Urbana: University of Illinois Press, 1987.

Kerr, Homer L. "Migration into Texas, 1860–1880." *Southwestern Historical Quarterly* 70 (October 1966):184–216.

Kimball, Justin F. *Our City—Dallas: A Community Civics.* Dallas: Kessler Plan Association, 1927.

Kolko, Gabriel. *The Triumph of Conservatism: A Re-Interpretation of American History.* Glencoe, Ill.: The Free Press, 1963.

Lancaster, Janice. "Dallas and the Early Railroads." Master's thesis, Southern Methodist University, 1971.

Larsen, Lawrence. *The Rise of the Urban South.* Lexington: University Press of Kentucky, 1985.

———. *The Urban West at the End of the Frontier.* Lawrence: The Regents Press of Kansas, 1978.

Larson, Robert W. *Populism in the Mountain West.* Albuquerque: University of New Mexico Press, 1986.

LaSalle, Patricia Ann. "Adelfa Callejo: An Impassioned Voice for Human Rights." *SMU Mustang*, Fall 1986, pp. 34–37.

Laurie, Bruce. *Working People of Philadelphia, 1800–1850.* Philadelphia: Temple University Press, 1980.

Leach, William R. "Transformations in a Culture of Consumption: Women and Department Stores, 1890–1925." *Journal of American History* 71 (1984):319–342.

Leggett, John C. *Class, Race, and Labor: Working-Class Consciousness in Detroit.* New York: Oxford University Press, 1968.

Leiby, James. *A History of Social Welfare and Social Work in the United States, 1815–1972.* New York: Columbia University Press, 1978.

Lerner, Gerda. "Placing Women in History: Definitions and Challenges." *Feminist Studies* 3 (Fall 1975):5–14.

Leslie, Warren. *Dallas Public and Private: Aspects of an American City.* New York: Grossman, 1964.

———. *The Starrs of Texas.* New York: Simon & Schuster, 1978.

Lewis, Willie Newbury. *Willie, a Girl from a Town Called Dallas.* College Station: Texas A&M University Press, 1984.

Lindsley, Philip. *A History of Greater Dallas and Vicinity.* Vol. 1. Chicago: Lewis Publishing, 1909.

———. *A History of Greater Dallas and Vicinity.* Vol. 2. Edited by L. B. Hill. Chicago: Lewis Publishing, 1909.

Livesay, Harold C. *Samuel Gompers and Organized Labor in America.* Boston: Little, Brown, 1978.

Logan, John R., and Harvey L. Molotch. *Urban Fortunes: The Political Economy of Place.* Berkeley: University of California Press, 1987.

Lotchin, Roger W. *Fortress California, 1910–1961: From Warfare to Welfare.* New York: Oxford University Press, 1992.

Lubove, Roy. *The Professional Altruist.* Cambridge: Harvard University Press, 1963.

———. "The Urbanization Process." *Journal of the American Institute of Planners* 33 (1967):33–39.

Luckingham, Bradford. *The Urban Southwest: A Profile History of Albuquerque, El Paso, Phoenix, Tucson.* El Paso: Texas Western Press, 1982.

McCarthy, Colman. *Disturbers of the Peace: Profiles in Nonadjustment.* Boston: Houghton Mifflin, 1973.

McCarthy, Kathleen D. *Noblesse Oblige: Charity and Cultural Philanthropy in Chicago, 1849–1929.* Chicago: University of Chicago Press, 1982.

McCarthy, Michael P. "Urban Optimism and Reform Thought in the Progressive Era." *The Historian* 51 (February 1989):239–262.

McComb, David G. *Houston: The Bayou City.* Austin: University of Texas Press, 1969.

McDonald, Terrence J. *The Parameters of Urban Fiscal Policy: Socioeconomic Change and Political Culture in San Francisco, 1860–1906.* Berkeley: University of California Press, 1986.

McDonald, William L. *Dallas Rediscovered: A Photographic Chronicle of Urban Expansion, 1870–1925.* Dallas: Dallas Historical Society, 1978.

McLaurin, Melton Alonza. *The Knights of Labor in the South.* Westport, Conn.: Greenwood Press, 1978.

McMath, Robert C., Jr. *Populist Vanguard: A History of the Southern Farmers' Alliance.* Chapel Hill: University of North Carolina Press, 1975.

Macune, Charles W., Jr. "The Wellsprings of a Populist: Dr. C. W. Macune before 1886." *Southwestern Historical Quarterly* 90 (October 1986): 139–158.

Manchester, William. *Death of a President*. New York: Harper & Row, 1967.

Maranto, Samuel Paul. "A History of Dallas Newspapers." Master's thesis, North Texas State University, 1952.

Marcus, Stanley. *Minding the Store*. Boston: Little, Brown, 1974.

Martin, Roscoe C. *The People's Party in Texas*. 1933; reprint ed., Austin: University of Texas Press, Texas History Paperback, 1970.

May, Martha. "The Historical Problem of the Family Wage: The Ford Motor Company and the Five Dollar Day." In *Families and Work*, pp. 111–131. Edited by Naomi Gerstel and Harriet Engel Gross. Philadelphia: Temple University Press, 1987.

Melosi, Martin V. "Dallas–Fort Worth: Marketing the Metroplex." In *Sunbelt Cities: Politics and Growth Since World War II*, pp. 162–195. Edited by Richard M. Bernard and Bradley R. Rice. Austin: University of Texas Press, 1983.

Members of the Texas Legislature 1846–1962. Austin, Texas, 1962.

Memorial and Biographical History of Dallas County, Texas. Chicago: Lewis Publishing, 1892.

Miller, Worth Robert. "Building a Progressive Coalition in Texas: The Populist-Reform Democrat Rapprochement, 1900–1907." *Journal of Southern History* 52 (May 1986):163–182.

Miller, Zane L., and Patricia M. Melvin. *The Urbanization of Modern America: A Brief History*, 2d ed. San Diego: Harcourt Brace Jovanovich, 1987.

Mills, C. Wright. *White Collar: The American Middle Classes*. New York: Oxford University Press, 1951.

Mohl, Raymond A., ed. *Searching for the Sunbelt: Historical Perspectives on a Region*. Knoxville: University of Tennessee Press, 1990.

Monkkonen, Eric H. *America Becomes Urban: The Development of U.S. Cities and Towns, 1780–1980*. Berkeley: University of California Press, 1988.

Montgomery, David. *The Fall of the House of Labor: The Workplace, the State, and American Labor Activism, 1865–1925*. Cambridge: Cambridge University Press, 1987.

Morrison, Andrew. *The City of Dallas and the State of Texas*. St. Louis: George W. Englehardt, n.d.

"North America Comes to Dallas." *Southwest Business*, October 1940, pp. 9–11, 14–15.

Norton, Wesley. "The Methodist Episcopal Church and the Civic Disturbances in North Texas in 1859 and 1860." *Southwestern Historical Quarterly* 68 (January 1965):317–341.

O'Connor, Robert F., ed. *Texas Myths*. College Station: Texas A&M University Press for the Texas Committee for the Humanities, 1986.

Payne, Darwin. *Dallas: An Illustrated History.* Woodland Hills, Calif.: Dallas Historic Preservation League and Windsor Publications, 1982.

———, ed. *Dissenting Opinion: Carl Brannin's Letters to the Editor, 1933–1976.* Austin: American Civil Liberties Foundation of Texas, 1977.

Pells, Richard H. *The Liberal Mind in a Conservative Age: American Intellectuals in the 1940s and 1950s.* New York: Harper & Row, 1985.

Perry, David, and Albert Watkins, eds. *The Rise of the Sunbelt Cities.* Beverly Hills: Sage Publications, 1977.

Peterson, Joyce Shaw. *American Automobile Workers, 1900–1933.* Albany: State University of New York Press, 1987.

Platt, Harold L. *City Building in the New South: The Growth of Public Services in Houston, Texas, 1830–1910.* Philadelphia: Temple University Press, 1983.

———. "Houston at the Crossroads: The Emergence of the Urban Center of the Southwest." *Journal of the West* 18 (1979):51–61.

Potter, Lester T. *Glitter, Glitter.* Dallas: Lester T. Potter, 1975.

Powers, Diane Curtis. "The Development and Expansion of the Street Railroad System in Dallas, Texas: 1871–1890." Master's thesis, Southern Methodist University, 1969.

Pred, Allan R. *The Spatial Dynamics of U.S. Urban-Industrial Growth, 1800–1914.* Cambridge: M.I.T. Press, 1966.

Ragsdale, Kenneth B. *The Year America Discovered Texas: Centennial '36.* College Station: Texas A&M University Press, 1988.

Rayback, Joseph G. *A History of American Labor.* New York: Macmillan, 1959.

Reese, James V. "The Early History of Labor Organizations in Texas, 1838–1876." *Southwestern Historical Quarterly* 72 (July 1968):1–20.

Reps, John W. *Cities of the American West: A History of Frontier Urban Planning.* Princeton: Princeton University Press, 1979.

———. *The Making of Urban America: A History of City Planning in the United States.* Princeton: Princeton University Press, 1965.

Rice, Bradley R. *Progressive Cities and the Commission Government Movement in America, 1901–1920.* Austin: University of Texas Press, 1977.

Rogers, John William. *The Lusty Texans of Dallas.* New York: E. P. Dutton, 1951; reprint ed. (expanded), Dallas: Cokesbury Book Store, 1965.

Rosenberg, Leon Joseph. *Sangers': Pioneer Texas Merchants.* Austin: Texas State Historical Association, 1981.

Safianow, Allen. "'Konklave in Kokomo' Revisited." *The Historian* 50 (May 1988):329–347.

Sale, Kirkpatrick. *Power Shift: The Rise of the Southern Rim and Its Challenge to the Eastern Establishment.* New York: Random House, 1975.

Santerre, George H. *Dallas' First Hundred Years, 1856–1956.* Dallas: Book Craft, 1956.

Saxon, Gerald D., ed. *Reminiscences: A Glimpse of Old East Dallas.* Dallas: Dallas Public Library, 1983.

Schnore, Leo F., ed. *The New Urban History: Quantitative Explorations by American Historians*. Princeton: Princeton University Press, 1975.

Schutze, Jim. "The Accommodation." *D Magazine*, March 1987, pp. 90–95, 126–132.

————. *The Accommodation: The Politics of Race in an American City*. Secaucus, N.J.: The Citadel Press, 1986.

Scott, Anne Firor. *Natural Allies: Women's Associations in American History*. Urbana: University of Illinois Press, 1991.

Scott, Elmer. *88 Eventful Years*. Dallas: Civic Federation of Dallas, 1954.

Scott, Mel. *American City Planning Since 1890*. Berkeley: University of California Press, 1969.

Seib, Philip. *Dallas: Chasing the Urban Dream*. Dallas: Pressworks, 1986.

Sharpe, Ernest. *G. B. Dealey of the Dallas News*. New York: Henry Holt, 1955.

Smith, Ralph. "The Farmers' Alliance in Texas, 1875–1900." *Southwestern Historical Quarterly* 48 (January 1945):346–369.

Smith, Richard Austin. "How Business Failed Dallas." *Fortune*, July 1964, pp. 156–163, 211–216.

————. "How Business Failed Dallas." In *Governing Texas*, pp. 278–286. Edited by Fred Gantt, Jr. New York: Crowell, 1966.

Smyrl, Frank H. "Unionism in Texas 1856–1861." *Southwestern Historical Quarterly* 68 (October 1964):172–195.

Stewart, Rick. *Lone Star Regionalism—The Dallas Nine and Their Circle*. Dallas: Dallas Museum of Art, 1985.

Stone, Harold, et al. *City Manager Government in Dallas*. Chicago: Public Administration Service, 1939.

Summaries of the Proposals for Achieving the Goals for Dallas. Dallas, 1969.

Susman, Warren I. *Culture as History: The Transformation of American Society in the Twentieth Century*. New York: Pantheon Books, 1973, 1984.

Teaford, Jon C. *The Twentieth-Century American City: Problem, Promise, and Reality*. Baltimore: Johns Hopkins University Press, 1986.

Terry, Marshall. "Willis Tate: Adventures of the Spirit." *SMU Mustang*, Fall 1986, pp. 27–29.

Texas Writers Project. *Dallas Guide and History*. Works Progress Administration, 1940.

Thernstrom, Stephan. *Poverty and Progress: Social Mobility in a Nineteenth Century City*. Cambridge: Harvard University Press, 1964; reprint ed., New York: Atheneum, 1977.

Thernstrom, Stephan, and Richard Sennett, eds. *Nineteenth Century Cities*. New Haven: Yale University Press, 1969.

Thometz, Carol Estes. *The Decision Makers: The Power Structure of Dallas*. Dallas: Southern Methodist University Press, 1963.

Thompson, E. P. *The Making of the English Working Class*. New York: Vintage Books, 1966.

Tilly, Charles. *The Contentious French*. Cambridge, Mass.: Belknap Press, 1986.

Tilly, Charles, Louise Tilly, and Richard Tilly. *The Rebellious Century, 1830–1930.* Cambridge: Harvard University Press, 1975.

Tilly, Louise, and Charles Tilly, eds. *Class Conflict and Collective Action.* Beverly Hills: Sage Publications, 1981.

Tinkle, Lon. *The Key to Dallas.* Keys to the Cities Series. Philadelphia: J. B. Lippincott, 1965.

Todes, Jay Littman. "Organized Employer Opposition to Unionism in Texas, 1900–1930." Master's thesis, University of Texas, 1949.

Trattner, Walter I. *From Poor Law to Welfare State: A History of Social Welfare in America.* New York: The Free Press, 1974.

———, ed. *Biographical Dictionary of Social Welfare in America.* Westport, Conn.: Greenwood Press, 1986.

Warner, Sam Bass, Jr. *The Urban Wilderness: A History of the American City.* New York: Harper & Row, 1972.

Weaver, Paul. *The Suicidal Corporation.* New York: Simon & Schuster, 1988.

Wedell, Marsha. *Elite Women and the Reform Impulse in Memphis, 1875–1915.* Knoxville: University of Tennessee Press, 1991.

Weinstein, James. *The Decline of Socialism in America, 1912–1925.* New York: Vintage Books, 1969.

Welter, Barbara. "The Cult of True Womanhood: 1820–1860." In *The American Family in Social-Historical Perspective,* 3d ed., pp. 372–392. Edited by Michael Gordon. New York: St. Martin's Press, 1983.

Wheeler, Kenneth W. *To Wear a City's Crown: The Beginnings of Urban Growth in Texas, 1836–1865.* Cambridge: Harvard University Press, 1968.

Widener, Ralph W., Jr. *William Henry Gaston: A Builder of Dallas.* Dallas: Historical Publishing, 1977.

Wiebe, Robert. *Businessmen and Reform: A Study of the Progressive Movement.* Cambridge: Harvard University Press, 1965.

Wiley, Nancy. *The Great State Fair of Texas—An Illustrated History.* Dallas: Taylor Publishing, 1985.

Williams, Roy H., and Kevin J. Shay. *Time Change: An Alternative View of the History of Dallas.* Dallas: To Be Pub., Co., 1991.

Wilson, L. A. *History and Opportunity.* Dallas, 1911.

Wilson, William H. "Adapting to Growth: Dallas, Texas, and the Kessler Plan, 1908–1933," *Arizona and the West* 25 (1983):245–260.

———. *The City Beautiful Movement.* Baltimore: Johns Hopkins University Press, 1989.

———. "Desegregation of the Hamilton Park School, 1955–1975." *Southwestern Historical Quarterly* 95 (1991):42–63.

———. "Private Planning for Black Housing in Dallas, Texas, 1945–1955." *Proceedings of the Second National Conference on American Planning History* 2 (1988):67–84.

Wood, E. A. "A City Looks to the Future: Dallas Believes in City Planning." *Southwest Review* 29 (Spring 1944): 301–311.

Wright, Lawrence. *In the New World: Growing Up With America, 1960–1984.*

New York: Alfred A. Knopf, 1988.

Yellowitz, Irwin. *The Position of the Worker in American Society, 1865–1896.* Englewood Cliffs, N.J.: Prentice-Hall, 1969.

Zunz, Olivier. *The Changing Pace of Inequality: Urbanization, Industrial Development, and Immigrants in Detroit, 1880–1920.* Chicago: University of Chicago Press, 1982.